Time Series Analysis with Spark

A practical guide to processing, modeling, and forecasting time series with Apache Spark

Yoni Ramaswami

Time Series Analysis with Spark

Portfolio Director: Sunith Shetty

Relationship Lead: Vaideeshwari Muralikrishnan

Project Manager: Hemangi Lotlikar

Content Engineer: Shrishti Pandey

Technical Editor: Gaurav Gavas

Copy Editor: Safis Editing

Proofreader: Shrishti Pandey

Indexer: Pratik Shirodkar

Production Designer: Gokul Raj S.T

Growth Lead: Bhavesh Amin

DevRel Marketing Coordinator: Ankur Mulasi

First published: March 2025

Production reference: 2051125

Published by Packt Publishing Ltd.
Grosvenor House
11 St Paul's Square
Birmingham
B3 1RB, UK

ISBN 978-1-80323-225-6

www.packtpub.com

*This book has been a long journey in the making, and I dedicate it to those who have shaped
and uplifted me along the way. To my loving wife, Mokshada, whose unwavering support and
partnership have been my greatest strength throughout this endeavor and our shared journey. To
my son, Aryan (aka Black Panther, aka ElectricMax), for inspiring me daily with his dedication to
improve his skills in tennis and violin. He motivates me to be the best role model I can be. In memory
of my late father, Vijay, and to my mother, Satya, for their sacrifices and love, and for bestowing on me
the passion for learning. They shared with me invaluable lessons of perseverance and determination.
Their unwavering belief in me has been a guiding light, pushing me toward greater heights,
no matter the challenges.*

– Yoni Ramaswami

Foreword

In the rapidly evolving landscape of data science and analytics, time series analysis stands as a critical yet often underutilized tool. Traditionally, this field has been constrained by proprietary technologies and specialist knowledge, limiting its application across diverse business domains. These constraints have resulted in static models ill-equipped to handle the dynamic, real-time challenges faced by modern enterprises.

Yoni Ramaswami's *Time Series Analysis with Spark* arrives at a pivotal moment, offering a fresh perspective on this vital discipline. By leveraging Apache Spark, Yoni democratizes time series analysis, transforming it from a niche skill into an accessible, scalable, and flexible approach applicable to a wide range of industries.

The impact of this democratization cannot be overstated. By blending time series analysis with other data types and enabling real-time applications, this book opens doors to more representative solutions for real-world challenges. Dynamic and complex domains such as supply chain management, logistics, and financial markets stand to benefit immensely from this approach, which breaks free from the limitations of proprietary technology and embraces evolving methodologies and AI-enabled techniques.

Yoni's talent shines through in his first-principles approach to the subject. He has crafted this book not just as a technical guide, but as a catalyst for evolving a field that is increasingly necessary in our data-driven world. Readers will find themselves equipped with the tools and understanding to apply time series analysis in ways that were previously out of reach, fostering innovation and driving efficiency across their organizations.

As we navigate an era where data flows ceaselessly and business landscapes shift at unprecedented speeds, the ability to extract meaningful insights from temporal data is more crucial than ever. *Time Series Analysis with Spark* is not just a book; it's a key that unlocks the potential of time series data for businesses of all sizes and sectors.

Yoni Ramaswami has delivered a book that is both timely and essential. It empowers data scientists, analysts, and business leaders to tackle real-world problems with cutting-edge tools and methodologies. In doing so, he has laid the groundwork for a new era of accessible, impactful time series analysis – one that promises to reshape how we understand and interact with the temporal dimensions of our data-rich world.

Dael Williamson

Field Chief Technology Officer, Databricks.

For centuries, humanity has been fascinated by the idea that even the simplest sequences - whether of numbers, events, or patterns - may hold the key to understanding a vast array of possibilities. This search for hidden meaning has fueled countless discoveries, from ancient astronomers charting the stars to the mysterious practice of reading the future in the flight patterns of birds. In fact, some of the earliest "data analysts" might have been soothsayers peering into the future through chicken bones or sheep entrails, convinced that the universe had secret messages waiting to be deciphered!

Today, in our digital age, we face an explosion of data unlike anything in history. Every moment, transaction, and action can be captured as a sequence of numbers. No longer do we need to rely on animal bones for our predictions - now, we look to massive datasets, believing that hidden patterns and trends might reveal the next big breakthrough. Across all scales, from the smallest dataset to the most complex, we are still driven by the same fundamental quest: to uncover the meaning that lies beneath the surface and gain insights into the world around us.

Since the early 2000s, companies have progressively realized that their data, when properly harnessed and structured (easier said than done... ask any Chief Data Officer!), represents a huge potential. Among all forms of data, those tied to time - sequences of events, measurements, or activities - are perhaps the most valuable. They tell stories, reveal trends, and, most interestingly, enable us to predict the future. Since the 1990s, factories have been equipped with sensors, monitoring systems, and databases, retailers have tried to standardize product identifiers across countries to consolidate their sales data, and more.

Imagine being able to predict when critical equipment is about to fail, saving a company from costly downtimes that would otherwise disrupt production. Or picture the ability to fine-tune an industrial process so that every batch of product meets the same high standard, day after day. Even in the most complex industrial systems, identifying anomalies before they spiral out of control can mean the difference between a minor issue and a major breakdown.

In the world of business, time series analysis can optimize inventory management, adjusting stock levels based on real-time consumption patterns, ensuring businesses are never overstocked or caught off guard by sudden demand. Similarly, the ability to detect fraudulent activity based on behavioral trends allows companies to respond quickly, minimizing financial loss and damage to their reputation.

On the healthcare front, time series data can play a crucial role in detecting early signs of heart issues from patient data, potentially saving lives before a condition becomes critical. And when it comes to market trends, analyzing historical data allows businesses to optimize strategic decisions, ensuring they stay one step ahead of their competition.

Yet, this wealth of data remains underutilized... and this is where Apache Spark comes in.

This tool is designed to process, analyze, and extract insights from massive data streams at speeds and scales once unimaginable. This book, Time Series Analysis with Spark, is an invitation to dive into this fascinating world. It will show you how to manipulate and analyze time series data to solve real-world problems in sectors as diverse as energy, finance, healthcare, and logistics.

This book is intended for data scientists, engineers, and technical decision-makers – those who understand that data is not only a source of power but also a responsibility. With clear explanations and concrete examples, this guide will equip you with the tools to transform raw data into actionable insights. You'll learn to unlock the full potential of time series data by harnessing the power of Apache Spark to fuel your ambitions.

In an era flooded with data, the companies that will succeed tomorrow won't simply be those that gather vast amounts of information. Rather, they will be the ones who understand it, share it, and use it to create lasting value.

But with this power comes responsibility. The goal is not merely to predict, but to foresee with awareness, acknowledging that every model - no matter how sophisticated - is just an imperfect projection of what we, as humans, choose to do with our future. Our ability to read the patterns and trends that emerge from time series data offers immense potential, but it also demands a careful approach. After all, in the end, the choices we make today shape the world we'll live in tomorrow.

This book, like much of Yoni's work, is guided by a deep sense of humanity. Over the 20 years that I have known him, from those early days of shared curiosity to this moment of collective insight, Yoni has always been a guide, not just in knowledge, but in human connection. His commitment to sharing his knowledge reflects a belief that true progress comes not just from accumulating insights, but from passing them on to others, so that together we can build a better tomorrow. His passion for learning, teaching, and empowering others serves as a reminder that knowledge is not only power, but also responsibility.

So, as we stand on the brink of this data-driven era, the question isn't just "What can you predict?" but also "What will you do with what you'll find?".

Jan Govaere

Chief Information Officer & IT leader.

Contributors

About the author

Yoni Ramaswami is a Senior Solutions Architect at Databricks with two decades of experience in IT, data, and AI. Recognized for his contributions to projects spanning digitally innovative technologies across industries, Yoni combines thought leadership, architecture, and implementation expertise. Originally from Mauritius, Yoni earned his Diplôme d'Ingénieur from UTC in France and Chalmers in Sweden, grounding his global perspective in both technical rigor and cultural insight. When not devising practical, high-impact solutions, he can be found exploring the lush landscapes of Mauritius with his son.

I would like to extend my thanks to Shrishti and the team at Packt, to the Technical Reviewers (Guillaume, Lorin, Mohammad, Sonali) and Ryuta, to the foreword writers (Dael and Jan), to Gita and Greg, Seeram and Sadna, Ammam and Baam, Manoj, François and Erika, Devind and Savita, Abdul, Manish, Chris, Gérard, Rushdee, Danny and JP. Your sound advice and encouragements have made this book possible.

About the reviewers

Guillaume Meister is an IT professional with over 25 years of experience in the tech industry, specializing in databases, big data, cloud architecture, and network infrastructures. Recognized for his leadership and problem-solving abilities, he has contributed to digital transformation and infrastructure migration projects for organizations such as Airbus, Amadeus, TSMC, and ANZ Bank. He holds a master's degree in computer science and has certifications from AWS and Microsoft. Guillaume has also authored publications on open-source software and is passionate about leveraging technology to drive impactful solutions.

Lorin Dawson is a technology professional with expertise in cloud architecture, platform and data engineering. As a member of the Digital Native Business team within Databricks Field Engineering, Lorin designs and optimizes secure, high-performance data and AI systems for enterprise-level applications. Lorin contributes to the time series project Tempo in Databricks Labs, enhancing Apache Spark's capabilities in advanced data analytics. When not working, Lorin enjoys mountaineering and exploring culinary arts. He resides in Denver, Colorado, with his wife.

Mohammad Shahedi is a Specialist Solutions Architect at Databricks, supporting data engineering and data warehousing use cases. He holds a Master's in Economics and Quantitative Finance from the University of Milan, where his thesis explored clustering financial time series. His Bachelor's in Civil Engineering provided a strong mathematical foundation, invaluable to his quantitative finance work.

Sonali Guleria is a recognized thought leader with over 12 years of professional experience in data, machine learning, and artificial intelligence. She helps organizations effectively scale their cloud data strategies with a strong focus on innovation. Sonali obtained her undergraduate degree in computer science from Amity University in India and later earned her master's degree in data and machine learning from Carnegie Mellon University in Pittsburgh. Currently, she serves as a Lead Solutions Architect at Databricks, specializing in financial services, machine learning, and artificial intelligence.

Join our community on Discord

Join our community's Discord space for discussions with the authors and other readers:

https://packt.link/ds

Table of Contents

2

Why Time Series Analysis?   27

3

Introduction to Apache Spark   49

Part 2: From Data to Models

4

End-to-End View of a Time Series Analysis Project   71

5

Data Preparation — 101

6

Exploratory Data Analysis — 123

7

Building and Testing Models — 149

Part 3: Scaling to Production and Beyond

8

Going at Scale · 181

9

Going to Production · 201

Preface

Time series are everywhere, at every time, ever-growing. With the right tools that can be scaled up, you can unleash their temporal insights with ease, giving you the edge over time.

Time series analysis—extracting insights from time series—is crucial for businesses and organizations to make informed decisions. This is achieved by analyzing patterns, trends, and anomalies in data collected at intervals of time. Apache Spark is a powerful big data processing framework that enables the efficient processing of large-scale time series data, making it an ideal tool for handling the volume and complexity of such data.

There are three main pillars for any time series analysis engagement with Apache Spark:

- Data Preparation and Processing: This involves collecting, cleaning, and transforming time series data into a format suitable for analysis.

- Modeling and Forecasting: This includes applying statistical models or machine learning algorithms to uncover patterns and predict future trends.

- Deployment and Maintenance: This involves integrating the models into operational systems and continuously monitoring and updating them to ensure accuracy and relevance.

This book, *Time Series Analysis with Spark*, aims to cover all these pillars. It will provide practical techniques for processing, modeling, and forecasting time series data using Apache Spark. The book is based on two main sources of information:

- Practical Experience: Drawing from real-world projects and experiences in handling large-scale time series data with Apache Spark.

- Industry Insights: Incorporating insights from experts and practitioners in the field of time series analysis and big data processing.

As the use of Apache Spark for time series analysis continues to grow, the demand for professionals skilled in this area is increasing rapidly. This book will guide you through the best practices and techniques necessary to leverage Apache Spark effectively for time series analysis, helping you to stay ahead in this rapidly evolving field.

Who this book is for

Professionals in data and AI, especially with time-dependent datasets, will find *Time Series Analysis with Spark* beneficial for enhancing their skills in leveraging Apache Spark and Databricks for time series analysis. The book caters to a broad audience, from those new to time series analysis and Apache Spark to experienced practitioners seeking to leverage Spark for temporal data analysis.

More specifically, data engineers will enhance their abilities in utilizing Spark and Databricks for the large-scale preparation of time series data. **Machine learning** (**ML**) engineers will find it easier to expand the scope of their ML projects. Data scientists and analysts will acquire fresh time series analysis skills to broaden their range of tools.

What this book covers

Chapter 1, *What Are Time Series?*, introduces the concept of time series data and the unique challenges in its analysis. This foundation is required to effectively analyze and forecast time-dependent data.

Chapter 2, *Why Time Series Analysis?*, elaborates on the importance of analyzing time-dependent data in enabling predictive modeling, trend identification, and anomaly detection. This is illustrated with real-world applications across industries.

Chapter 3, *Introduction to Apache Spark*, dives into Apache Spark and its distributed computing capabilities for processing large-scale time series data.

Chapter 4, *End-to-End View of a Time Series Analysis Project*, guides us through the entire process of a time series analysis project. Starting with use cases, it covers key stages such as data processing, feature engineering, model selection, and evaluation.

Chapter 5, *Data Preparation*, delves into the critical steps of organizing, cleaning, and transforming time series data. It covers techniques for handling missing values, dealing with outliers, and structuring data, enhancing the reliability of subsequent analytical processes.

Chapter 6, *Exploratory Data Analysis*, goes through exploratory data analysis to uncover patterns and insights in time series data. These steps are crucial for identifying characteristics such as trends and seasonality, informing subsequent modeling decisions.

Chapter 7, *Building and Testing Models*, focuses on constructing predictive models for time series data, covering the diverse types of models, which one to choose, and how to train, tune, and evaluate models.

Chapter 8, *Going at Scale*, addresses the considerations for scaling time series analysis in large and distributed computing environments. It covers the different ways that Apache Spark can be used to scale feature engineering, hyperparameter tuning, and single- and multi-model training.

Chapter 9, *Going to Production*, explores the practical considerations and steps involved in deploying time series models into production, while ensuring the reliability and effectiveness of time series models in operational environments.

Chapter 10, Going Further with Apache Spark, provides answers to the challenges of setting up and managing the platform by using Databricks as a cloud-based, managed, platform-as-a-service solution to go further with Apache Spark.

Chapter 11, Recent Developments in Time Series Analysis, explores recent developments in the field of time series analysis, including an approach from the exciting field of generative AI applied to time series forecasting, as well as new approaches to making the outcome of time series analysis accessible to them in non-technical ways.

To get the most out of this book

This book requires you to have a basic understanding of the Python programming language along with a fundamental knowledge of data science and machine learning concepts.

- *Chapters 1, 2, 5, 6,* and *7* use the Databricks Community Edition.

- *Chapters 3, 4,* and *9* use local containerized environments. The examples in this book were tested with Docker on macOS. They should work with Docker or Podman on Windows or Linux with adaptation. You can skip the hands-on part of these chapters if you do not intend to build your own environment locally and prefer to use a managed platform such as Databricks.

- *Chapters 8, 10,* and *11* use the Databricks platform.

Additional installation instructions and information for getting set up are documented in the individual chapters.

Software/hardware covered in the book	Operating system requirements
Databricks Community Edition	
Databricks on Amazon Web Services (AWS) or Microsoft Azure	
Docker v4.48 or Podman v1.16	Windows, macOS, or Linux

Additional software packages required for the code examples are installed automatically at code execution. As software packages and User Interfaces are subject to changes, refer to the corresponding package or product documentation for information on changes.

If you are using the digital version of this book, we advise you to type the code yourself or access the code from the book's GitHub repository (a link is available in the next section). Doing so will help you avoid any potential errors related to the copying and pasting of code.

If there is an update to instructions, it will be added to the README.md of the individual chapters on the GitHub repository to the extent possible.

Download the example code files

You can download the example code files for this book from GitHub at `https://github.com/PacktPublishing/Time-Series-Analysis-with-Spark`. If there's an update to the code, it will be updated in the GitHub repository.

We also have other code bundles from our rich catalog of books and videos available at `https://github.com/PacktPublishing/`. Check them out!

Conventions used

There are a number of text conventions used throughout this book.

`Code in text`: Indicates code words in text, database table names, folder names, filenames, file extensions, pathnames, dummy URLs, user input, and Twitter handles. Here is an example: "Mount the downloaded `WebStorm-10*.dmg` disk image file as another disk in your system."

A block of code is set as follows:

```
#### Summary Statistics
# Code in cell 10
df.summary().display()
```

When we wish to draw your attention to a particular part of a code block, the relevant lines or items are set in bold:

```
sns.boxplot(x='dayOfWeek', y='Global_active_power', data=pdf)
```

Any command-line input or output is written as follows:

```
Test SMAPE: 41.193985580947896
Test WAPE: 0.35355667972102317
```

Bold: Indicates a new term, an important word, or words that you see onscreen. For instance, words in menus or dialog boxes appear in **bold**. Here is an example: "Other sections of the report cover **Alerts**, shown in *Figure 6.8*, with outcomes of tests run on the dataset, including time-series-specific ones, and a **Reproduction** section with details on the profiling run."

> **Tips or important notes**
> Appear like this.

Get in touch

Feedback from our readers is always welcome.

General feedback: If you have questions about any aspect of this book, email us at `customercare@packtpub.com` and mention the book title in the subject of your message.

Errata: Although we have taken every care to ensure the accuracy of our content, mistakes do happen. If you have found a mistake in this book, we would be grateful if you would report this to us. Please visit `www.packtpub.com/support/errata` and fill in the form.

Piracy: If you come across any illegal copies of our works in any form on the internet, we would be grateful if you would provide us with the location address or website name. Please contact us at `copyright@packtpub.com` with a link to the material.

If you are interested in becoming an author: If there is a topic that you have expertise in and you are interested in either writing or contributing to a book, please visit `authors.packtpub.com`.

Share Your Thoughts

Once you've read *Time Series Analysis with Spark*, we'd love to hear your thoughts! Please click here to go straight to the Amazon review page for this book and share your feedback.

Your review is important to us and the tech community and will help us make sure we're delivering excellent quality content.

Free Benefits with Your Book

This book comes with free benefits to support your learning. Activate them now for instant access (see the "*How to Unlock*" section for instructions).

Here's a quick overview of what you can instantly unlock with your purchase:

PDF and ePub Copies

Next-Gen Web-Based Reader

Access a DRM-free PDF copy of this book to read anywhere, on any device.

Use a DRM-free ePub version with your favorite e-reader.

Multi-device progress sync: Pick up where you left off, on any device.

Highlighting and notetaking: Capture ideas and turn reading into lasting knowledge.

Bookmarking: Save and revisit key sections whenever you need them.

Dark mode: Reduce eye strain by switching to dark or sepia themes

How to Unlock

UNLOCK NOW

Scan the QR code (or go to `packtpub.com/unlock`). Search for this book by name, confirm the edition, and then follow the steps on the page.

Note: Keep your invoice handly. Purchase made directly from packt don't require one.

Part 1:
Introduction to Time Series and Apache Spark

In this part, you will be introduced to time series analysis and Apache Spark. Starting with the foundational concepts of time series data, we will dive into the practical significance of time series analysis and use cases across industries with some hands-on examples. You will then get introduced to Apache Spark to understand how it is used, its architecture, and how it works, and conclude by installing it in your own environment.

This part has the following chapters:

- *Chapter 1, What Are Time Series?*
- *Chapter 2, Why Time Series Analysis?*
- *Chapter 3, Introduction to Apache Spark*

1

What Are Time Series?

"Time is the wisest counselor of all." – Pericles

History is fascinating. It offers a profound narrative of our origins, the journey we are on, and the destination we strive toward. History equips us with learnings from the past to better face the future.

Let's take, for example, the impact of meteorological data on history. Disruptions in weather patterns, starting in the Middle Ages and worsened by the Laki volcanic eruption in 1783, caused widespread hardship in France. This climatic upheaval contributed to the social unrest that ultimately led to the French Revolution in 1789. (Find out more about this in the *Further reading* section.)

Time series embody this narrative with numbers echoing our past. **They are history quantified**, a numerical narrative of our collective past, with lessons for the future.

This book takes you on a comprehensive journey with time series, starting with foundational concepts, guiding you through practical data preparation and model building techniques, and culminating in advanced topics such as scaling, and deploying to production, while staying abreast of recent developments for cutting-edge applications across industries. By the end of this book, you will be equipped to build robust time series models, in combination with Apache Spark, to meet the requirements of the use cases in your industry.

As a start on this journey, this chapter introduces the fundamental concepts of time series data, exploring its sequential nature and the unique challenges it poses. The content covers key components such as trend and seasonality, providing a foundation to embark on time series analysis at scale using the Spark framework. This knowledge is crucial for data scientists and analysts as it forms the basis for leveraging Spark's distributed computing capabilities in effectively analyzing and forecasting time-dependent data and making informed decisions in various domains such as finance, healthcare, and marketing.

We will cover the following topics in this chapter:

- Introduction to time series

- Breaking time series into their components

- Additional considerations with time series analysis

Free Benefits with Your Book

Your purchase includes a free PDF copy of this book along with other exclusive benefits. Check the *Free Benefits with Your Book* section in the Preface to unlock them instantly and maximize your learning experience.

Technical requirements

In the first part of the book, which sets the foundations, you can follow along without participating in hands-on examples (although it's recommended). The latter part of the book will be more practice-driven. If you want to get hands-on from the beginning, the code for this chapter can be found in the GitHub repository of this book at:

```
https://github.com/PacktPublishing/Time-Series-Analysis-with-Spark/
tree/main/ch1
```

Note

Refer to this GitHub repository for the latest revisions of the code, which will be commented on if updated post-publication. The updated code (if any) might differ from what is presented in the book's code sections.

The following hands-on sections will give you further details to get started with time series analysis.

Introduction to time series

In this section, we will develop an understanding of what time series are and some related terms. This will be illustrated by hands-on examples to visualize time series. We will look at different types of time series and what characterizes them. This knowledge of the nature of time series is necessary for us to choose the appropriate time series analysis approach in the upcoming chapters.

Let's start with an example of a time series with the average temperature in Mauritius every year since 1950. A short sample of the data is shown in *Table 1.1*.

Year	Average temperature
1950	22.66
1951	22.35
1952	22.50
1953	22.71
1954	22.61
1955	22.40
1956	22.22
1957	22.53
1958	22.71
1959	22.49

Table 1.1: Sample time series data – average temperature

While visualizing and explaining this example, we will be introduced to some terms related to time series. The code to visualize this dataset is covered in the hands-on section of this chapter.

In *the following figure*, we see the change in temperature over the years since 1950. If we focus on the period after 1980, we can observe the variations more closely, with similarly increasing temperatures over the years (trend – shown with a dashed line in both figures) to the current temperature.

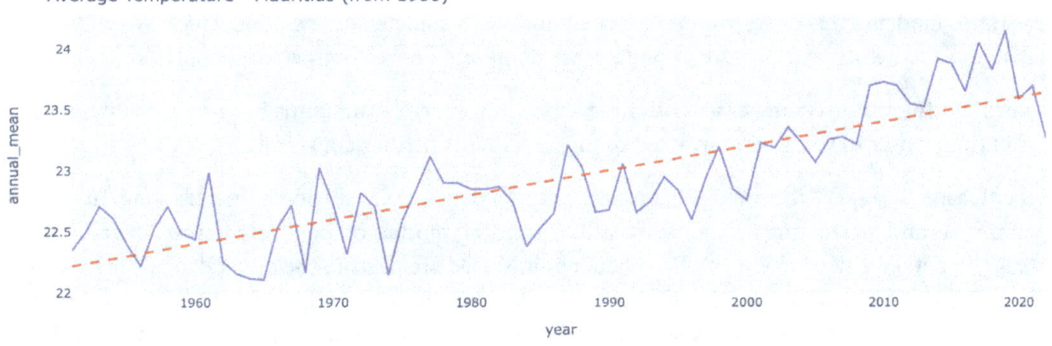

Figure 1.1: Average temperature in Mauritius since 1950

If the temperature continues to increase in the same way, we are heading to a warmer future, a manifestation of what is now widely accepted as global warming. At the same time as the temperature has been increasing over the years, it also goes up every summer and down during the winter months (**seasonality**). We will visualize this and other components of temperature time series in the hands-on section of this chapter.

With the temperatures getting warmer over the years (**trend**), global warming has an impact (**causality**) on our planet and its inhabitants. This impact can also be represented with time series – for example, sea level or rainfall measurements. The consequences of global warming can be dramatic and irreversible, which further highlights the importance of understanding this trend.

These time-over-time readings of temperature form what we call a time series. Analysis and understanding of such a time series is critical for our future.

So, what is a time series in more general terms? It is simply a *chronological series of measurements together with the specific time at which it was generated by a source system*. In the example of temperature, the source system is the thermometer at a specific geographical location.

Time series can also be represented in an aggregated form, such as the average temperature every year, as shown in *Table 1.1*.

From this definition, illustrated with an example, let's now probe further into the nature of time series. We will also cover in further detail in the rest of this book the terms introduced here, such as trend, seasonality, and causality.

Chronological order

At the beginning of the chapter, we mentioned chronological order while defining time series, this is because it is a major factor that differentiates the approach when working with time series data compared to other datasets. One of the main reasons why order matters is due to potential auto-correlation within time series, where measurement at time t is related to measurement at n time steps earlier (**lag**). Ignoring this order will make our analysis incomplete and even incorrect. We will look at the method to identify auto-correlation later, in *Chapter 6* on exploratory data analysis.

It is worth noting that, in many cases with time series, auto-correlation tends to make measurements closer in time closer in value, as compared to measurements further apart in time.

Another reason to respect chronological order is to avoid data leakage during model training. In some of the analysis and forecasting methods, we will be training models on past data to predict value at a future target date. We need to ensure that all data points used are prior to the target date. Data leakage during training, often tricky to spot with time series data, will invalidate the integrity of the approach and create models that perform misleadingly well during development, then not so well when faced with new unseen data.

Terms introduced here, such as auto-correlation, lags, and data leakage, will be further explained in the rest of the book.

Chronological order, discussed here, is one defining characteristic of time series. In the next section, we will highlight regularity or the lack of it, which is another characteristic.

Regular and irregular

Time series can be regular or irregular with regard to the interval of their measurements.

Regular time series have values expected at regular intervals in time, say every minute, hour, month, and so on. This is usually the case for source systems generating a continuous value, which is then measured at a regular interval. This regularity is expected, but not guaranteed, as these time series can have gaps or values at zero, due to missing data points or just the measurement itself being zero. In this case, they will still be considered of a regular nature.

Irregular time series are when measurements are not generated at regular intervals at the source. This is usually the case of events occurring at irregular points in time, for which events some type of value is then measured. These irregular interval values can be resampled to a regular interval with a lower frequency—effectively turning into a regular time series. For example, an irregular event not occurring every minute may have a likelihood of occurring every hour and be considered regular in nature at the hourly rate.

This book will primarily focus on regular time series. After the regularity of time series, another characteristic we will consider in the next section is stationarity.

Stationary and non-stationary

Considering the statistical properties of time series over time, they can be further categorized as stationary or non-stationary.

Stationary time series are those for which statistical properties such as mean and variance do not vary over time.

Non-stationary time series have changing statistical properties. These time series can be converted to stationary by a combination of methods: for example, one or more orders of differencing to stabilize the mean and using the log value to stabilize the variance. This distinction is important as it will determine which analysis method can be used. For instance, if an analysis method is based on the assumption of stationary series, the above conversion can be applied to non-stationary data first. You will learn about the method to identify stationarity in *Chapter 6* on exploratory data analysis.

> **Note**
>
> Converting a non-stationary time series to a stationary one removes the trend and seasonal components, which may not be what we want if we want to analyze these components.

This section was an important one to understand the underlying nature of time series, which is a prerequisite to identifying the right analysis method to use in the later part of this book. *Figure 1.2* summarizes the types of time series and conversation operations that can be used.

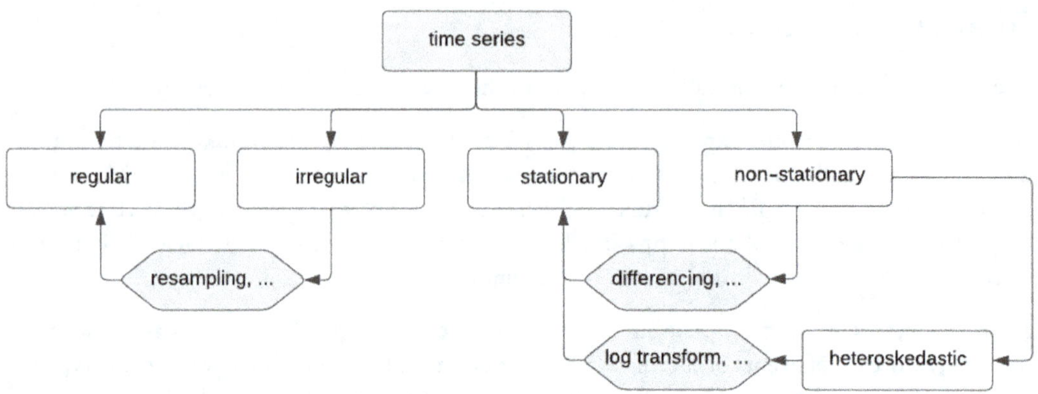

Figure 1.2: Types of time series

This concludes the theoretical part of this chapter. In the next section, we will have our first hands-on experience, setting up the coding environment along the way. We will start with visualizing and decomposing time series in this chapter. We will get into different types of time series analysis and when they are used in the next chapter.

Hands-on: Loading and visualizing time series

Let's go through the hands-on exercise to load a time series dataset and visualize it. We will try to create the visual representation we've already seen in *Figure 1.1*.

Development environment

In order to run the code, you will need a Python development environment where you can install Apache Spark and other required libraries. Specific libraries will be detailed, together with installation instructions, in the corresponding chapters when required.

PaaS

An easy way to get going with these requirements is by using Databricks Community Edition, which is free. This comes with a notebook-based development interface, as well as compute with pre-installed Spark and some other libraries.

The instructions to sign up for Databricks Community Edition can be found here:

```
https://docs.databricks.com/en/getting-started/community-edition.html
```

Community Edition's compute size is limited as it is a free cloud-based PaaS. You can also sign up for a 14-day free trial of Databricks, which, depending on the signup option you choose, may require you to first have an account with a cloud provider. Some cloud providers may have promotions with some free credits at the start. This will give you access to more resources than on Community Edition, for a limited time.

Sign up for the free trial to Databricks at the following URL: `https://www.databricks.com/try-databricks`

The folks at Databricks are the original creators of Apache Spark, so you will be in a good place there.

The examples in the early chapters will use Community Edition and the open source version of Apache Spark. We will use the full Databricks platform in *Chapter 8* and *Chapter 10*.

Custom

Alternatively, you can build your own environment, setting up the full stack, for instance, in a Docker container. This will be covered in *Chapter 3, Introduction to Apache Spark*.

Code

The code for this section is in the following notebook file titled `ts-spark_ch1_1.dbc` in the `ch1` folder of this book's GitHub repository, as per the *Technical requirements* section.

The location URL is as follows: `https://github.com/PacktPublishing/Time-Series-Analysis-with-Spark/raw/main/ch1/ts-spark_ch1_1.dbc`

Dataset

Once the development and runtime environment are chosen, the other consideration is the dataset. The one we will be using is the observed annual average mean surface air temperature of Mauritius, available on the Climate Change Knowledge Portal at `https://climateknowledgeportal.worldbank.org/country/mauritius`.

A copy of the dataset (in the file titled `ts-spark_ch1_ds1.csv`) is available in the `ch1` GitHub folder. It can be downloaded using the code mentioned earlier.

Next, you will be working on the Databricks Community Edition workspace, which will be your own self-contained environment.

Step-by-step: Loading and visualizing time series

Now that we have everything set up, let's get our hands on the first coding exercise. First, log in to Databricks Community Edition to import the code, create a cluster, and finally run the code:

1. Log in to Databricks Community Edition, shown in *Figure 1.3*, using your credentials as specified during the signup process. Access the login page at the following URL: `https://community.cloud.databricks.com/`

Refer to the *Development environment* section on how to sign up if you have not already done so.

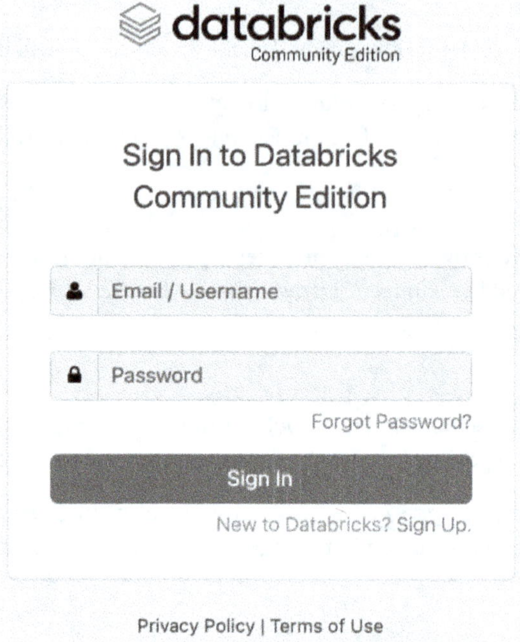

Figure 1.3: Sign in to Databricks Community Edition

2. Once in the workspace, click on **Create a notebook**. See *Figure 1.4*.

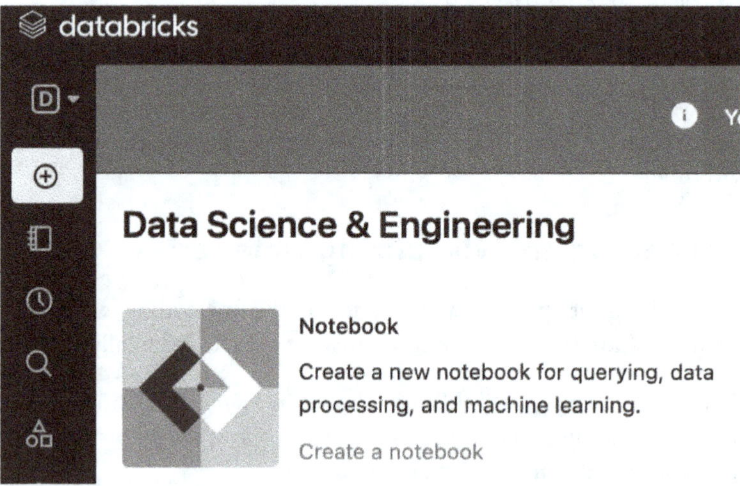

Figure 1.4: Create a notebook

3. From here, we will get into the code, first importing the `ts-spark_ch1_1.dbc` notebook provided for *Chapter 1* on GitHub, as per *Figure 1.5*.

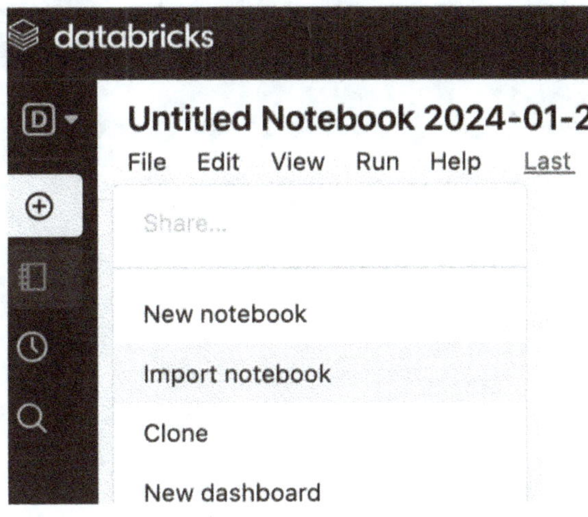

Figure 1.5: Import a notebook

4. Note that you can either download the file from the GitHub URL for *Chapter 1*, provided in the *Technical requirements* section, to your local machines and then import it from there, or you can specify the following raw file URL for the import, as per *Figure 1.6*: `https://github.com/PacktPublishing/Time-Series-Analysis-with-Spark/raw/main/ch1/ts-spark_ch1_1.dbc`

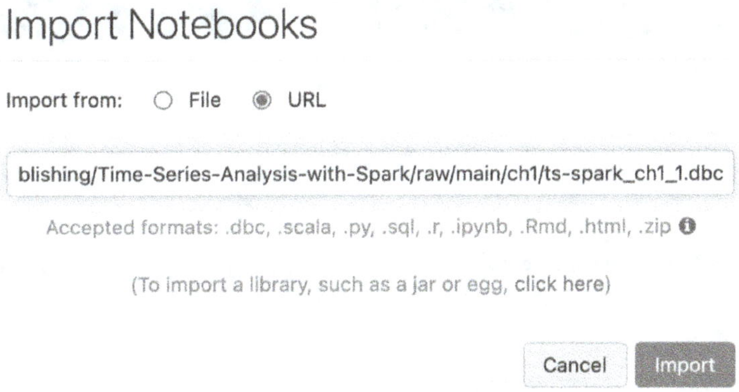

Figure 1.6: Import a notebook from the file or URL

5. We get to the actual code at this point. You should now have a notebook with code as per *Figure 1.7*.

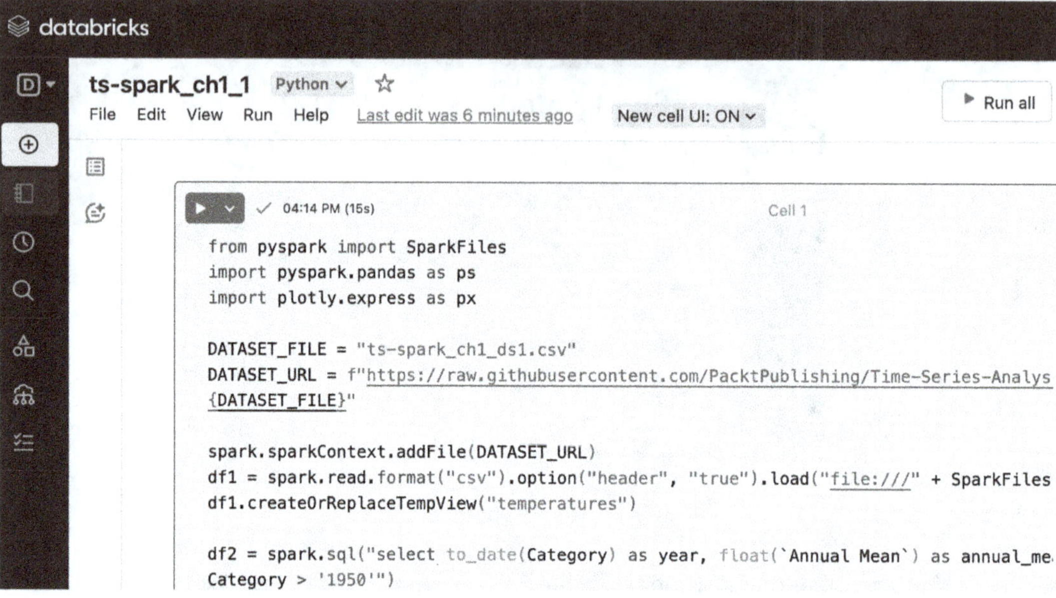

Figure 1.7: Notebook with code

6. Finally, let's run the code. Click on **Run all** as per *Figure 1.8*.

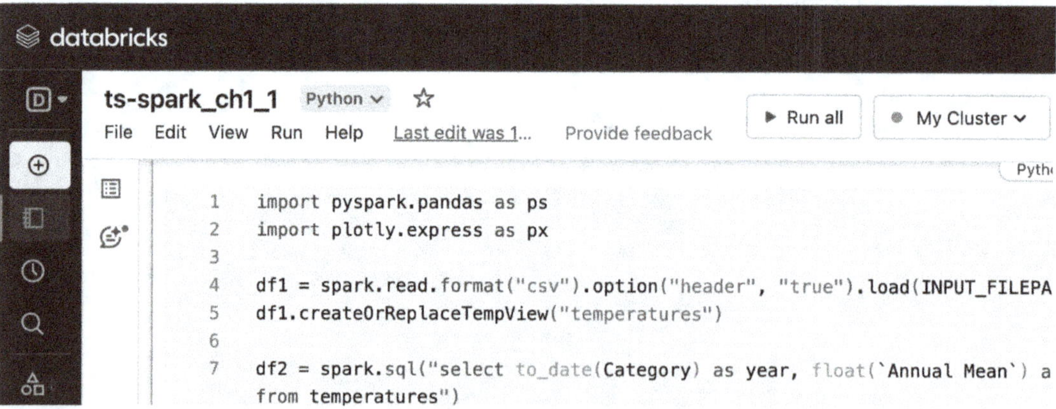

Figure 1.8: Run all code in the notebook

7. In case you do not have a cluster already started, you will have to create and start a new one. Note that clusters are automatically terminated when not in use on Databricks Community Edition, in which case you will see the **Attached cluster is terminated** message, as per *Figure 1.9*, and you will have to select another resource.

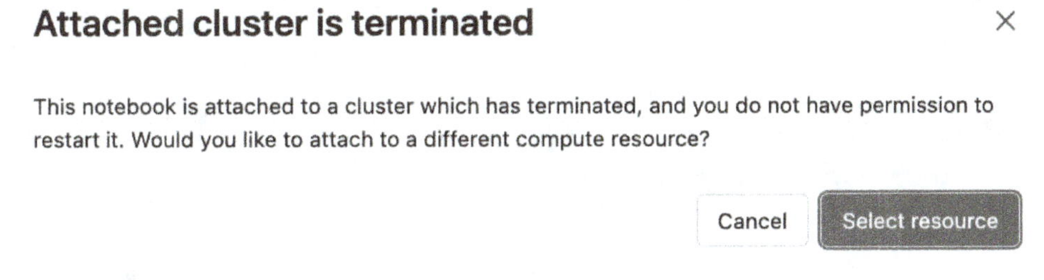

Figure 1.9: Attached cluster is terminated

8. From this point, you can either attach to another active cluster (non-terminated one) or choose to create a new resource as per *Figure 1.10*.

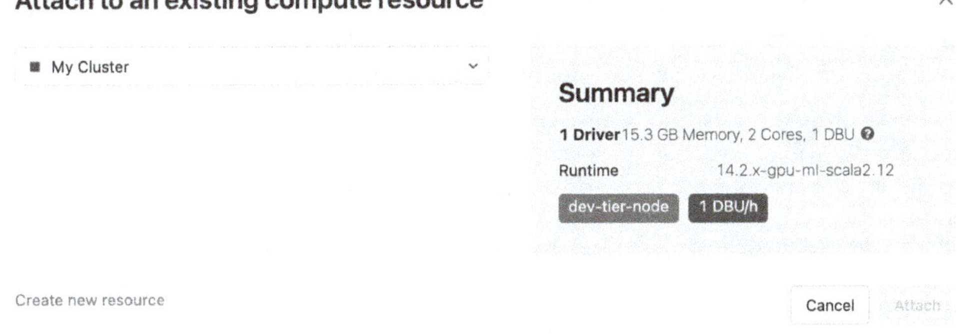

Figure 1.10: Compute – Create new resource

9. Next, you will need to specify a name for the cluster and which version of Spark you want to use, as per *Figure 1.11*. The recommendation here is to use the latest version unless, for portability to another environment reasons, you need the code to work with an earlier version.

Attach to a compute resource   ✕

Your notebook must be attached to a compute resource to execute commands. Create new
compute to run your command.

Name

My Cluster

Runtime

Runtime: 14.2 ML (GPU, Scala 2.12, Spark 3.5.0)   ⌄

Advanced Configuration   Cancel   Create, Attach, & Run

Figure 1.11: Compute – Create, Attach, & Run

10. Once the cluster is created and started, which may take a few minutes in this free environment, the code will run, and you will see the chart in *Figure 1.1*, toward the beginning of the chapter, as output. The graphical library used to create and display the chart provides you with an interactive interface, allowing you – for instance – to zoom into a specific time period.

11. As this is the first hands-on, we have gone into the step-by-step details. In future hands-on sections, we will be focusing on specific datasets and code as the rest will be very similar. Additional instructions will be provided whenever they differ.

Now that we have executed the code, let's go over the main sections. We will keep it high level in this introductory section and go into further details in upcoming chapters once Apache Spark concepts have been introduced:

1. The `import` statements add libraries for date format conversion and for drawing graphs:

```
import pyspark.pandas as ps
import plotly.express as px
```

We are using pandas, which is an open source data manipulation Python library – more specifically, the PySpark version, which is optimized for Spark.

`Plotly`, a graphing library that enables interactive visualization, converts data points into graphs.

2. We then use `spark.read` to read the CSV data file into a table:

```
df1 = spark.read.format("csv") \
    .option("header", "true") \
    .load("file:///" + SparkFiles.get(DATASET_FILE))
df1.createOrReplaceTempView("temperatures")
```

3. The `spark.sql` statement chooses a subset of the dataset based on the year column, named `Category` in the source dataset:

```
df2 = spark.sql("select to_date(Category) as year, float(`Annual
Mean`) as annual_mean from temperatures where Category >
'1950'")
```

4. Finally, we plot the time series as well as the trendline based on **Ordinary Least Squares** (**OLS**) regression, as per *Figure 1.1*:

```
fig = px.scatter(
    df2_pd, x="year", y="annual_mean",
    trendline="ols",
    title='Average Temperature - Mauritius (from 1950)'
)
```

5. The plotting library used, `plotly`, allows interactivity on the user interface, such as mouseover information on the data points and zooming in and out.

From this point on, feel free to experiment with the code and the Databricks Community Edition environment, which we will be using for most of the initial chapters of this book.

In this section, you had your first introduction to time series and the coding environment, starting with a simple exercise. In the next section, we will go into detail about some of the concepts introduced so far and break down a time series into its components.

Breaking a time series down into its components

This section aims to further your understanding of a time series by analyzing its components and detailing several terms introduced so far. This will set you on track for the rest of the book, to use the right methods based on the nature of the time series you are analyzing.

Time series models can be broken down into three main components: trend, seasonality, and residuals:

$$Time\ Series = Trend + Seasonality + Residuals$$

> **Note**
>
> The mathematical representations in this book will follow a simplified English notation, in favour of a broad audience. Refer to the following great resource on time series for mathematical formulations: *Forecasting: Principles and Practice*: `https://otexts.com/fpp3/`.

As you will see in the next hands-on section, this breakdown into components is derived from the model fitted to the time series data. For most real-life datasets, the breakdown is only an approximation of reality by the model. As such, each model will come up with its own identification and approximation of the components. The whole idea is to find the best model that fits the time series. This is what we will be building up to and covering in *Chapter 7* on building and testing models.

Let's go over each of the components, defining what they mean and visualizing them based on an example dataset, as in *Figure 1.12*.

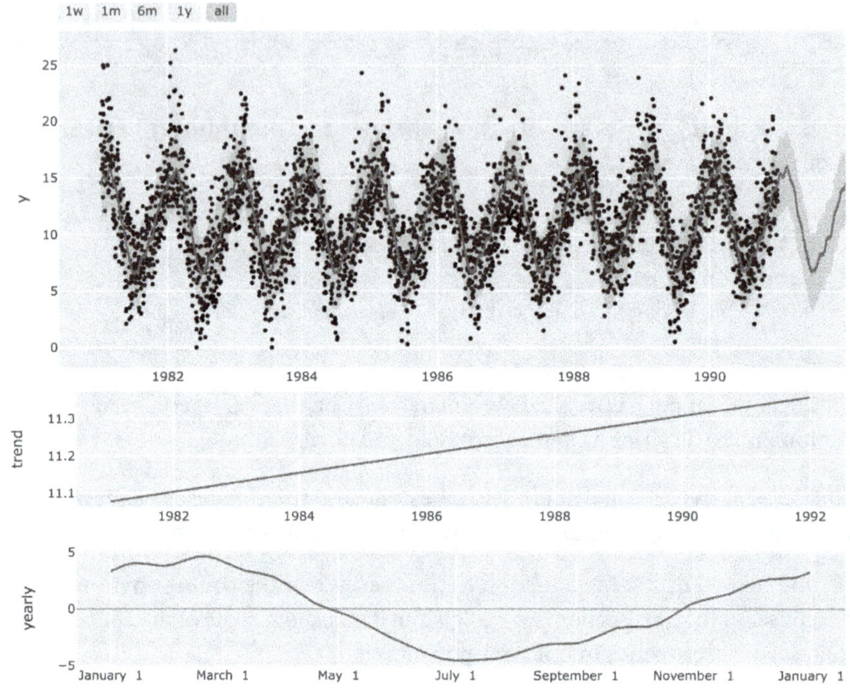

Figure 1.12: Time series decomposition

Systematic and non-systematic components

The level, trend, seasonality, and cycle are called the **systematic** components. They represent the underlying structure of the time series, which can be modeled and hence forecast.

In addition to the systematic components, there is a **non-systematic** part that cannot be modeled, which is called residual, noise, or error. The goal of time series modeling is to find the model with the best match for the systematic components while minimizing the residuals.

We will now go into the details of each of the systematic and non-systematic parts.

Level

Level, also referred to as the base level, is the mean of the series, acting as a baseline on which the effects of the other components are added. Sometimes, it is explicitly added to the preceding formula as an additional component. However, the level is not always shown in the formula, as it may not be the primary focus of the analysis, or the decomposition method may implicitly account for it within other components.

Trend

Trend is the component indicating the general direction in which the values in the time series go over a time period: increasing, decreasing, or flat. This change can be linear, as in *Figure 1.1* and *Figure 1.12*, or non-linear. The trend itself can change at different points in time, as what we can refer to as trend changepoints. More broadly, changepoints refer to points on the timeline when the statistical properties of the time series change. This can have a significant impact on the model parameters or even the model we use to analyze the time series.

Seasonalities and cycles

Seasonality indicates changes to a time series at regular time intervals. This is usually due to seasonal calendar events. Using our example with temperature, every summer month the temperature goes up compared to the rest of the year, and down during the winter months, as can be seen in *Figure 1.12*. Similarly, a time series for sales of gift items will likely show an increase in sales every Christmas period in its seasonality pattern.

Multiple seasonalities (intervals and amplitudes) can have a combined effect within the same time series, as illustrated in *Figure 1.13*. For example, with temperatures, in addition to the ups and downs of summers and winters, the temperature goes up during the day and down every night.

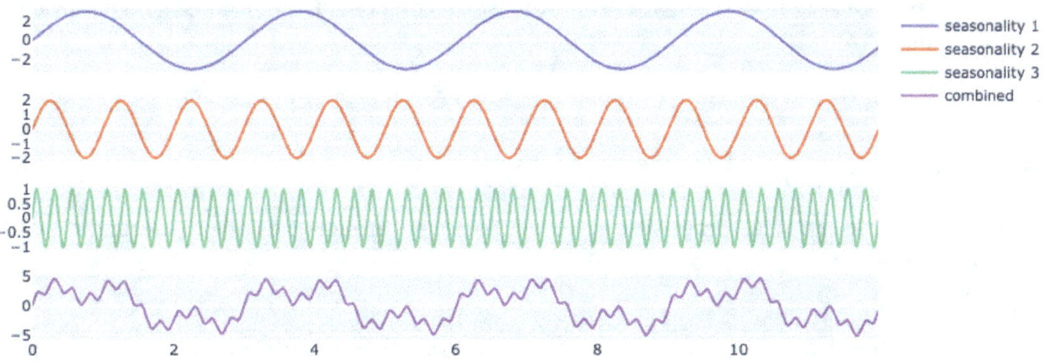

Figure 1.13: Multiple overlapping seasonalities (synthetic data)

Cycles are changes that happen at intervals, similar to seasonality, with the difference of being at irregular intervals. Cycles in time series are reflective of external cycles impacting the series. For example, recessions occur every certain number of years and have an impact on economic indicators. We don't know when in advance and it is different from the seasonality of Christmas, which just occurs predictably every December 25.

Remainders or residuals

Remainders or **residuals** are what remains once the model has accounted for trends, seasonalities, and cycles. Remainders can be modeled using **autoregression** (**AR**) or **moving average** (**MA**) methods. What is still residual at this point, also referred to as noise or error, is random in nature and is the part that can't be modeled. You can visualize residuals in the topmost graph of *Figure 1.12*, as the distance between the data points and the modeled line. We will look at the method to test for residuals in *Chapter 6* on exploratory data analysis.

> **Note**
>
> While with residuals only a component of the time series is random, a whole series can be completely random or can be a random walk. A completely random series will have no dependency on earlier time values, whereas for a random walk, the value at time t is dependent on the value at t-1 (plus some drift and a random component).

Additive or multiplicative

Time series can be **additive** (the preceding formula) or **multiplicative**. In the first case, the seasonality and residual components are not dependent on the trend. In the second case, they change with the trend and can be seen as changing amplitude of the seasonal component – for example, higher peaks and lower troughs.

Now that we have gone through the components of time series, let's put this into practice with code.

Hands-on: Decomposing time series

To demonstrate **time series decomposition**, we will be going through the code to create the data visualization in *Figure 1.12*. The code for this section is in the notebook file titled `ts-spark_ch1_2fp.dbc`.

The location URL is as follows: `https://github.com/PacktPublishing/Time-Series-Analysis-with-Spark/raw/main/ch1/ts-spark_ch1_2fp.dbc`

The dataset we will be using is the daily minimum temperature from 1981 to 1990 in Melbourne, Australia, originally from the Australian Bureau of Meteorology, and available on Kaggle at the following URL: `https://www.kaggle.com/datasets/samfaraday/daily-minimum-temperatures-in-me`

A copy of the dataset is provided in the GitHub folder under the name `ts-spark_ch1_ds2.csv`.

We will keep it high-level in this chapter, with selected extracts from the notebook, and go into further details in upcoming chapters once further concepts of forecasting models have been introduced:

1. The `import` statements add libraries for forecasting models and for drawing graphs:

    ```python
    from prophet import Prophet
    from prophet.plot import plot_plotly, plot_components_plotly
    ```

    The forecasting library used is `Prophet`, which is an open source library by Facebook. It is accessible to both experts and non-experts, providing automatic forecasting for time series data.

2. We then use `spark.read` to read the CSV data file into a table:

    ```python
    df1 = spark.read.format("csv") \
        .option("header", "true") \
        .load("file:///" + SparkFiles.get(DATASET_FILE))
    df1.createOrReplaceTempView("temperatures")
    ```

3. The `spark.sql` statement converts the `date` and `daily_min_temperature` columns into the correct format and column name, which is required by `Prophet`:

    ```python
    df2 = spark.sql("select to_date(date) as ds, float(daily_min_
    temperature) as y from temperatures sort by ds asc")
    ```

4. We then use the `Prophet` library to create a forecasting model on the basis of a seasonality of 12 months and fit it to the data:

    ```python
    model = Prophet(
        n_changepoints=20,
        yearly_seasonality=True,
        changepoint_prior_scale=0.001)
    model.fit(df2_pd)
    ```

5. The model is then used to predict temperatures for future dates:

    ```python
    future_dates = model.make_future_dataframe(
        periods=365, freq='D')
    forecast = model.predict(future_dates)
    ```

6. Finally, we plot the components of the time series as identified by the model, as shown in *Figure 1.12*:

    ```python
    plot_components_plotly(model, forecast)
    ```

Now that we have had a basic discussion on components and forecasting, let's explore the case of overlapping seasonalities.

Multiple overlapping seasonalities

We will be going through the code to create the data visualization in *Figure 1.13*. The code for this section is in the notebook file named `ts-spark_ch1_3.dbc`.

The location URL is as follows: `https://github.com/PacktPublishing/Time-Series-Analysis-with-Spark/raw/main/ch1/ts-spark_ch1_3.dbc`

The dataset is synthetic and generated as three different sine curves representing three overlapping seasonalities.

The following code is an extract from the notebook. Let's look at it at a high level:

1. The `import` statements add libraries for numerical calculations and for drawing graphs:

   ```python
   import numpy as np
   from plotly.subplots import make_subplots
   ```

   NumPy is an open source Python library for scientific computing significantly more efficient in terms of computation and memory use than standard Python. We will use it here for its mathematical functions.

2. We then generate a number of sine curves, using `np.sin`, to represent different seasonalities and add them together:

   ```python
   (amp, freq) = (3, 0.33)
   seasonality1 = amp * np.sin(2 * np.pi * freq * time_period)
   (amp, freq) = (2, 1)
   seasonality2 = amp * np.sin(2 * np.pi * freq * time_period)
   (amp, freq) = (1, 4)
   seasonality3 = amp * np.sin(2 * np.pi * freq * time_period)
   combined = seasonality1 + seasonality2 + seasonality3
   ```

3. Finally, we plot the individual seasonalities as well as the combined one, as per *Figure 1.13*:

   ```python
   fig = make_subplots(rows=4, cols=1, shared_xaxes=True)
   fig.add_scatter(
       x=time_period, y=seasonality1,
       row=1, col=1, name=f"seasonality 1")
   fig.add_scatter(
       x=time_period, y=seasonality2,
       row=2, col=1, name=f"seasonality 2")
   fig.add_scatter(
       x=time_period, y=seasonality3,
       row=3, col=1, name=f"seasonality 3")
   fig.add_scatter(
       x=time_period, y=combined,
       row=4, col=1, name=f"combined")fig.show()
   ```

From here on, feel free to experiment with the full code in the notebooks.

In this section, we started our journey analyzing time series, probing the underlying structure, and paving the way for further analysis with the most appropriate method based on their nature. In the next section, we will cover several key considerations and challenges to factor into our journey.

Additional considerations with time series analysis

This section is probably the most important in this early part of the book. In the introductory section, we mentioned some key considerations for time series, such as the preservation of chronological order, regularity, and stationarity. Here, we map out the key challenges and additional considerations when analyzing time series in real-life projects. In doing so, it allows you to plan your learning and practice accordingly, with guidance in the relevant sections of this book as well as further reading.

According to *Hidden Technical Debt in Machine Learning Systems* a well-known paper published in 2015, only a fraction of the effort is with the code in advanced analytics projects. The rest of the time is mostly spent on other considerations such as data preparation and infrastructure.

The solutions to these challenges are very specific to your context. The aim in this chapter is to bring these considerations, as summarized in *Figure 1.14*, to your awareness.

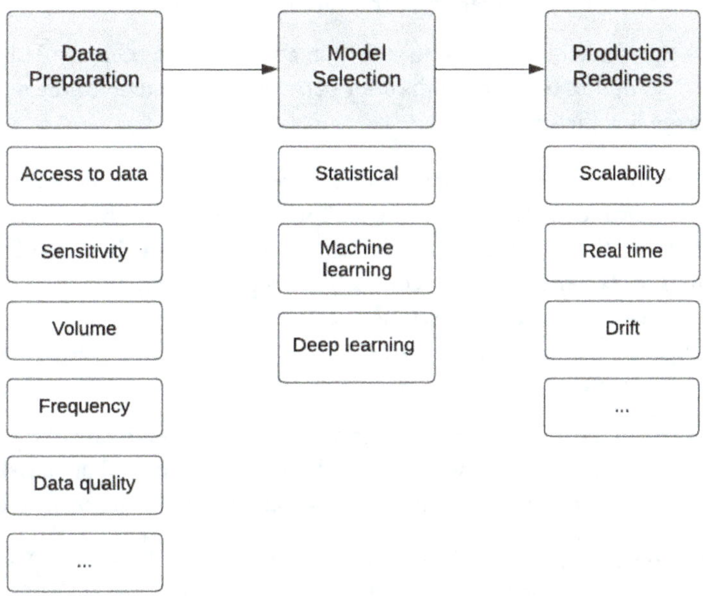

Figure 1.14: Considerations and challenges with time series analysis

While the majority of these considerations are shared in common with non-time-series analytics such as machine learning, time series analysis tends to be the most challenging of advanced analytics methods. We will go into detail on some of the solutions to these challenges in the rest of the book.

Facing data challenges

As with all data science and machine learning projects, data is key. The analysis you run and the model you build are going to be only as good as the data. Data challenges are varied and very dependent on your own specific context and dataset.

We will list some of the common ones here:

- **Access** to data is probably where it all starts. For the purpose of this book, we will be using several freely accessible datasets, so this will not be an issue. In real-life projects, the ownership of the dataset you need may sit in another part of your organization or even with another organization altogether. In this case, you will have to go through the process of acquiring the dataset, potentially at a financial cost, and transferring it reliably, with acceptable speed and freshness. The transfer pipeline will have its own cost to build as well as the transfer cost itself. The transfer mechanism will have to be production grade to support operational requirements: robust, recoverable, monitored, and so on.

  Initially, your data access requirement will be for exploratory data analysis and model training. A batch dump may be sufficient. Moving to production, you may need access to the data in real or near-real time. The considerations then are vastly different.

Once data is ingested, the next requirement is to store it in a secure and usable way. Using a specialized time series database is an option that is optimized for performance, though for the majority of cases, general-purpose storage is sufficient:

- **Sensitivity** is another key aspect. Again, here, there will likely be different requirements in development and production. In many cases, though, a subset of production data is used in development and testing. Certain columns with **Personally Identifiable Information** (**PII**) will require masking or encryption to comply with regulations such as GDPR in Europe. In highly sensitive cases, the whole dataset may be encrypted. This can be a challenge for large-scale processing, as every access to data may require decryption and re-encryption. This will have a processing overhead.

  In summary, end-to-end security and data governance will be high on your requirement list, and this starts from day one. You want to avoid security and compliance risks at all stages, including during development, even more so if you are dealing with sensitive data.

- The **volume** and **frequency** of data feeds at high volume in real or near-real time will require the right platform to enable quick processing without data loss. This may not be initially apparent in a pre-production environment due to the smaller scale. Performance and reliability issues then tend to surface late when ramping up in production. We will discuss scaling and streaming once we have introduced Apache Spark, which will help you avoid such issues.

- **Data quality** is a challenge we will face very early on, as soon as data access is resolved, and we start working with the data during the exploratory phase and in development. Challenges include gaps in data, corrupt data, noisy data, and – even more pertinent for time series – delayed and out-of-order data. As mentioned in the earlier section, it is important to preserve the chronological order for time series data. We will go further into resolving data quality issues when we discuss data preparation.

Moving on from the data challenges, the next area of focus is choosing the right approach and model for the problem that needs solving.

Using the right model

This may be more of a challenge for those new to time series. As we have seen so far, time series have different statistical properties. Some analysis and modeling methods are created based on assumptions about the statistical properties of time series, with stationarity as a common assumption. The method used will not work as intended or lead to misleading results if used with the incorrect type of time series. Handling multiple overlapping seasonalities, assuming you have identified them in the first place, can also be a challenge for some methods. *Figure 1.14* gives a recap of the types of time series and analytical models. The choice of model will be discussed further in *Chapter 7, Building and Testing Models*.

Selecting the right model is also very much dependent on what we want to achieve as an outcome, whether it is forecasting one or many time steps into the future, or analyzing one (univariate) or more (multivariate) series at the same time. For some domains, such as regulated industries, there is usually an additional requirement for explainability, which can be difficult with some models, such as black-box models. We will go further into the outcomes of time series analysis and choosing the right model, including for anomaly and pattern detection, in addition to predictive modeling, in the next chapter on why time series matter.

Maintaining spatial and temporal hierarchy

Note that another key consideration is the hierarchy in which the data is collected and analyzed. This needs to be consistent between different levels. To illustrate this point, let's use an example of time series forecasting of the sales volume of different products by a multi-store retailer. Spatial hierarchies here will likely be at product and product category levels, as well as at specific stores and regional levels. Temporal hierarchies will correspond to sales every hour, every day, every quarter, and so on. The challenge in this case is to ensure the consistency of forecasts for individual products and product categories, as well as, say, daily forecasts adding up and being consistent with the quarterly forecast.

Finally, the right model depends on the volume of data as we will see in our discussion on building models in later chapters.

Tackling scalability

There are primarily two factors impacting scalability: data volume and processing complexity. Earlier, we discussed data volume as a data challenge. Let's consider processing complexity here. **Complexity** can arise from the extent of data transformations required to prepare the data for use, as well as the number, hierarchy, and size of models that need to be managed:

- **Large number and complex hierarchy of models**: As you work on actual projects, it will not be uncommon for you to have to run tens to even thousands of models in parallel within a relatively short time period – say, if you work in a store and need to forecast the next day's sales and stock level for each of the thousands of items sold in the store. This need for parallelism is one of the key reasons for using Apache Spark, as we will see further in this book.

- **Size of the model**: Another requirement for scalability comes from the size of the model itself, which can be very large and have high compute requirements if we are using deep learning techniques with many layers and nodes.

We will dedicate a whole chapter to scaling later in the book.

Approaching real time

Earlier, we identified high-frequency data as a significant data challenge. Approaching real time requires not just data-level adjustments but also a processing pipeline designed to handle such demands. Typically, models are trained on a batch of data collected over time, before being deployed for tasks such as forecasting or anomaly detection, where real-time processing becomes critical. For instance, in detecting fraudulent transactions, it's essential to identify anomalies as close to the event occurrence as possible. A viable solution for near-instant data processing is Apache Spark Structured Streaming, a topic we'll explore when we discuss Apache Spark later in the book.

Managing production

The preceding considerations apply to the production environment as well. In addition, moving the developed solution into a production environment has several specific requirements. These can cause challenges if not managed properly.

Once the right model has been trained and is ready for use, the next step is to package it together with any required API wrapper, as well as the data pipeline and model-consuming application code. This means an end-to-end process involving DataOps, ModelOps, and DevOps. We will go into more on these in *Chapter 9* when we discuss production.

Monitoring and addressing drift

Once a model is in use, changes happen over time, resulting in the model not being fit for purpose anymore. These changes are broadly categorized as follows:

- Changes in the nature of the dataset (**data drift**)

- Changes in the relationship between input and output (**concept drift**)

- Unexpected events such as COVID, or impactful events missed out during the modeling process (**sudden drift**, a type of concept drift)

These drifts will impact the model's performance and, as such, need to be monitored. The solution in this case is usually to retrain the model on the new data or find a new model with better performance on the updated dataset.

This section gave an overview of the considerations and challenges when working with time series. There are lots of commonalities with working on other datasets, so the guidance here will be useful in a broader context. As we saw in the introductory section, though, time series have their own set of specific considerations.

Summary

Time series are everywhere, and this chapter gave us an introduction to what they are, their components, and the challenges in working with them. We started with some simple code to explore time series, setting the foundation for further practice in upcoming chapters. The concepts discussed in this first chapter will be built upon to get us to the point of analyzing time series at scale by the end of this book.

Now that you understand the "what" for time series, in the next chapter, we will be looking at the "why," which will pave the way to applications in various domains.

Further reading

This section serves as a repository of sources that can help you build on your understanding of the topic:

- *Climate Chaos Helped Spark the French Revolution*: `https://time.com/6107671/french-revolution-history-climate/`

- Databricks Community Edition: `https://docs.databricks.com/en/getting-started/community-edition.html`

- Climate Change Knowledge Portal: `https://climateknowledgeportal.worldbank.org/country/mauritius`

- *Forecasting: Principles and Practice* by Rob J Hyndman and George Athanasopoulos: `https://otexts.com/fpp3/`

- *Hidden Technical Debt in Machine Learning Systems* (Sculley et al., 2015): `https://papers.neurips.cc/paper/5656-hidden-technical-debt-in-machine-learning-systems.pdf`

Get This Book's PDF Version and Exclusive Extras

Scan the QR code (or go to `packtpub.com/unlock`). Search for this book by name, confirm the edition, and then follow the steps on the page.

Note: Keep your invoice handly. Purchase made directly from packt don't require one.

Why Time Series Analysis?

This chapter delves into the practical significance of analyzing time-dependent data. It elucidates how time series analysis enables predictive modeling, trend identification, and anomaly detection. By illustrating real-world applications across industries, the chapter emphasizes the critical role of temporal insights in decision-making. Grasping the importance of time series analysis is crucial for professionals, as it highlights the impact on forecasting accuracy, resource optimization, and strategic planning, fostering a comprehensive appreciation for the utility of time-oriented data analysis.

We will cover the following topics in this chapter:

- The need for time series analysis

- Industry-specific use cases

- Hands-on with selected use cases

Technical requirements

Following the first chapter, we will go one notch up with the code here. The objective will be to showcase the use of time series for selected use cases. The code for this chapter can be found in the `ch2` folder of the GitHub repository of this book: `https://github.com/PacktPublishing/Time-Series-Analysis-with-Spark/tree/main/ch2`.

Refer to this GitHub repository for the latest revisions of the code, which will be commented on if updated post-publication from what is presented in the code sections of this book.

The hands-on section of this chapter will go into further detail.

Understanding the need for time series analysis

As we discussed in the previous chapter, time series are present in all avenues of life and across all industries. Hence, the need for analyzing time series is everywhere. We will explore the different use cases for different industries in this chapter. Before we get to that, in this section, we will look at the underlying approaches. These can be broadly categorized as forecasting, pattern detection and categorization, and anomaly detection. *Figure 2.1* shows several key time series analysis concepts that will be discussed in this chapter.

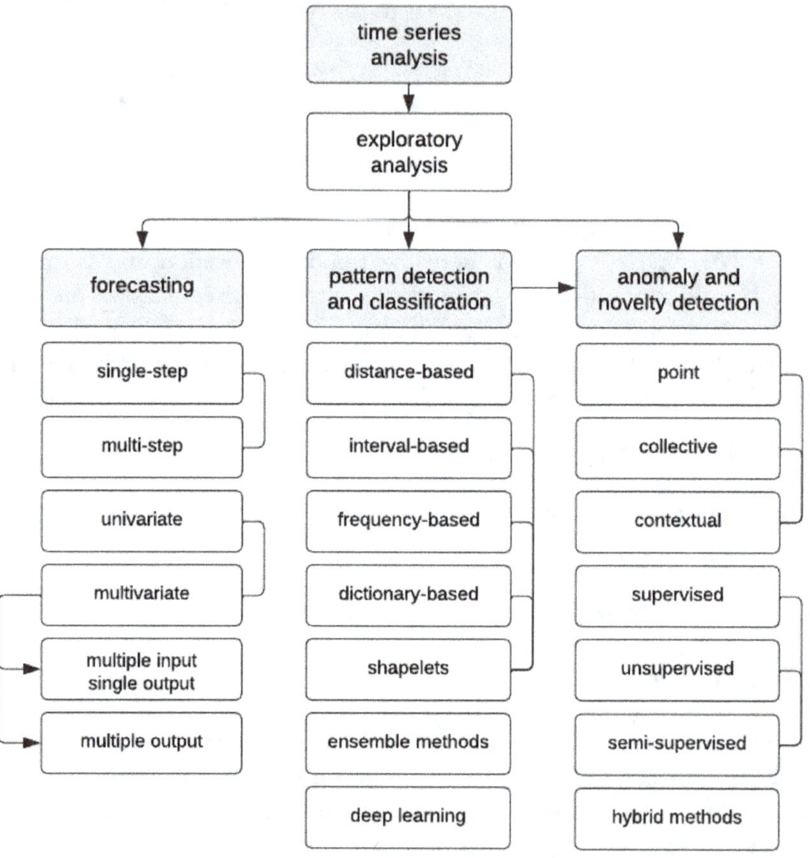

Figure 2.1: Concepts in time series analysis

Let's now go into further detail on each of these.

Forecasting

Forecasting time series is the prediction of future values based on previously observed values. This is achieved by modeling the underlying patterns in the time series data – such as trends, seasonality, and cycles – to make predictions about future data points. For example, in the case of the temperature time series we visualized in *Chapter 1*, we can use forecasting models to predict next month's temperatures based on the pattern learned from previous months. Forecasting is the most common approach used for time series analysis, and we will spend the most time on it in this book. This can be single-step, multi-step, univariate, or multivariate.

Single-step forecasting

With single-step forecasting, we predict the next occurrence in the time series based on our analysis of the historical data points, and the model built accordingly. The granularity of the step is usually the same as in the dataset from which we are learning the historical patterns. For example, if in our historical time series, we have daily temperatures, then the next step will be the next day. If we have aggregated the data points to, for example, monthly averages, and modeled the pattern of monthly changes, then the next step will be the average temperature for the next month.

While single-step forecasting is usually the most reliable forecast we can get, it is, unfortunately, insufficient for many requirements because, in real life, we plan way more ahead than just one (time) step at a time. If we are doing daily forecasts, we want to forecast not just for tomorrow. We want to predict days, weeks, and even months into the future. A single step is just not sufficient for planning.

Multi-step forecasting

With muti-step forecasting, we predict multiple next steps in the time series using the model built from the historical data points. We also use the forecasted prior steps as input. With our daily temperature example, this could mean forecasting day by day for the entire upcoming week.

Challenges

The challenge with multi-step forecasting is that further predictions are built upon prior predictions, which contrasts with single-step forecasting, where predictions are based on actual data points. Practically, this means recursively applying the forecasting algorithm one step at a time, each step adding the forecast to the dataset, and using the historical and forecasted data points to predict the next step. Hence, inaccuracies in the forecast are cumulated further and further as we go each step into the future.

> **Note**
>
> This cumulation of forecasting errors with multi-step forecasting is the kind of limitation you want to be upfront about with the business or anyone you are building the forecast for. You want to be sure to set the expectations on longer-term forecasting.

Solutions

There are a few ways to address the multi-step forecast challenge, besides limiting it to a very short horizon:

- First and foremost, build as accurate a model as possible so that the initial step forecasted is close to reality

- Another approach is to use a combination of models, aiming to average out the forecasting errors

- Finally, limit the forecasting interval or number of steps and recalculate the forecast when new measurements come in

Univariate forecasting

So far, with the temperature time series in *Chapter 1*, we have considered only one variable (univariate) at a time, that is, the temperature at a specific location. Another example of a univariate time series, this time in the economic sector, is the rate of unemployment for a specific region or country. A single time series is univariate by definition, be it for temperature or unemployment rate. In real-world scenarios, the requirement is likely going to be to forecast multiple time series at the same time so that we can get a more comprehensive view of the future than just one time series can give us. In the case of temperature, this can mean taking multiple locations into account or additionally forecasting the level of pollutants in the air. For economic forecasting, it can be about forecasting the **Gross Domestic Product (GDP)** in addition to the level of unemployment. This leads us to multivariate forecasting.

Multivariate forecasting

While univariate is about a single time series, there are a couple of ways to characterize multivariate forecasting:

- **Multiple input** dimensions are the case when we provide several variables (time series and non time series) as input to the forecasting model – for example, using past temperatures and pollutant levels to predict future temperatures.

- **Multiple output** prediction uses the forecasting model to predict multiple variables. With the preceding temperature example, this means forecasting both the temperature and the pollutant level.

As we have seen with the preceding examples, there can be several scenarios with multiple time series. These series can be **correlated**, and if they have the same underlying cause (which can itself be represented by yet another time series), can have **co-movement**. They can have **causal dependency**, where one time series has a causality relationship to another. They can also be **independent**, and we just predict them simultaneously. We will address some of these considerations in *Chapter 6* on exploratory data analysis.

In summary, forecasting is rarely done in isolation, and the number of time series that we need to analyze at the same time can be in the hundreds or even thousands. This need to scale to multiple time series is a good reason to use a parallel execution tool such as Apache Spark, as we will see in later chapters.

Now that we have discussed forecasting, let's see another type of analysis, which will enable us to classify time series.

Pattern detection and categorization

Pattern detection and categorization is about identifying and classifying time series based on certain patterns. In general, time series follow a certain pattern, which we can identify and label. These labels allow us to classify time series by matching the labeled pattern to new occurrences of time series. We can follow different approaches to achieve this, broadly categorized as distance-based, interval-based, frequency-based, dictionary-based, shapelets, ensembles, and deep learning. These approaches will now be detailed.

Distance-based

Distance-based time series classification using **k-Nearest Neighbors** (**kNN**) and **Dynamic Time Warping** (**DTW**), which will be explained here, is a proven method for analyzing time-sequential data. Due to shifts and distortions in time series data, standard Euclidean distance is a poor metric for similarity measurement. DTW offers an alternative by aligning the sequences in time. It calculates the minimum distance between two time series, considering all possible alignments, which makes it compute-intensive. kNN is then used to classify the time series based on the similarity of their shapes.

The following chart shows the outcome of DTW to calculate the distance between the shares of Google (lower, black) and Amazon, and the shares of Google and Meta. We will execute this example in the hands-on section of this chapter.

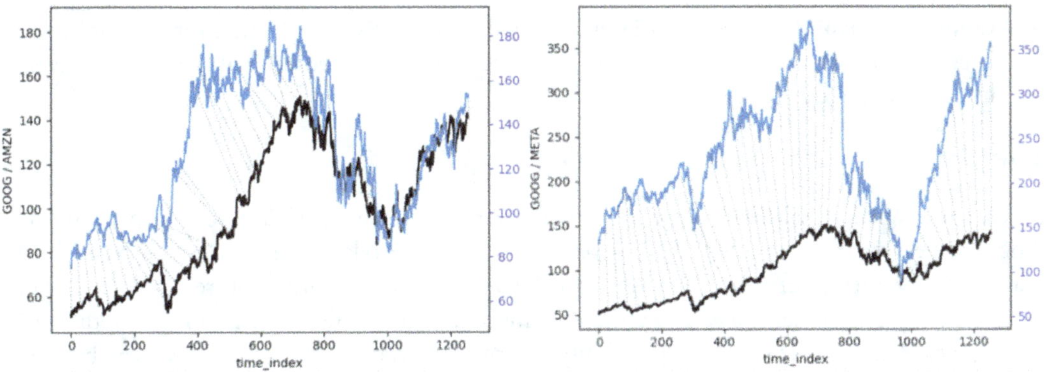

Figure 2.2: DTW distance (GOOG – black line)

Interval-based

With this approach, the time series is first partitioned into intervals, for which descriptive statistics are calculated. These intervals are then used as feature vectors together with classifiers such as random forests or support vector machines. The advantage of this method is that it captures the properties of time series over different phases, which works well for time series with non-uniform patterns over time. This summarization of the time series into intervals with statistical features is also a great way to reduce complexity and improve interpretability.

Frequency-based

This classification method, such as **Random Interval Spectral Ensemble** (**RISE**), involves first transforming the time series to the frequency domain, using, for example, the Fourier transform. RISE is an ensemble approach based on classifiers, such as decision trees, built from random intervals and spectral features extracted for these intervals. The advantage of this method is in identifying frequency-related or periodic characteristics, and as an ensemble approach, it is robust while providing accuracy.

Dictionary-based

Dictionary-based time series classification methods convert time series into symbolic representations, allowing the use of text-based techniques for classification. Prominent methods following this approach are these:

- **Bag of Patterns** (**BoP**): BoP creates a "bag" of patterns by applying a sliding window to capture local patterns. This is then hashed into a frequency histogram, which is used as the feature vector for classification.

- **Bag of SFA Symbols** (**BOSS**): BOSS is a variation that is more robust to noise and effective at capturing key patterns. It uses **Symbolic Fourier Approximation** (**SFA**) to capture the time series at different resolutions.

- **RandOm Convolutional KErnel Transform** (**ROCKET**): ROCKET offers further speed and efficiency for large datasets. It generates and uses random convolutional kernels to convert time series into feature vectors.

Shapelets

These are sub-sequences within the time series, which are representative of class-specific patterns. By finding shapelets that match within the time series or another correlated time series, it is possible to classify the time series accordingly. This works well when the class-defining features are localized in time – for example, a sudden spike in transaction amount, which could correspond to a credit card theft. Shapelets can also help with interpretability—once it is well understood, a shapelet can be used to explain the time series at the points in time where they match.

Ensembles

The ensemble classification methods mentioned so far group a similar type of classifier. Another approach, such as the **Hierarchical Vote Collective of Transformation-based Ensembles (HIVE-COTE)**, is with different types of classifiers. The idea is to have an ensemble based on different aspects of the time series as captured by the different nature of classifiers used. These are trained independently, and the predictions are combined based on a hierarchical voting method. As with other ensemble methods, this can yield greater robustness and accuracy. Also, due to the various techniques used, HIVE-COTE is a good candidate for complex multi-pattern time series. This does, however, come with a high compute cost.

Deep learning

Methods such as **TimeNet** leverage deep neural networks to automatically extract features, patterns, and relationships within time series. TimeNet is pre-trained, which makes it quickly usable. It combines layers of **Convolutional Neural Networks (CNNs)** for local features and **Recurrent Neural Networks (RNNs)** for sequential patterns. This allows TimeNet to capture both low-level and high-level patterns, effectively learning the hierarchical representation. The benefit is adaptability to various time series classification problems while limiting the need for manual feature engineering. The cons, similar to other deep learning approaches, are the high volume of data needed for pre-training, the computing resources required, and the lack of interpretability. Despite these, they are state-of-the-art in performance in several complex cases.

While we will not spend as much time on the classification of time series in this book as on forecasting, this is a promising area for further research, together with its own set of operational challenges.

This brings us to the final type of analysis, which is about detecting anomalies from time series data.

Anomaly detection

The third category of use cases for time series analysis is anomaly detection, which is about flagging unexpected patterns or occurrences. While this is related to pattern detection and forecasting, the purpose here is different: to identify an unexpected deviation in the behavior of the source system. Anomaly detection is crucial in various domains, such as finance, healthcare, and industrial systems. These anomalies can be indicative of critical incidents, such as system failures, financial fraud, or network intrusions.

In addition to being uni- or multivariate, an anomaly can be as follows:

- **Point**: This is the case when a single data point is identified as an anomaly

- **Collective**: It can be that multiple data points as a group of near measurements are all flagged

- **Contextual**: A data point or a collective can be anomalous in the context of surrounding measurements, and the same point or collective may not be an issue in another context

Anomalies can also be distinguished as outliers and novelties, where outliers may indicate errors or faults, and novelties are previously unseen patterns that may not be problematic.

> **Note**
>
> For anomaly detection to work, the prior data preparation stage must keep the outliers in the dataset, which is the opposite of what is usually done during the data curation process.

In addition to traditional statistical and rule-based approaches, there are newer machine learning techniques. The methods for anomaly detection in time series data can be categorized into unsupervised, supervised, and semi-supervised approaches, each with its own set of techniques and algorithms. An anomaly score is usually calculated with a threshold configured to flag anomalies.

Unsupervised anomaly detection

Unsupervised anomaly detection does not need labeled data. This assumes that anomalies are different enough from the normal that they can be detected without prior knowledge. Common methods include the following:

- **Statistical** methods such as **z-score** and **box plot analysis** are used to identify outliers based on statistical properties

- **Clustering-based** methods such as **DBSCAN** or **k-means** cluster similar data points, with anomalies as points that do not fit into any cluster

- **Density-based** methods such as kNN and **Local Outlier Factor** (**LOF**) use the density of the local neighborhood to identify anomalies

- **Isolation forest** is a tree-based model that works well for high-dimensional data, isolating anomalies

The chart in *Figure 2.3* shows the outcome of an isolation forest model, used to detect anomalies in a household's energy consumption.

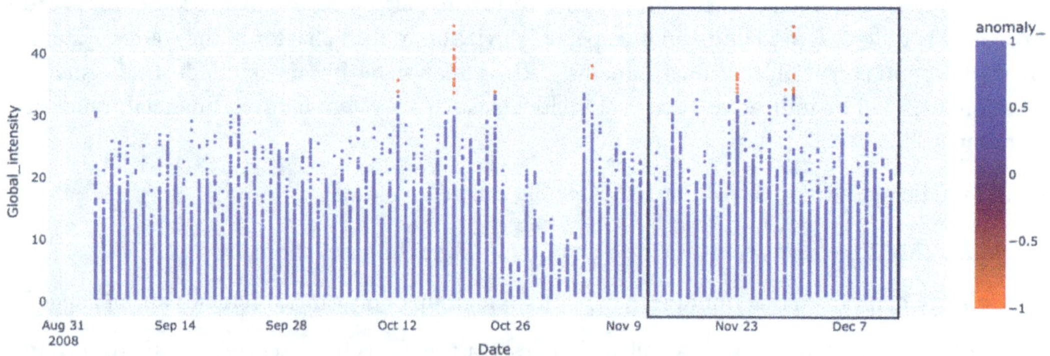

Figure 2.3: Anomaly detection on energy consumption

The model was fitted to consumption data up to November 9 and thereafter used on previously unseen data in the box. The anomalies are shown in red/paler color. We will run this example in the hands-on section of this chapter.

Supervised anomaly detection

Supervised anomaly detection works with a labeled dataset having both normal and anomalous cases. Better at detecting anomalies, it does, however, require labeled data, which can be difficult to obtain. Techniques include the following:

- **Classification models** such as traditional classifiers such as logistic regression, **Support Vector Machines (SVMs)**, or more complex models such as CNNs and RNNs, trained to distinguish between normal and anomalous instances

- **Ensemble methods** such as random forest or gradient boosting can be used with improved detection accuracy as they combine multiple models

Semi-supervised anomaly detection

Semi-supervised anomaly detection needs a smaller amount of labeled data together with a larger set of unlabeled data. An example is the case of industrial monitoring when we have limited data points from sensor readings. These measurements correspond mostly to normal operations of the equipment and can be labeled as such. New readings falling out of the normal label can then be flagged as anomalous.

Also useful when labeling a large dataset is expensive, semi-supervised techniques include the following:

- Modifying unsupervised techniques to include the limited available labels – for example, modifying density-based or clustering methods for added sensitivity to labeled anomalies.

- **Novelty detection** trains a model on the normal data to find its distribution, akin to unsupervised statistical approaches, and then deviation from this distribution is flagged. One-class SVMs and autoencoders are examples of techniques in this case.

Advanced deep learning methods

Methods using deep learning techniques include the following:

- **Autoencoders** are neural networks that compress and then reconstruct the input data. The idea is that these models will reconstruct normal data well and have higher reconstruction errors with anomalous data.

- Sequence types of models such as **Long Short-Term Memory (LSTM)**, **RNNs**, and **Transformers** identify temporal dependencies in time series data, hence are useful for anomaly detection in sequences.

> **Note**
>
> From an operational point of view, an anomaly detection system is part of a comprehensive monitoring and alerting architecture. Note that Kalman filters are used in cases where low-latency or real-time detection and alerting are required.

This summarizes the various methods for anomaly detection. The choice of method for anomaly detection depends on the characteristics of the time series and anomalies that need to be detected, the availability of labeled data, the computational resources available, and the requirement for real-time detection. Hybrid and advanced methods, especially those based on deep learning, have shown promising results in various applications due to their ability to model complex patterns and dependencies in time series data.

Moving on from an overview of the landscape of time series analysis, let's now consider how they are used and their impact in various sectors.

Industry-specific use cases

We looked at different types of time series analysis in the previous section. The question remains on their applicability across different sectors, which we will now dive into. But before we do that, the chart in *Figure 2.4* gives you a sense of the multitude of applications across industries.

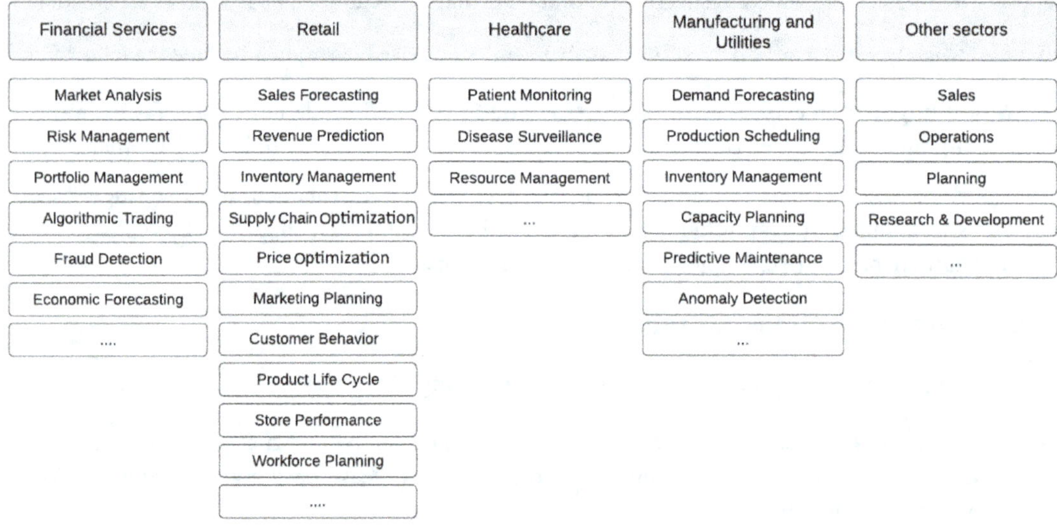

Figure 2.4: Application of time series analysis across industries

Let's look at the application of time series analysis in each of these sectors in detail.

Financial services

Time series analysis in financial services is crucial for understanding trends, patterns, and future behaviors. The applications are diverse, offering valuable insights for decision-making, strategic planning, risk management, and regulatory compliance. The following is how time series analysis is used across various functions within financial services:

- **Market analysis**: The future prices of assets are forecast by analyzing their historical prices, including trends and seasonality. This helps traders and investors decide on which asset to trade and when.

- **Risk management**: In addition to the preceding, another important aspect of financial instruments' prices is their volatility, which needs to be analyzed to better manage risks and design mitigation strategies. This includes **Value at Risk (VaR)** modeling, which estimates the potential loss for an investment over a period based on historical volatility and correlations. Another area of risk management is credit risk, which covers time series data on repayment histories, defaults, and economic conditions. This helps assess the likelihood of future defaults and losses. The counter to this, estimation for provisioning, ensures enough funds are set aside to cover potential loan losses, while liquidity management ensures sufficient liquidity is maintained. Finally, at the macro-economic level, stress testing involves analyzing historical worst-case scenarios.

- **Portfolio management**: The two main aspects here are optimizing asset allocation and related performance evaluation of the portfolio. By analyzing the historical returns and correlations between assets, portfolio managers can define the asset allocation to meet the desired risk-return profiles. Looking back at their performance over time, the portfolio can then be adjusted as needed.

- **Algorithmic trading**: At its core, this involves using time series data on a microseconds or milliseconds scale to make high-frequency trading decisions. The complete cycle includes developing strategies, doing backtesting, and then, once strategies are in active use, generating the correct signals for trading.

- **Fraud detection**: The idea here is to analyze transactions to identify and flag patterns that could indicate fraudulent activities, including market manipulation or insider trading.

- **Economic forecasting**: This is used to project, for example, interest rates and other economic indicators with an impact on policymaking by central banks, governments, and financial institutions.

In essence, time series analysis in financial services is foundational to support a wide range of activities, from trading decisions to portfolio management and regulatory compliance. It leverages historical data to forecast future events, manage risks, and uncover valuable insights. Thus, time series analysis drives informed decision-making across the financial ecosystem.

Retail

Time series analysis in the retail industry uses chronological data for decision-making, to optimize operations, and to enhance customer experiences. Retailers can gain insights into trends, seasonal variations, and cyclical behaviors that affect their business. The following are some of the key use cases:

- **Sales forecasting and revenue prediction**: Predicting future sales based on historical data, considering seasonal variations, trends, and external factors such as holidays and economic conditions, helps plan inventory, staffing, and marketing activities. This is crucial for financial planning and investment decisions.

- **Inventory management and supply chain optimization**: Retailers can optimize stock levels by analyzing purchasing patterns and lead times. Better demand planning and scheduling of replenishment minimizes stockouts and reduces excess inventory. Forecasting can be done at each product level, facilitating efficient inventory replenishment. This has also a positive impact on supply chain management. A related use case in retail that is growing in adoption is food waste prediction and reduction.

- **Price optimization and marketing planning**: Optimal pricing strategies over time, maximizing sales and profits, can be determined by analyzing the impact of price changes on sales volumes. This includes insight into seasonal price sensitivities, impacts of promotions and marketing campaigns, and competitive pricing. This also optimizes marketing spend, while better aligning to seasonal patterns.

- **Customer behavior analysis and product life cycle management**: Retailers can inform marketing strategies and product development by understanding changes in customer buying habits over time. This analysis helps identify trends, such as changes in purchasing channels or increasing interest in product categories. This, in turn, improves decisions about product introductions, discontinuation, or relaunches. With better customer behavior analysis, it is also possible to develop effective loyalty projects, resulting in improved customer retention.

- **Store performance analysis and workforce planning**: By comparing the sales trends across different locations, this analysis identifies high-performing stores and those needing help. This informs decisions about store expansions or closures and aligns staffing levels to the right store and busy times. The impact here is both on operational efficiency and improved customer service.

The use of time series analysis in retail influences every aspect of the business, from inventory and pricing to marketing and workforce management. By leveraging historical data, retailers can make informed decisions that enhance operational efficiency, customer satisfaction, and profitability.

Healthcare

Time series analysis in healthcare is an essential tool for tracking health-related data over chronological intervals. This method allows for the observation of patterns, trends, and changes in health metrics, which can be critical in improving patient care, operational efficiency, and clinical outcomes. Here's an overview of applications in healthcare:

- **Patient monitoring**: In the continuous monitoring of vital signs (heart rate, blood pressure, etc.), time series analysis can be used for real-time assessment of patient health and early detection of acute medical events. Similarly, by analyzing data from wearable devices, one can monitor trends in physical activity, sleep patterns, and other health indicators over time. This can be either in a clinical setting or for personal health awareness.

- **Epidemiology and disease surveillance**: The significance of this requirement was highlighted by COVID-19. The spread of infectious diseases must be tracked over time to understand transmission patterns, identify outbreaks, and plan public interventions accordingly. At the individual level, patients with a chronic disease may need to adjust their treatment plans based on the progression of the disease. Though similar, this is different from monitoring vitals in terms of the timescale of interventions.

- **Management of hospital resources**: With most public hospitals stretched thin, it is a huge benefit to be able to predict hospital admission rates in order to optimize bed allocation and staffing.

There are numerous other applications of time series analysis in healthcare, such as healthcare quality monitoring, drug development, and medical research, and with the COVID-19 pandemic, public health monitoring, analysis, and policy-making.

By using time series analysis, the healthcare sector can enhance patient care, improve operational efficiencies, and contribute to medical research, ultimately leading to better health outcomes and more informed healthcare policies.

Manufacturing and utilities

Time series analysis is important in the manufacturing and utilities sectors for ensuring safety, optimizing operations, and improving efficiency. Here's an overview of its use cases in these industries:

- **Manufacturing**: First, in terms of planning, with demand forecasting, scheduling production, and inventory management, time series help meet market demand without overproduction. Then, to keep production going, machine sensors send data to predictive maintenance models to generate warnings of potential failures, resulting in prompt maintenance. This can significantly reduce downtime while saving on unnecessary preventive maintenance. Anomaly detection further helps with early detection and limitation of quality issues.

- **Oil and gas**: As in manufacturing, predictive maintenance and anomaly detection ensure reduced downtime, while maximizing output. Also, with the significant upfront investment required in infrastructure in this sector, it is crucial to have good forecasting of demand and prices to guide planning.

- **Utilities**: The primary use cases in the utilities sector are demand and load forecasting, which result in planning, grid management, and development. This further leads to optimal grid utilization, with improved customer service, while preventing outages. Finally, time series analysis and forecasting of new renewal energy sources ensures they can be optimally integrated into the overall energy mix.

In all these sectors, time series analysis contributes to resource optimization, cost reduction, and strategic planning, ultimately leading to more resilient and efficient operations.

> **Note**
>
> A predominant and fast-growing source of time series data is **Internet of Things (IoT)** devices and sensors. This is due to the explosion in the number of connected devices. This data is collected, stored, and analyzed – usually in real time – with use cases across industries, some of which have been discussed, from machine sensor data used for predictive maintenance to energy meter data to forecast consumption to health trackers, and many more.

This concludes the section on industry-specific use cases, on the many applications of time series analysis to different sectors of activity. The list is ever-expanding with frequent innovation on new use cases, driven by new analysis methods and new business requirements. Next, we will see some of the time series analysis methods in action with industry-specific datasets.

Hands-on with selected use cases

In this hands-on section, we will go through some selected use cases with industry-specific datasets.

Forecasting

For the forecasting use case, we started with an example on temperatures in *Chapter 1*, where we loaded the dataset, analyzed its components, and visualized the result. The focus was on the past – that is, historical data. In the following steps, we will highlight the specific part of the code related to the future – that is, forecasting. This is based on the code in `ts-spark_ch1_2fp`, which we imported into Databricks Community Edition in *Chapter 1*.

The forecasting steps are as follows:

1. Load the dataset, which was covered in *Chapter 1*.

2. Using the `Prophet` library, the model is created and trained (fit) on the data:

```
model = Prophet(
    n_changepoints=20,
    yearly_seasonality=True,
    changepoint_prior_scale=0.001)
model.fit(df2_pd)
```

3. We then use a very handy function in Prophet to generate future dates, `make_future_dataframe`. These will be required as input, and passed as parameters, to do the prediction part, which is with the `predict` function:

```
future_dates = model.make_future_dataframe(
    periods=365, freq='D')
forecast = model.predict(future_dates)
```

4. The call to `plot_plotly` generates *Figure 2.5*. The right-most part of the graph does not have any collected data points as it is for the forecasted dates:

```
plot_plotly(model, forecast, changepoints=True)
```

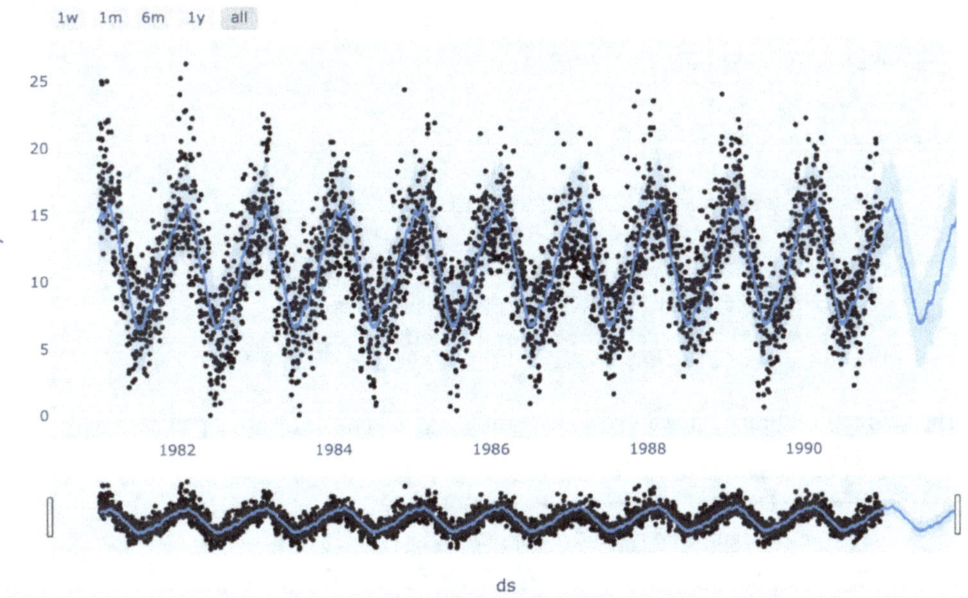

Figure 2.5: Forecasting temperature

This was a brief hands-on introduction to forecasting. We will be doing more forecasting, including with other libraries in addition to Prophet, in the rest of this book.

Pattern classification

For pattern classification, we will use financial time series – more specifically, share prices of technology companies. We will explore the use of two different open source libraries for DTW, `fastdtw` and `dtw-python`. This is based on the code in `ts-spark_ch2_1.dbc`, which we can import from the GitHub location for *Chapter 2* into Databricks Community Edition, as per the approach explained in *Chapter 1*.

The code URL is as follows:

```
https://github.com/PacktPublishing/Time-Series-Analysis-with-Spark/
raw/main/ch2/ts-spark_ch2_1.dbc
```

Let's start with `fastdtw` with the following code steps:

1. First, we import the necessary libraries:

    ```python
    import yfinance as yf
    import numpy as np
    from fastdtw import fastdtw
    import plotly.express as px
    ```

2. We'll use the `yfinance` library to download the share prices from Yahoo Finance for several technology companies for a date range:

    ```python
    from_date = "2019-01-01"
    to_date = "2024-01-01"
    yftickers = [
        "AAPL", "AMZN", "GOOG", "META",
        "MSFT", "NVDA", "PYPL", "TSLA"]
    yfdata = {
        yftick: yf.download(
            yftick, start=from_date, end=to_date, multi_level_
    index=False)['Close'].tolist() for yftick in yftickers}
    ```

3. The `fastdtw` library is used to calculate the DTW distances for each pair of stocks:

    ```python
    for i in range(num_tickers):
        for j in range(num_tickers):
            dtwdistance, _ = fastdtw(X[i], X[j])
            dtwmatrix[i, j] = float(dtwdistance)
    ```

4. We then plot the distance matrix using a heatmap with the following code:

    ```python
    fig = px.imshow(
        dtwmatrix,
        labels=dict(x="Tickers", y="", color="DTW distance"),
        x=yftickers,
        y=yftickers
    )
    fig.update_xaxes(side="top")
    fig.show()
    ```

This creates the visualization in *Figure 2.6*, where the value of the DTW distance between AMZN and GOOG share prices is highlighted. Of the combination of shares analyzed, these two are the nearest to each other compared to the other DTW distances.

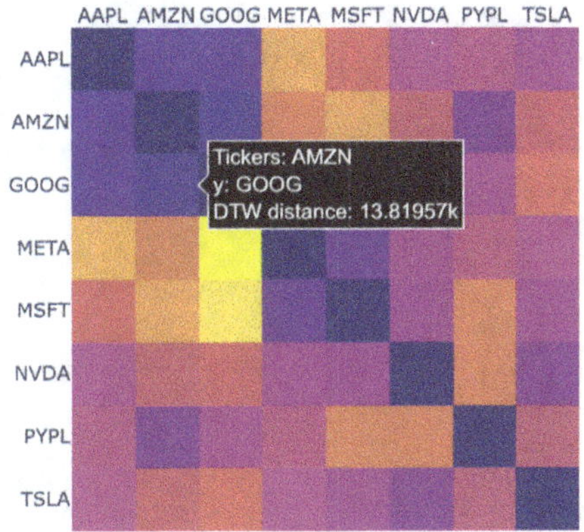
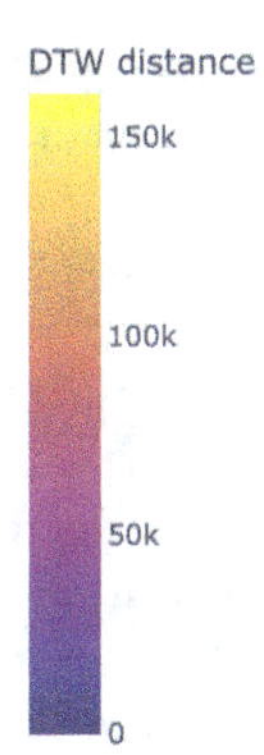

Figure 2.6: DTW distance heatmap

The line showing the DTW distance measurement between the two time series, AMZN and GOOG, is visualized in *Figure 2.2*.

5.   The plot of the time series for all the tickers is simply done with the following:

```
fig = px.line(yfdata, y=yftickers)
fig.show()
```

This creates *Figure 2.7*:

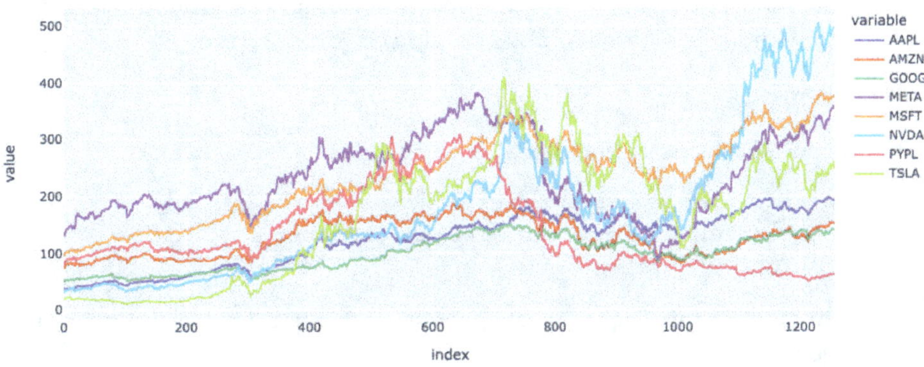

Figure 2.7: Selected technology share prices

6.   We use the following code with the `dtw-python` library to generate the alignment plot in *Figure 2.2*:

```
from dtw import *
alignment = dtw(
    yfdata['GOOG'], yfdata['AMZN'],
```

```
            keep_internals=True,
            step_pattern=rabinerJuangStepPattern(6, "c"))
    alignment.plot(
            type="twoway", offset=-2,
            xlab="time_index", ylab="GOOG / AMZN")
    alignment = dtw(
            yfdata['GOOG'], yfdata['META'],
            keep_internals=True,
            step_pattern=rabinerJuangStepPattern(6, "c"))
    alignment.plot(
            type="twoway", offset=-2,
            xlab="time_index", ylab="GOOG / META")
```

This concludes a brief hands-on introduction to pattern classification – more specifically, the initial step of distance calculation for the distance-based method using DTW, as applied to financial time series. Following this step, you can then apply the kNN classification algorithm.

Anomaly detection

In the final hands-on example of this chapter, we will explore an anomaly detection use case applied to energy consumption for a household. This is based on the code in `ts-spark_ch2_2.dbc`, and the dataset in `ts-spark_ch2_ds2.csv`. We import the code into Databricks Community Edition, as per the approach explained in *Chapter 1*.

The code URL is as follows: `https://github.com/PacktPublishing/Time-Series-Analysis-with-Spark/raw/main/ch2/ts-spark_ch2_2.dbc`

The code steps follow:

1. First, we import the necessary libraries:

    ```
    from pyspark import SparkFiles
    from sklearn.ensemble import IsolationForest
    import plotly.express as px
    ```

    As discussed earlier in this chapter, isolation forest is a tree-based model that can be used for isolating anomalies.

2. Spark is used to read the dataset:

    ```
    df = spark.read.csv(
        "file:///" + SparkFiles.get(DATASET_FILE),
        header=True, sep=";", inferSchema=True
    )
    ```

Note that this is a different yet equivalent syntax to `spark.load()`, which we used in *Chapter 1*.

3. To enable calculations on the columns' value, we need to change the data types of the columns from string to double:

```
df = df.dropna() \
    .withColumn(
        'Global_active_power',
        df.Global_active_power.cast('double')) \
    .withColumn(
        'Global_reactive_power',
        df.Global_reactive_power.cast('double')) \
    .withColumn(
        'Voltage', df.Voltage.cast('double')) \
    .withColumn(
        'Global_intensity',
        df.Global_intensity.cast('double')) \
```

4. We then choose the first part of the dataset to use for training the model:

```
df_train = df_pd.iloc[:35000, :]
```

5. The Isolation Forest model can then be created and fitted to the training dataset:

```
isoforest_model = IsolationForest(
    n_estimators=100,
    max_samples='auto',
    contamination=float(0.0025),
    random_state=123)


isoforest_model.fit(feature_col_train)
```

You can use the `contamination` level to specify the expected proportion of outliers in the dataset.

6. The model can then be used to flag the anomalies in the full dataset:

```
df_pd['anomaly_'] = isoforest_model.predict(feature_col)
```

7. Finally, to show the result in *Figure 2.3*:

```
fig = px.scatter(
    df_pd, x='Date', y=feature_name,
    color='anomaly_',
    color_continuous_scale=px.colors.sequential.Bluered_r)
fig.update_traces(marker=dict(size=3))
fig.add_vrect(x0=df_train_lastdate, x1=df_lastdate)
fig.show()
```

This completes the hands-on introduction to anomaly detection using an energy consumption time series. As discussed in this chapter, Isolation Forest, used here, is just one of many methods available.

Summary

In this chapter, we focused on the practical significance of analyzing time series data for predictive modeling, trend identification, and anomaly detection. We viewed real-world applications across industries, highlighting the importance of time series analysis while getting some practice with two different sector-specific datasets.

Before we can scale these and other use cases, we need an additional key component, Apache Spark, to which you will be introduced in the next chapter.

Further reading

This section serves as a repository of sources that can help you build on your understanding of the topic:

- *Time Series Analysis - Data, Methods, and Applications*, edited by Chun-Kit Ngan: `https://www.intechopen.com/books/8362`

- **Financial services:**

  - *Essentials of Time Series for Financial Applications* by Massimo Guidolin and Manuela Pedio: `https://www.sciencedirect.com/book/9780128134092/essentials-of-time-series-for-financial-applications`

  - *Time-Series Forecasting Techniques for Banking Variables* by Arindam Bandyopadhyay: `https://academic.oup.com/book/43110/chapter-abstract/361614151?redirectedFrom=fulltext&login=false`

- **Retail:**

  - *A profit prediction model with time series analysis for retail store* by Sridevi U. K. and Shanthi P: `https://www.researchgate.net/publication/325882164_A_profit_prediction_model_with_time_series_analysis_for_retail_store`

  - *A Comparative Study on Forecasting of Retail Sales* (Hasan et al., 2022): `https://arxiv.org/pdf/2203.06848.pdf`

- **Healthcare:**

  - *AI in Healthcare: Time-Series Forecasting Using Statistical, Neural, and Ensemble Architectures* (Kaushik et al., 2020): `https://www.frontiersin.org/articles/10.3389/fdata.2020.00004/full`

- *Time Series Forecasting for Healthcare Diagnosis and Prognostics with the Focus on Cardiovascular Diseases* (Bui et al., 2018): `https://www.researchgate.net/publication/320002542_Time_Series_Forecasting_for_Healthcare_Diagnosis_and_Prognostics_with_the_Focus_on_Cardiovascular_Diseases`

- **Manufacturing and utilities:**

  - *Time Series Prediction in Industry 4.0: A Comprehensive Review and Prospects for Future Advancements* (Kashpruk et al., 2023): `https://www.mdpi.com/2076-3417/13/22/12374`

  - *Time-series pattern recognition in Smart Manufacturing Systems: A literature review and ontology* (Farahani et al., 2023): `https://www.sciencedirect.com/science/article/pii/S0278612523000997`

  - *Measuring the energy intensity of domestic activities from smart meter data* (Stankovic et al., 2016): `https://www.sciencedirect.com/science/article/pii/S0306261916313897`

- **Libraries:**

  - FastDTW: `http://cs.fit.edu/~pkc/papers/tdm04.pdf`

  - dtw-python: `https://dynamictimewarping.github.io/python/`

Join our community on Discord

Join our community's Discord space for discussions with the authors and other readers:

`https://packt.link/ds`

3

Introduction to Apache Spark

This chapter provides an overview of Apache Spark, explaining its distributed computing capabilities and suitability for processing large-scale time series data. It explains how Spark addresses the challenges of parallel processing, scalability, and fault tolerance. This foundational knowledge is essential as it sets the stage for leveraging Spark's strengths in handling vast temporal datasets, facilitating efficient time series analysis. Practical knowledge of Spark's role enhances practitioners' ability to harness its power for complex computations, making it a valuable resource for scalable, high-performance time series applications.

We're going to cover the following main topics:

- Apache Spark and its architecture

- How Apache Spark works

- Installation of Apache Spark

Technical requirements

The hands-on focus of this chapter will be to deploy a multi-node Apache Spark cluster to get familiar with important components of a deployment. The code for this chapter can be found in the `ch3` folder of this book's GitHub repository at this URL: `https://github.com/PacktPublishing/Time-Series-Analysis-with-Spark/tree/main/ch3`.

The hands-on section of this chapter will go into further detail. This requires some skills in building an open source environment. If you do not intend to build your own Apache Spark environment and your focus is instead on time series and using but not deploying Spark, you can skip the hands-on section of this chapter. You can use a managed platform such as Databricks, which comes pre-built with Spark, as we will do in future chapters.

What is Apache Spark?

Apache Spark is a distributed computing system that is open source, with a programming interface and clusters for parallel data processing at scale and with fault tolerance. Started as a project at Berkeley's AMPLab in 2009, Spark became open source in 2010 as part of the Apache Software Foundation. The original creators of Spark have since founded the Databricks company, which provides a managed version of Spark on their multi-cloud platform.

Spark can handle both batch and stream processing, making it a widely usable tool for big data processing. Bringing significant performance improvement over existing big data systems, Spark uses in-memory computing and optimized query execution for very fast analytic queries on data of any size. It is built on the concept of **Resilient Distributed Datasets (RDDs)** and DataFrames. These are collections of data elements distributed across a cluster of computers that can be operated on in parallel with fault tolerance. We will expand further on these concepts in the rest of this chapter.

Why use Apache Spark?

There are numerous benefits to using Spark, which explains its popularity as a large-scale data processing solution, as shown in *Figure 3.1* based on Google Trends. We can see here the increasing interest in Apache Spark software in line with the big data topic, while the trend for Hadoop software had been increasing, then decreased when it was overtaken by Apache Spark software in March 2017.

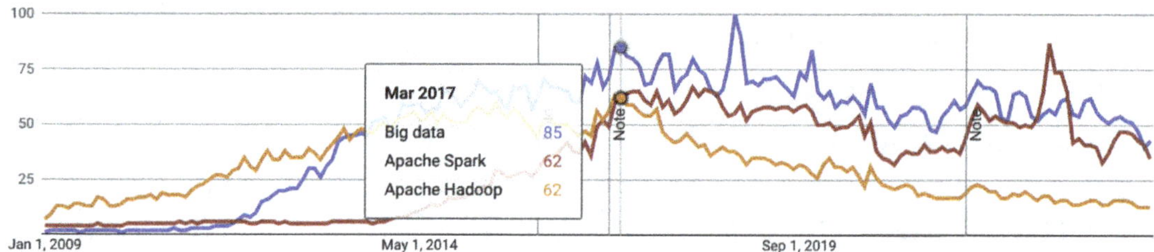

Figure 3.1: Increasing interest in Apache Spark compared to Hadoop and big data

This surge in interest can be explained by some key benefits, as follows:

- **Speed:** Spark runs up to 100 times faster in memory and up to 10 times faster even when running on disk, when compared to non-Spark Hadoop clusters.

- **Fault tolerance:** With the use of distributed computing, Spark provides a fault-tolerant mechanism with recovery on failure.

- **Modularity:** Spark includes support for SQL and structured data processing, machine learning, graph processing, and stream data processing. With libraries for diverse tasks, it can handle a wide range of data processing tasks.

- **Usability**: With APIs in Python, Java, Scala, and R, as well as Spark Connect, Spark is accessible to a wide range of developers and data scientists.

- **Compatibility**: Spark can run on different platforms – including Databricks, Hadoop, Apache Mesos, and Kubernetes, standalone, or in the cloud. It can also access diverse data sources, which will be discussed in the *Interfaces and integrations* section.

The growing popularity of Spark, and the numerous benefits explaining it, came over several years of evolution, which we will look at next.

Evolutions

Apache Spark has gone through several evolutions over the years, with the following major release versions:

- **1.x**: These were early versions of Spark, starting with RDDs and some distributed data processing capabilities.

- **2.x**: Spark 2.0, in 2016, had significant improvements with the introduction of Spark SQL, structured streaming, and the Dataset API, which is more efficient than RDDs.

- **3.x**: From 2020, Spark 3.0 had further improvements, with **Adaptive Query Execution** (**AQE**), which dynamically adjusts query plans based on runtime statistics, enhanced performance optimizations, and dynamic partition pruning. It also included support for newer Python versions as well as additions to the **machine learning library** (**MLlib**).

As of the time of writing, the latest version is 3.5.3. To understand the direction the project is going in, let's now zoom in on the highlights of some of the most recent versions, which are as follows:

- **PySpark** gains user-friendly support for Python-type hints, the pandas API on Spark, and enhanced performance thanks to optimizations.

- Adaptive Query Execution improvements drive more efficient query execution and resource utilization.

- **Structured Streaming** enhancements give better stability and performance.

- Kubernetes supports better integration and resource management capabilities for running Spark on Kubernetes. This results in greater efficiency and ease of use.

- API and SQL enhancements bring more efficient data processing and analysis, with new functions and improvements to existing ones. The key themes here are better usability and performance.

As we can see from the preceding, the recent focus is on support for modern infrastructure, performance, and usability. As a tool for large-scale data processing and analysis, this is turning Spark into an even more widely adopted tool.

Distributions of Spark

With its popularity and wide adoption have come several distributions of Spark. These have been developed by different organizations, with Apache Spark, at its core, providing different integration capabilities, usability features, and enhancements to functionalities. Bundled with other big data tools, these distributions often offer improved management interfaces, enhanced security, and different storage integrations.

The following distributions are the most common ones:

- **Apache Spark** is the original open source version maintained by the Apache Software Foundation. It is the basis for the other distributions.

- **Databricks Runtime** is developed by Databricks, the company founded by the creators of Spark. It is optimized for cloud environments, with a unified analytics platform facilitating collaboration between data engineers, data scientists, and business analysts. Databricks provides optimized Spark performance with a C++ rewritten version called **Photon**, interactive notebooks, integrated workflows for data engineering with **Delta Live Tables** (**DLT**), and machine learning with MLflow, along with enterprise-grade compliance and security as part of its Unity Catalog-based governance capabilities.

- **Cloudera Data Platform** (**CDP**) includes Spark as part of its data platform, which includes Hadoop and other big data tools.

- **Hortonworks Data Platform** (**HDP**), before merging with Cloudera, offered its own distribution that included Spark.

- **Microsoft Azure** includes Spark as part of **Azure Databricks**, which is a first-party service on Azure, HDInsight, Synapse, and, moving forward, Fabric.

- **Amazon Web Services** (**AWS**) offers Databricks in its Marketplace, as well as **Elastic MapReduce** (**EMR**) running as a cloud service to run big data frameworks such as Apache Spark on AWS.

- **Google Cloud Platform** (**GCP**) hosts Databricks, as well as **Dataproc**, which is Google's managed service for Apache Spark and Hadoop clusters in the cloud.

From on-premises to cloud-native solutions to those that integrate with other data platforms, each distribution of Apache Spark answers different needs. When organizations choose a distribution, factors typically considered are performance requirements, ease of management, the existing technology stack, and specific capabilities provided by each distribution.

Now that we have gone through what Apache Spark is, its benefits, and its evolutions, let's dive deeper into its architecture and components.

Apache Spark architecture

The primary objective of an architecture with Apache Spark is to process large datasets across distributed clusters. Architectures can vary based on the specific requirements of the application, whether it is batch processing, stream processing, machine learning, querying for reports, or even a combination of these. A typical Spark architecture includes several key components that contribute to the data processing requirements. An example of such architecture is represented in *Figure 3.2.*

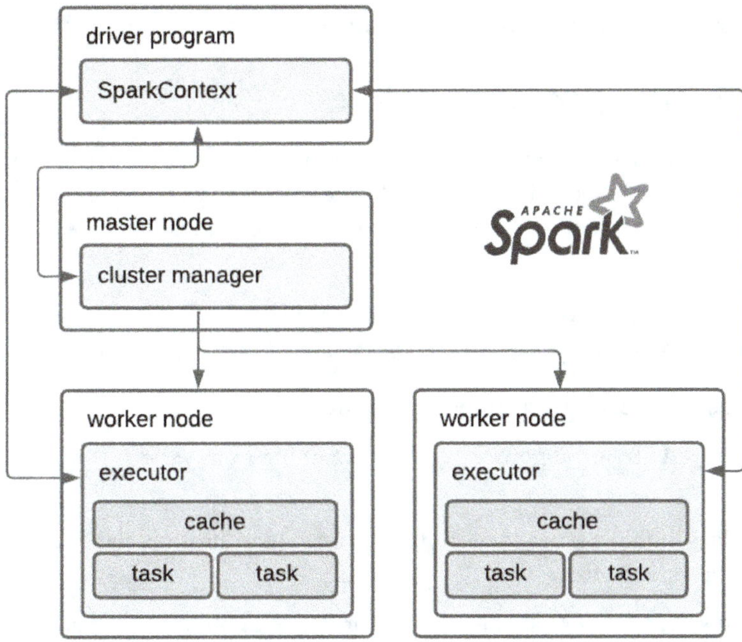

Figure 3.2: Example of Apache Spark-based architecture (standalone mode)

Let's now drill down into what each of these parts does.

Cluster manager

Cluster managers are responsible for allocating resources to the clusters, which are the operating system environments on which the Spark workloads execute. These include the following:

- **Standalone**: A basic cluster manager is included with Spark, making it easy to set up a cluster to get started. This cluster manager node is also known as the master node:

- **Kubernetes**: Spark can be deployed to Kubernetes, which is an open source container-based system that automates the deployment, management, and scaling of containerized applications.

- **Apache Mesos**: As a cluster manager, Mesos supports Spark, in addition to running Hadoop MapReduce.

- **Hadoop YARN**: Spark can share clusters and datasets with other Hadoop components when running with YARN.

- **Proprietary and commercial**: The solutions that incorporate Spark have their own cluster managers – usually a variation and improvement of the preceding open source versions.

Next, we will look at what is within these Spark clusters.

Spark Core, libraries, and API

Once we have one or more clusters provided by the cluster manager, Spark Core then manages memory and fault recovery, as well as everything related to Spark jobs, such as scheduling, distributing, and monitoring. Spark Core abstracts storage read and write, using RDDs and, more recently, DataFrames as the data structure.

On top of (and working very closely with) Core, several libraries and APIs provide additional functionalities specific to the data processing requirements. These are as follows:

- **Spark SQL** allows querying structured data via SQL

- **Spark Structured Streaming** processes data streaming from various sources, such as Kafka and Kinesis

- **MLlib** provides multiple types of machine learning algorithms for classification, regression, and clustering, among others

- **GraphX** allows the use of graph algorithms for the creation, transformation, and querying of graphs

Spark is about data processing, and as such, an important part of the solution is the data structure, which we will discuss next.

RDDs, DataFrames, and Datasets

We have mentioned RDDs and DataFrames a few times since the start of the chapter without going into detail, which we will do now, as well as introducing Datasets.

In short, these are the in-memory data structures representing the data and providing us with a programmatic way, more formerly termed an abstraction, to manipulate the data. Each of these data structures has its use cases, as follows:

- An **RDD** is Spark's fundamental data structure. Immutable and distributed, it can store data in memory across a cluster. Fault-tolerant, an RDD can automatically recover from failures. Note that in case of insufficient memory on the cluster, Spark does store part of the RDD on disk, but as this is managed behind the scenes, we will keep referring to RDDs as being in memory.

You are less and less likely to use RDDs, as more operations become possible with easier-to-use DataFrames, which we will see next. RDDs are more suitable for low-level transformations with direct manipulation of data, useful when you need low-level control over computations.

- A **DataFrame** is built upon an RDD as a distributed collection of data with named columns. This is like a table in a relational database. In addition to the more user-friendly higher-level API, which makes code more concise and easier to understand, DataFrames benefit from performance gain over RDDs thanks to Spark's Catalyst optimizer, which we will discuss later in the chapter.

  We have already started using DataFrames as part of the hands-on exercises done so far. You may have noticed pandas DataFrames in addition to Spark DataFrames while doing the exercises. While similar in concept, they are part of different libraries and have their underlying implementation differences. Fundamentally, pandas DataFrames are on single machines while Spark DataFrames are distributed. pandas DataFrames can be converted to pandas-on-Spark DataFrames, with the benefit of pandas DataFrame API support in addition to parallelism.

- A **Dataset** provides the type safety of RDDs with the optimizations of DataFrame. Type safety means that you can catch data type errors at compilation time, resulting in more runtime reliability. This is, however, dependent on the programming language supporting data type definition at the time of coding and verification and enforcement during compilation. As such, Datasets are only supported in Scala and Java, with Python and R, being dynamically typed, using DataFrames.

In summary, you will get low-level control with RDDs, optimized higher-level abstraction with DataFrames, and type safety with Datasets. Which data structure to use depends on the specific requirements of your application.

So far, we have considered the internal components. We will next go into the external facing parts and how Spark integrates in the backend with storage and in the frontend with applications and users.

Interfaces and integrations

When considering interfacing and integrating with the environment, there are a few ways in which this is fulfilled with Apache Spark. These are the following:

- **Storage**: The first one (and one that is key) is integration with storage to read the source data to be processed and write back the results. Apache Spark supports several native and third-party connectors, including to local file systems, **Hadoop Distributed File System** (**HDFS**), and cloud storage, among many others. The data itself can be read and stored in different file formats such as `csv`, `json`, `xml`, `orc`, `avro`, `parquet`, and `protobuf`. Of these, Parquet is the most common as it gives good performance with snappy compression. In addition, Spark can be extended with packages to support several storage protocols and external data sources. Delta is one of these, which we will discuss further in *Chapter 4* and *Chapter 5*. Other formats include Iceberg and Hudi. Note that we are talking here about the disk representation of the data, which is loaded into the memory-based data structures in RDDs and DataFrames discussed previously.

We already have some experience with Spark and storage as part of the hands-on exercises done so far, where we have been reading CSV files from the local storage on the Databricks Community Edition's Spark clusters.

- **Applications**: This is the code with the logic for data processing, calling the Spark APIs and libraries for tasks such as data transformations, streaming, SQL queries, or machine learning. Developers can write in Python, R, Scala, or Java. The code is then executed on the Spark clusters.

  Our experience with the application side has started as well, with the hands-on code used so far.

- **Platform user interface**: In addition to the web interface for Databricks Community Edition, which we have seen in the hands-on exercises, open source Apache Spark has a web **user interface** (**UI**) for monitoring the cluster and Spark applications. This provides insights into stages of job execution, resource usage, and the execution environment. Other data platforms that incorporate Apache Spark have their own UIs.

- **Application end user interface**: Another type of UI is for end users consuming the outcome of the processing by Apache Spark. This can be reporting tools or, for example, an application using Apache Spark in the backend for data processing.

In this section on Apache Spark architecture, we saw how the architecture enables data to be ingested from various sources into the Spark system, to be processed using Spark's libraries, and then stored or served to users or downstream applications. The chosen architecture is dependent on requirements, such as latency, throughput, data size, and the complexity and type of data processing tasks. In the next section, we will focus on how Spark performs distributed processing at scale.

How Apache Spark works

So far in this chapter, we have viewed the components and their roles, but not so much about their interactions. We will now cover this part, to understand how Spark manages distributed data processing across a cluster, starting with transformations and actions.

Transformations and actions

Apache Spark does, at a high level, two types of data operations:

- **Transformations** are operations on RDDs, DataFrames, or Datasets, returning another RDD, DataFrame, or Dataset. The original data structure is not altered, that is, it is immutable. Transformations are not executed immediately and are called lazy operations, and as such, enable Spark to optimize the execution plan. They are part of a **Directed Acyclic Graph** (**DAG**) of transformations and get executed when an action, which we will define next, is called. Examples of transformations are `filter` and `groupBy`.

- **Actions** are eager, that is, executed immediately. Examples of actions are `count` and `save` types of operations, such as writing to Parquet files or using the `saveAsTable` operation. Actions trigger the execution of all transformations defined as prior steps in the DAG. This results in Spark computing the result of the series of transformations.

The distinction between transformations and actions is an important consideration when writing efficient Spark code. This enables Spark to use its execution engine for high-performance processing of jobs, which will be explained next.

Jobs, stages, and tasks

Spark applications are executed as jobs, which are split into stages, and further into tasks, as follows:

- **Job**: Spark submits a job when an action is called on an RDD, DataFrame, or Dataset. The job is converted into a physical execution plan with several stages, which we will explain next. The purpose of a Spark job is to execute a sequence of computational steps as a logical unit of work to achieve a specific goal, such as aggregating data or sorting, with the aim of producing an output.

- **Stage**: A job can have multiple stages, as defined in its physical execution plan. A stage is a group of contiguous tasks that can be completed without moving data across the cluster. The data movement between stages is referred to as shuffle. The separation of a job into stages is beneficial as shuffling is costly in terms of performance impact. A stage is further broken down into tasks, which we will look at next.

- **Task**: As the most granular unit of processing, a task is a single operation on a Spark in-memory partition of data. Each task processes a different set of data and can run in parallel with other tasks. These run on worker nodes, which we will look at next.

In summary, jobs, stages, and tasks are related hierarchically. Spark applications can have multiple jobs, which are divided into stages based on data shuffling boundaries. Stages are further broken down into tasks, which run on different partitions in parallel on the cluster. This execution hierarchy allows Spark to efficiently distribute the workload across several nodes in a cluster, thus efficiently processing data at scale.

Now that we have seen the units of processing, the next consideration is how these units are run on compute resources with driver and worker nodes.

Driver and worker nodes

Driver and worker nodes are the compute resources created by the cluster manager to form part of a Spark cluster. They work together for Spark to process large datasets in parallel, using the resources of multiple machines.

Let's discuss these resources in detail:

- **Driver nodes**: The driver node is where the main process of a Spark application runs. It principally does the following:

    - **Resources**: The driver requests resources from the cluster manager for processes to run on the worker nodes.

    - **SparkSession**: This is an object created by the driver and used to programmatically access Spark for data processing operations on the cluster.

    - **Tasks**: The driver translates code into tasks, schedules the tasks on worker nodes, and thereafter manages the tasks' execution.

- **Worker nodes**: The worker node is where the data processing happens, via what is called the executor process. The executors interact with the storage and keep the data in their own memory space, as well as having their own set of CPU cores. The tasks are scheduled by the driver nodes to execute on the executors with direct communication between drivers and executors. They communicate on task status and results.

Driver and worker node interaction: *Figure 3.3* summarizes the sequence of interactions between driver and worker nodes.

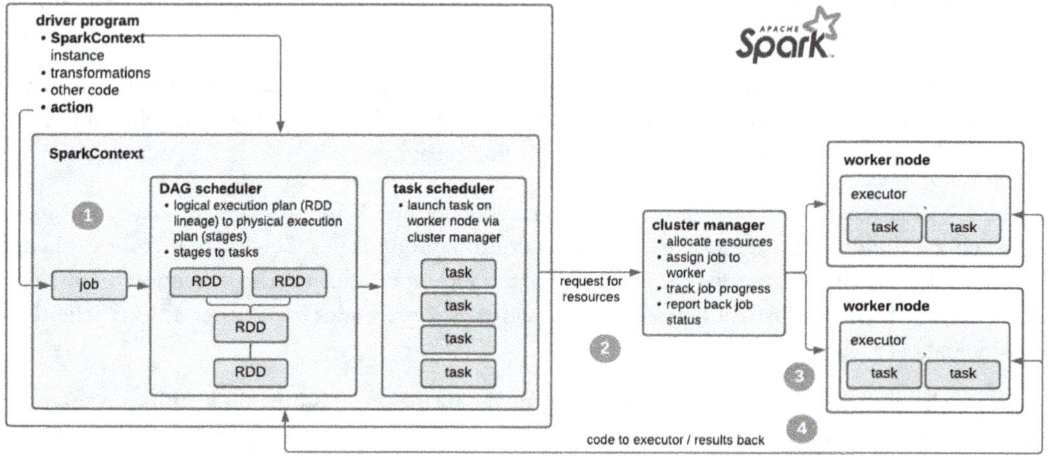

Figure 3.3: Driver and worker nodes in action

The steps are as follows:

1. **Initialization**: When the Spark application is started, the driver converts jobs into stages, further broken into tasks.

2. **Scheduling**: The driver node schedules tasks on executors on the worker nodes, keeping track of status and rescheduling in case of failure.

3. **Execution**: The tasks assigned by the driver are run by the executor on the worker node. In addition, the driver coordinates between executors when data needs to be shuffled across executors. This is required for certain operations such as joins.

4. **Result**: Finally, the results of processing tasks by the executors are sent back to the driver node, which aggregates the results and sends them back to the user.

This cooperative process between the driver and worker nodes is at the core of Spark, enabling data processing at scale, in parallel across a cluster, while handling fault tolerance.

Now that we have seen the workings of Spark clusters, let's zoom in on what makes it even more performant and efficient.

Catalyst optimizer and the Tungsten execution engine

So far we've discussed that among the successive improvements brought to Apache Spark over the different versions, two notable ones are the Catalyst optimizer and the Tungsten execution engine. They play crucial roles in ensuring the Spark processes are optimized for fast execution time and efficient use of resources.

Catalyst optimizer

Introduced in Spark SQL, the Catalyst optimizer is a query optimization framework that significantly improves the performance of queries by using tree transformation on the **abstract syntax tree (AST)** of queries. It does this through several stages, as follows:

1. **Analysis**: The query is transformed into a tree of operators called a logical plan.

2. **Logical optimization**: The optimizer uses rule-based transformations to optimize the logical plan.

3. **Physical planning**: The logical plan is converted to physical plans, which are based on the choice of algorithm to use for the query operation.

4. **Cost model**: The physical plans are then compared based on a cost model to find the most efficient one in terms of time and resources.

5. **Code generation**: As a final stage, the physical plan is converted to executable code.

With these stages, the Catalyst optimizer ensures that the most performant and efficient code is run.

Tungsten execution engine

Another area of focus is the efficient use of CPU and memory by Spark processes. The Tungsten execution engine achieves this in the following ways:

- **Code generation**: Tungsten works in conjunction with the Catalyst optimizer to generate optimized, compact code, which reduces runtime overhead while maximizing speed.

- **Cache-awareness**: Reducing cache misses improves the computation speed. Tungsten achieves this by making algorithms and data structures cache-aware.

- **Memory management**: Tungsten manages memory efficiently, improving the impact of the cache while reducing the overhead of garbage collection.

Working together, the Catalyst optimizer and the Tungsten execution engine significantly contribute to Spark's performance by optimizing query plans, generating efficient code, and reducing computation overhead. This improves Spark's efficiency for big data processing, at scale and fast.

Now that we understand how Apache Spark works, we will move on to how to set up our own Spark environment.

Installing Apache Spark

So far, in the previous chapters, we have successfully executed Spark code on Databricks Community Edition. This has, however, been on a single-node cluster. If we want to make full use of Spark's parallel processing power, we will need multiple nodes. We have the option of using a Databricks-managed **Platform as a Service (PaaS)** cloud solution, another equivalent cloud PaaS, or we can build our own Apache Spark platform. This is what we will do now to deploy the environment as per *Figure 3.2* shown in the section on *Apache Spark architecture*.

> **Note**
>
> If you do not intend to build your own Apache Spark environment, you can skip the practical part of this section and use a managed Spark platform such as Databricks, as we will do in future chapters.

Using a container for deployment

We can install Apache Spark directly on our local machine, but this will give us only one node. By deploying it in containers, such as Docker, we can have multiple containers running on the same machine. This effectively provides us with a way to have a multi-node cluster. Other advantages of this method include maintaining separation with the local execution environment, as well as providing a portable and repeatable way to deploy to other machines, including to cloud-based container services such as Amazon **Elastic Kubernetes Service (EKS)**, **Azure Kubernetes Service (AKS)**, or **Google Kubernetes Engine (GKE)**.

In what follows, we will be using Docker containers, starting by first installing Docker, then building and starting the containers with Apache Spark, and finally validating our deployment.

> **Alternative to Docker**
>
> You can use Podman as an open source alternative to Docker. See more information here: `https://podman.io/`.

Docker

The following instructions guide you on how to install Docker:

1. Refer to the following link to download and install Docker to your local environment, based on your OS:

   `https://docs.docker.com/get-docker/`

   For macOS users, follow the instructions here:

   `https://docs.docker.com/desktop/install/mac-install/`

2. Once Docker is installed, launch it as shown in *Figure 3.4*.

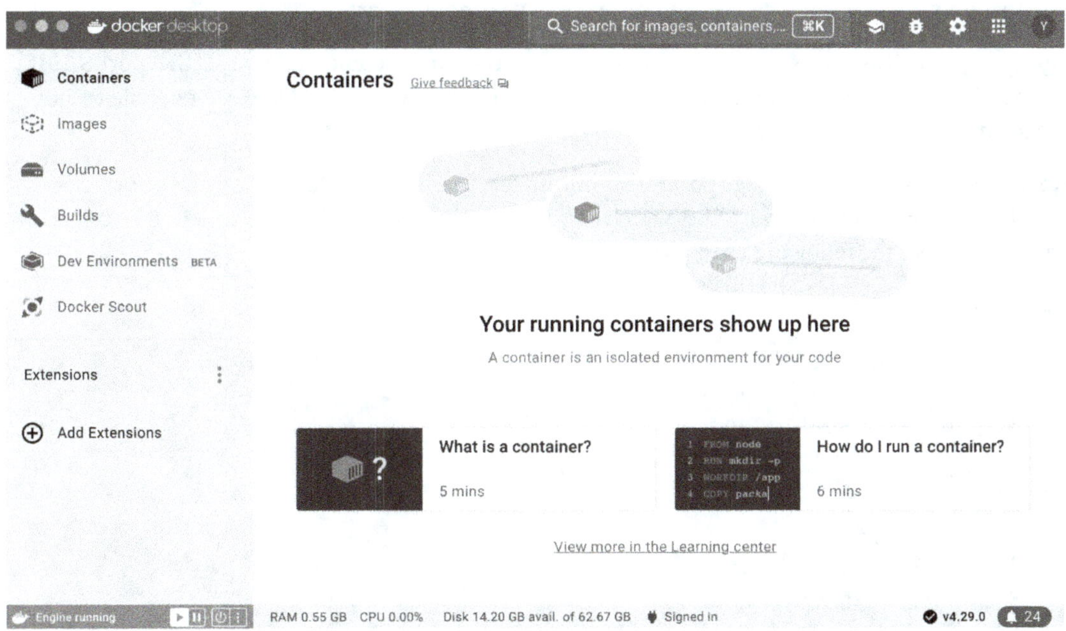

Figure 3.4: Docker Desktop

On macOS, you may see a Docker Desktop warning: "**Another application changed your Desktop configurations**". Depending on your setup, the following command may resolve the warning:

```
ln -sf /Applications/Docker.app/Contents/Resources/bin/docker-
credential-ecr-login /usr/local/bin/docker-credential-ecr-login
```

Once Docker Desktop is up and running, we can build the containers with Apache Spark.

Network ports

The following network ports need to be available on your local machine or development environment:

- Apache Spark: 7077, 8080, 8081

- Jupyter Notebook: 4040, 4041, 4042, 8888

You can check for the current use of these ports by existing applications with the following command, run from the command line or terminal:

```
% netstat -an | grep LISTEN
```

If you see the required ports in the list of ports already in use, you must either stop the application using that port or change the docker-compose file to use another port.

As an example, let's assume that the output of the above `netstat` command reveals that port 8080 is already in use on your local machine or development environment, and you are not able to stop the existing application using this port.

In this case, you will need to change port 8080 (meant for Apache Spark) in the `docker-compose.yaml` file to another, unused port. Just search and replace 8080 on the left of : to, say, 8070 if this port is free, as per the following example:

- From:

    ```
    ports:
      - '7077:7077'
      - '8080:8080'
    ```

- To:

    ```
    ports:
      - '7077:7077'
      - '8070:8080'
    ```

Keep note of the new port and use this instead of the existing one whenever you need to type the corresponding URL. In this example, port 8080 is changed to 8070, and the matching URL change for the Airflow web server is as follows:

- From: `http://localhost:8080/`

- To: `http://localhost:8070/`

> **Note**
>
> You will need to change the network port in all URLs in the following sections that you had to modify as per this section.

Building and deploying Apache Spark

The following instructions guide you on how to build and deploy the Docker images:

1. We first download the deployment script from the Git repository for this chapter, which is at the following URL:

    `https://github.com/PacktPublishing/Time-Series-Analysis-with-Spark/tree/main/ch3`

    We will be using the git clone-friendly URL, which is the following:

    `https://github.com/PacktPublishing/Time-Series-Analysis-with-Spark.git`

    To do this, start a terminal or command line and run the following commands:

    ```
    git clone https://github.com/PacktPublishing/Time-Series-
    Analysis-with-Spark.git
    cd Time-Series-Analysis-with-Spark/ch3
    ```

    Note that the preceding is for a macOS or Linux/Unix-based system, and you will need to run the equivalent for Windows.

2. On macOS, you may see the following error when you run this command:

    ```
    xcrun: error: invalid active developer path (/Library/Developer/
    CommandLineTools), missing xcrun at: /Library/Developer/
    CommandLineTools/usr/bin/xcrun
    ```

    In this case, you will need to reinstall the command-line tools with the following command:

    ```
    xcode-select --install
    ```

3. We can now start the container build and startup. A makefile is provided to simplify the process of starting and stopping the containers. The following command builds the Docker images for the containers and then starts them:

```
make up
```

> **Windows environment**
>
> If you are using a Windows environment, you can install a Windows version of Make, as per the following documentation: `https://gnuwin32.sourceforge.net/packages/make.htm`

This will give the following or equivalent output:

```
docker-compose up -d
[+] Running 4/4

...

✔ Container ts-spark-env-spark-master-1    Started
✔ Container ts-spark-env-jupyter-1         Started
✔ Container ts-spark-env-spark-worker-1-1  Started
✔ Container ts-spark-env-spark-worker-2-1  Started
```

By the end of the process, you will have a running Spark cluster with a master node (`ts-spark-env-spark-master-1`), which is where the cluster manager runs, and two worker nodes (`ts-spark-env-spark-worker-1-1` and `ts-spark-env-spark-worker-2-1`). In addition, there is a separate node (`ts-spark-env-jupyter-1`) for a notebook environment, called Jupyter Notebook, similar to what you have used in the previous chapters on Databricks Community Edition. In this deployment, this Jupyter node is also the driver node.

Let's now validate the environment that we have just deployed.

Accessing the UIs

We will now access the UIs of the different components as a quick way to validate the deployment:

1. We start with Jupyter Notebook at the following local URL: `http://localhost:8888/lab`

> **Note**
>
> You will need to change the network port in the preceding URL if you need to modify it as discussed in the *Network ports* section.

This will open the web page as per *Figure 3.5*.

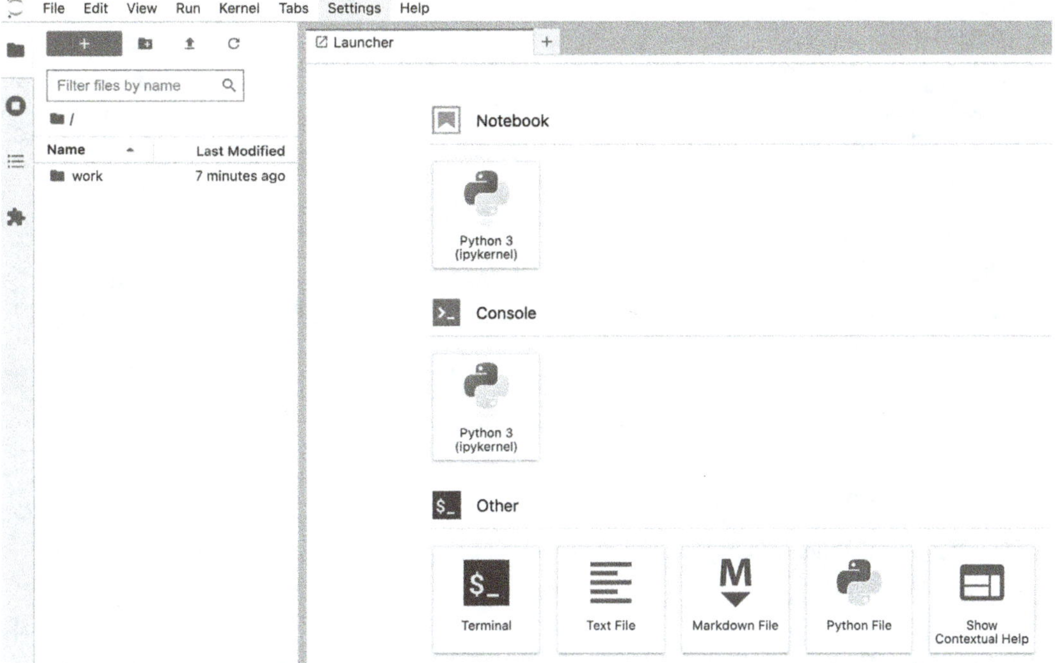

Figure 3.5: Jupyter Notebook

2. The next (and important) UI is for the Apache Spark master node, accessible via the following
    local URL: `http://localhost:8080/`

    Figure 3.6 shows this master node UI, as well as the worker nodes connected.

URL: spark://7ca952eea60a:7077
Alive Workers: 2
Cores in use: 2 Total, 0 Used
Memory in use: 4.0 GiB Total, 0.0 B Used
Resources in use:
Applications: 0 Running, 0 Completed
Drivers: 0 Running, 0 Completed
Status: ALIVE

▾ Workers (2)

Worker Id	Address	State	Cores	Memory	Resources
worker-20250119165517-172.19.0.3-46883	172.19.0.3:46883	ALIVE	1 (0 Used)	2.0 GiB (0.0 B Used)	
worker-20250119165517-172.19.0.4-34087	172.19.0.4:34087	ALIVE	1 (0 Used)	2.0 GiB (0.0 B Used)	

Figure 3.6: Spark master node UI

We now have our own Apache Spark cluster running.

As a final step to conclude this chapter, you can stop the containers with the following command:

```
make down
```

If you do not intend to use it further, you can additionally delete the Docker containers created with the Delete action as explained here: `https://docs.docker.com/desktop/use-desktop/container/#container-actions`

Summary

In this chapter, we dove deep into the Apache Spark architecture, its key components, and its features. The key concepts, how it works, and what makes it such a great tool were explained. We then deployed a multi-node cluster representing an example architecture. The concepts presented in this chapter, while essential, cover only a part of an Apache Spark project. We will view such a project end to end in the next chapter.

Further reading

This section serves as a repository of sources that can help you build on your understanding of the topic:

- Apache Spark official web page: `https://spark.apache.org/`

- *Mastering Apache Spark* (Packt Publishing) by Timothy Chen, Mike Frampton, and Tim Seear

- *Azure Databricks Cookbook* (Packt Publishing) by Phani Raj and Vinod Jaiswal

- Google Trends comparison: `https://trends.google.com/trends/explore?date=2009-01-01%20 2024-08-28&q=%2Fm%2F0bs2j8q,%2Fm%2F0ndhxqz,%2Fm%2F0fdjtq&hl=en`

- Cluster Overview: `https://spark.apache.org/docs/latest/cluster- overview.html`

- Spark Connect: `https://spark.apache.org/docs/latest/spark-connect- overview.html`

- Docker Compose: `https://docs.docker.com/compose/`

- Make and Makefile: `https://www.gnu.org/software/make/manual/make.html`

- Jupyter: `https://jupyter.org/`

Get This Book's PDF Version and Exclusive Extras

Scan the QR code (or go to `packtpub.com/unlock`). Search for this book by name, confirm the edition, and then follow the steps on the page.

Note: Keep your invoice handly. Purchase made directly from packt don't require one.

Part 2: From Data to Models

Building on the foundations, in this part, you will get a holistic view of all the stages involved in a time series analysis project, with a focus on the data and models. Starting with the ingestion and preparation of time series data, we will then do exploratory analysis to understand the nature of the time series. The data readiness and analysis will then lead us to the choice of model for analysis, development, and testing.

This part has the following chapters:

- *Chapter 4, End-to-End View of a Time Series Analysis Project*
- *Chapter 5, Data Preparation*
- *Chapter 6, Exploratory Data Analysis*
- *Chapter 7, Building and Testing Models*

4

End-to-End View of a Time Series Analysis Project

Building on the foundation set in the previous chapters in which we were introduced to time series analysis, its multiple use cases, and Apache Spark, a key tool for such analysis, this chapter guides us through the entire process of a time series analysis project. Starting with use cases, we will move on to the end-to-end approach with DataOps, ModelOps, and DevOps. We will cover key stages such as data processing, feature engineering, model selection, and evaluation, offering practical insights into building a time series analysis pipeline with Spark and other tools.

This holistic view of a time series analysis project will equip us with a structured approach to handling real-world projects, enhancing our ability to implement end-to-end solutions. The information here will guide us as practitioners through a framework for using Spark in a cohesive manner and ensuring the successful execution of time series analysis projects. We will conclude with two approaches for implementation.

We will cover the following topics in this chapter:

- Driven by use cases

- From DataOps to ModelOps to DevOps

- Implementation examples and tools

Let's get started!

Technical requirements

The hands-on part of this chapter will be to implement end-to-end examples for a time series analysis project. The code for this chapter can be found in the `ch4` folder of the GitHub repository at the following link:

```
https://github.com/PacktPublishing/Time-Series-Analysis-with-Spark/
tree/main/ch4
```

The hands-on section of this chapter (*Implementation examples and tools*) will go into further detail. This requires some skills in building an open source environment. If you do not intend to build your own Apache Spark environment and your focus is instead on time series and using but not deploying Spark and other tools, you can skip the hands-on section of this chapter. You can use a managed platform such as Databricks, which comes pre-built with Spark, MLflow, and tools for workflows and notebooks, as we will do in future chapters.

Driven by use cases

Before we get into the *how* of doing an end-to-end time series analysis project, as always, it is good to start with the *why*. There can be many reasons, often a combination, to justify the inception of a time series analysis project. Some of the reasons are as follows:

- **Technology refresh**: The emphasis can be on the technology due to an aging platform needing replacement and not being able to meet requirements anymore, or when a new technology is available, offering better performance, lower costs, or more capabilities, such as advanced machine learning models or scalable cloud-based resources.

- **Research on methods**: For organizations or departments focused on research, the main driver is finding new and better methods such as developing and testing new algorithms for analyzing time series.

- **Data exploration**: Similar to research in its nature, but requiring to be nearer to the data, this is usually embedded within businesses' data teams. The need here is to understand time series data without necessarily a predefined end application. The objective is to uncover patterns, trends, and anomalies in the data.

- **Use case**: With this approach, we begin with the end in mind, first identifying specific needs and expectations of the end users or stakeholders. We then set the project to answer those needs based on the analysis of time series data.

While all the preceding reasons have their merit and are certainly valid, over the years, I have seen the business-driven use case approach as the one with the highest return on investment. We started the discussion on time series-based use cases across various industries in *Chapter 2*, such as inventory forecasting, predicting energy usage, financial market trend analysis, or anomaly detection in sensor data; here, we will focus on this use case-driven approach and take it further.

The use case approach first identifies and defines real-world specific business applications or challenges. It then chooses the technical solution best fit to address these requirements. At first glance, this does not sound very different from any project in a business setup. The key difference here is highlighted by the word "specific" in that the use case approach is about a specific, measurable business outcome. This follows a lean approach in the sense that we want to avoid features that do not contribute to the business outcome.

Use cases can be compared to user stories in the agile approach to software development. As a matter of fact, the agile methodology is often how the use cases are implemented, with a streamlined iterative development process involving users all the way.

The following *Figure 4.1* gives an overview of the use case driven approach, based on what has been discussed so far, including their key characteristics.

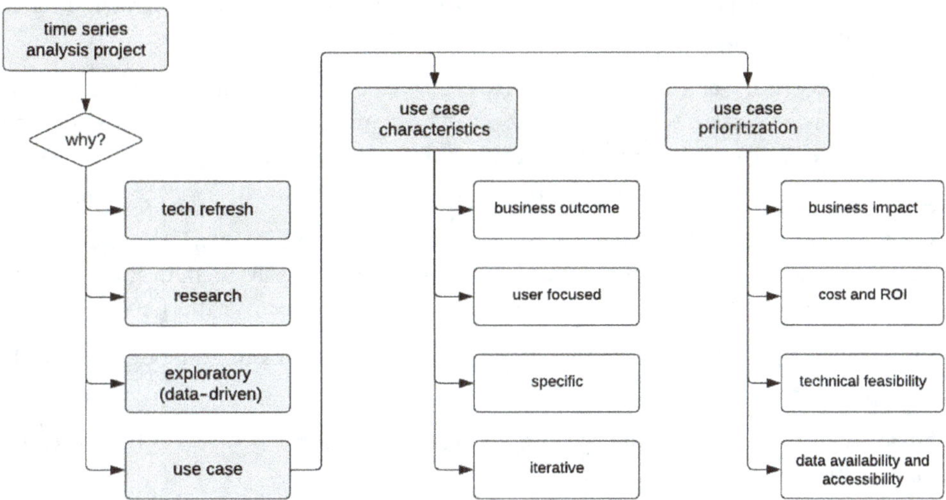

Figure 4.1: Use case driven approach

Now that we have defined the use case-driven approach, we will look at the key characteristics of this approach, as follows:

- **Business outcome**: Project success is measured by the outcome in terms of business metrics on higher revenue, cost reduction, efficiency gain, and better and quicker decision-making.

- **User-focused**: Working from the start with the end users and stakeholders to identify their specific needs, the project's objectives include answering those needs, in addition to the preceding business outcomes.

- **Specific**: We've discussed this term a couple of times. The specificity of a project provides a focused direction to its scope, making its execution more agile. We want to address a specific need, for example, sales forecasting, and this can be even more granular, such as forecasting for a specific line of product or region.

- **Iterative**: Feedback and refinement loops involving end users and stakeholders ensure the project remains on track to meet the expected business outcomes. This again highlights the similarity to an agile approach with its short development cycles, incremental delivery, continuous feedback, and adaptability.

Adhering to these characteristics, the use cases are scoped small enough to be achievable and bring value within a few months, if not even weeks. These smaller use cases usually mean that there are several of them competing in parallel for development resources. This requires prioritization to ensure that resources are well invested. The following criteria are commonly used to prioritize use cases:

- **Impact**: This is a measurement of the expected business impact of the use case, preferably calculated in monetary value. If the outcome is a reduction in time, the equivalent monetary value of the time saving is estimated.

- **Cost**: We need to account for all costs related to the use case from the moment of use case ideation to the time the use case is live in production and bringing value to the business. Costs can be related to development, infrastructure, migration, training, support, and production operations.

- **Return on investment (ROI)**: This can be simply estimated by dividing the impact by the cost. As an example, for a retailer who wants to better forecast stocks in stores, if the total cost to get the stock forecasting use case in production is $50k, and the improvement in stock forecasting is estimated to bring $200k in savings over 3 years, the ROI is 4x over this period.

- **Technical feasibility**: The technical solution for the use case exists and can be achieved within time and budget.

- **Data availability and accessibility**: Data is available and accessible to build the use case and then operationalize it.

Using the preceding criteria, in the case of competing need for resources, a use case with a high impact and an ROI of 10x that is feasible and has data available is done before another use case with a lower impact and an ROI of 3x, or before one that does not have data access.

In summary, starting with a clear understanding of the user's needs, a use case-based project ensures applicability and relevance to the business, closely aligning with the stakeholders' objectives, with measurable impact. Having a good use case is only the start, though. We will now deep-dive into the next steps, from the use case to the successful completion of a time series analysis project that delivers business outcomes.

From DataOps to ModelOps to DevOps

Once a significant use case has been identified, a few phases play a crucial role, starting from **data operations (DataOps)** to **model operations (ModelOps)** and finally to **deployment (DevOps)** to a live business environment delivering value. A solid end-to-end process covering these phases ensures that we can consistently deliver from one use case to the next while ensuring that the results are reproducible. *Figure 4.2* gives an overview of these phases, which will be detailed in this section.

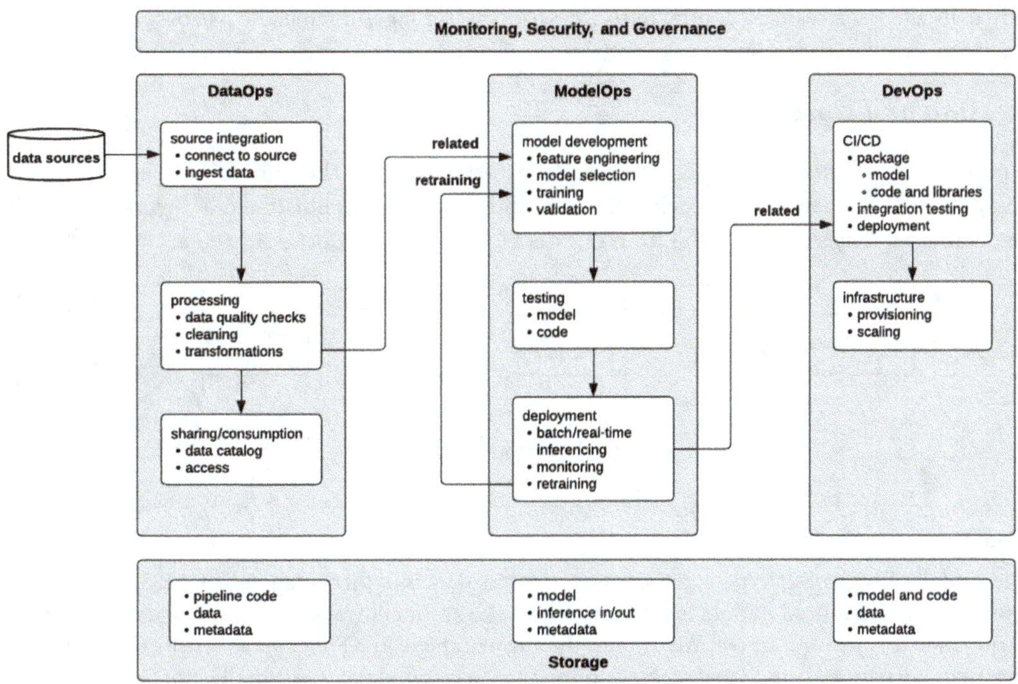

Figure 4.2: DataOps, ModelOps, and DevOps

DataOps

DataOps for a time series analysis project encompasses best practices and processes to ensure the flow, quality, and access to time series data as part of its life cycle. The aim is for timely, efficient, and accurate time series analysis and modeling to derive actionable business insights.

DataOps practices follow the complete data and metadata life cycle and can be broken down broadly into data source integration, data processing, data governance, and data sharing.

Source integration

Data source integration involves first identifying the data source and gaining access, and then ingesting data from the source.

Data sources can be internal or external. Internal sources are primarily databases such as transactional records, system logs, or sensor data for telemetry. External sources include examples such as market data, weather data, or social media, which is now becoming predominant. Sources vary greatly across industries in volume, frequency of updates, and data format. Once the sources have been identified and accessed, **data ingestion** is the process of bringing the data into the platform for processing. This is usually achieved with automated ingestion pipelines, running in batches at specific frequencies (hourly, daily, etc.) or streaming continuously. Mechanisms for ingestion include database connections, API calls, or web-based scraping, among others.

Processing and storage

Data processing includes cleaning up the data, transforming it into the right format, and storing it for analysis. A recommended approach is the medallion approach, as illustrated in *Figure 4.3*, which involves multiple stages of processing from raw data to curated to report-ready data.

Figure 4.3: Medallion stages of processing

> **Medallion approach**
>
> The medallion approach to data processing organizes data into three stages: Bronze, Silver, and Gold. This is often used in data lakes and Delta Lake architecture. Raw data is ingested from various sources without transformation in the Bronze stage. The Silver stage results from data cleaning, enrichment, and transformation to create a curated dataset. Finally, the Gold stage represents the highest quality data, cleansed, aggregated, and read-optimized for advanced analytics, reporting, and business intelligence. This multi-tiered structure augments data quality and facilitates data management.

Once the data has been ingested from sources, **data quality checks and cleaning** are the first steps to building trustworthiness in the data. These involve the handling of missing values, detecting and correcting errors, removing duplicates, and filtering outliers. These improve the data quality and give confidence that the analysis is built on a solid foundation. The specific requirement at this stage for time series data is to verify and maintain temporal integrity due to the sequential nature of the data.

The raw data from sources is usually not apt for direct analysis use and requires several **transformations** to be appropriate for time series analysis. This involves, among other transformations, changing semi-structured data to a structured format for quicker access. Data at granular or irregular intervals is aggregated to a higher-level interval such as from every minute to hourly, from hourly to daily, and so on. Date and time fields may require special processing to be in a sortable format and used to set a time index for faster retrieval. Different time zones need to be handled accordingly.

Frequently disregarded in smaller projects, **metadata** is an essential requirement in an enterprise environment to enable data traceability and lineage for governance. This data about the data captures, for example, source identifier, ingestion and update times, changes made, as well as historical versions. Metadata is captured as part of the data ingestion and transformation pipelines, and natively with storage protocols such as Delta.

While all the data processing described so far can be done in memory, there is a requirement for longer-term **storage** and retrieval for analysis over time. This storage needs to be cost-effective, scalable, and secure while providing the high performance required for timely analysis. Based on the volume and velocity of data, options include dedicated time series databases such as InfluxDB, or cloud-based storage in combination with a storage protocol such as Delta.

We will delve deeper into data processing in *Chapter 5* on data preparation. For now, let's shift our focus to governance and security, which are among the most critical considerations for DataOps from a risk perspective.

Monitoring, security, and governance

Data monitoring, security, and governance encompass several overlapping data practice areas, including data quality, privacy, access control, compliance, and policies. To appreciate the importance of these practices, let's consider the following in the news at the time of this writing:

A cybersecurity breach just impacted major organizations, including Ticketmaster, Banco Santander, and Ticketek. A hacking group called ShinyHunters gained access to Ticketmaster's database, and in doing so, compromised the personal information of 560 million users. This includes names, addresses, phone numbers, email addresses, and payment details. Reports are that this data is being sold on hacking forums for substantial amounts. Banco Santander had a similar breach, affecting customers and employees.

- [Source: `https://www.wired.com/story/snowflake-breach-ticketmaster-santander-ticketek-hacked/`]

These breaches, linked to a third-party cloud data warehouse service, highlight the challenges in cybersecurity and the need for strong measures for monitoring, security, and governance.

Monitoring

The goal here is to promptly identify issues and be able to take corrective measures, ideally before it has a negative consequence. The monitoring is of the data itself, of the execution status of transformation pipelines, as well as for security and governance breaches. For data monitoring, this means tracking the data quality by measuring its accuracy and completeness while catching data gaps and anomalies. One way to achieve this is by comparing against a range or specific time series pattern, as we have seen in the anomaly detection example in *Chapter 2*. As for the data pipeline monitoring, these are tracked for performance to ensure data freshness, **service-level agreements (SLAs)** are honored, and lineage to track provenance and integrity. From a security point of view, we want to catch any attempt at a data breach in time to act upon it. The monitoring should be an automated process, with alerting in place.

Security

Related to both data at rest and in transit, we need to define roles and related permissions to ensure access control. Some time series data is sensitive and only authorized personnel should be able to view or manipulate the data.

In regulated industries, when handling personal data, we need to ensure that data handling and storage practices comply with relevant regulations (HIPAA, GDPR, etc.). This also involves ensuring privacy and managing consent for personal data.

Governance

In addition to the preceding, the data governance practice is responsible for assigning roles and responsibilities to manage data. As part of this, the data stewards oversee data quality, compliance, and policies.

By establishing the right processes, people, and tools in place, we can ensure the prevention of data breaches and effective mitigation if they do occur.

We have now covered the process of ingesting and transforming data into trustworthy and useful data in a governed and secure way. The step left now as part of DataOps is to share the data for analysis and consumption by users or other systems.

Sharing and consumption

After ingestion and processing the data, we want the curated data and outcome of analytics to be visible and available to users. A centralized **data catalog**, complete with descriptions and usage guidelines, allows users to easily discover and access available datasets.

Finally, as part of the DataOps phase, we want data scientists, analysts, and other users to be able to consume the data for exploration, analysis, and reporting. Ideally, we want to tie this to governance to ensure that the right set of users are accessing and consuming permitted datasets only. Access and methods for consumption include file-based access, database connection, and APIs, among others.

As discussed in this section, DataOps is the set of processes to ensure that data is available, accessible, and usable. It is iterative, with feedback from consumers and continuous improvement to data, pipelines, and practices. By establishing a scalable and flexible infrastructure with Apache Spark's processing power and versatility at its core, DataOps ensures that data scientists and analysts have the high-quality data they need when they need it, to derive insights and drive decisions.

We will cover the practical considerations for DataOps in *Chapter 5, Data Preparation*. For now, let's focus on ModelOps, which is the next phase after DataOps.

ModelOps

While DataOps is about the data life cycle, ModelOps is about the model life cycle – more specifically, statistical and machine learning models. The objective is to manage the models from development to deployment, ensuring that they are reliable, accurate, and scalable while delivering actionable insights based on the use cases' requirements.

ModelOps, MLOps, and LLMOps

These terms have overlapping definitions and are sometimes used interchangeably. In this book, we will refer to ModelOps as the broader life cycle management practice for different types of models, including simulations, statistical, and machine learning models. We will use **machine learning operations** (**MLOps**) more specifically for machine learning models and **large language model operations** (**LLMOps**) for the specific considerations that apply to the life cycle of LLMs. As such, ModelOps will refer to the superset of practices.

ModelOps practices can be categorized broadly into model development and testing, and model deployment.

Model development and testing

Model development and testing involves creating and fine-tuning time series analysis models based on historical data. This process starts with feature engineering, selecting appropriate algorithms, such as Autoregressive Integrated Moving Average (ARIMA) or Long Short-Term Memory (LSTM), and splitting the data into training and testing sets. Then, models are iteratively trained and evaluated using performance metrics. This ensures accuracy. After that, by testing the model on unseen data, we can ensure that the model can generalize well to new, real-world scenarios.

We will now detail further each of these steps:

1. **Feature engineering**: Overlapping with the DataOps phase, feature engineering is the initial stage of model development, concerned with the identification of existing and creation of new features from the time series data. These include creating lags and rolling averages features, where information from previous time steps is used to calculate new features, and creating temporal features that capture the time-based characteristics such as specific time of day, day of the week, month, or holidays. In addition, the feature engineering stage covers transformations to make time series stationary, such as differencing or log transformation, or resampling to make time series regular, as discussed in *Chapter 1*. We will see how Apache Spark can be used for feature engineering in *Chapter 8*, on model development.

2. **Model selection**: The model to choose is from an ever-growing list of candidate models for time series: ARIMA, Prophet, machine learning, deep learning models such as LSTM, and many others. The right time series model depends on the data available and the use case we are implementing, as we have seen with the use case examples in *Chapter 2*. **Exploratory data analysis** (**EDA**), detailed in *Chapter 6*, guides us in this process by providing an understanding

of the data's trends, seasonality, and underlying patterns. Finding the best model, however, is part of an iterative process, refined by model validation, which we will now present as the next step.

3. **Dataset splitting**: Once we have candidate models, the first step before training the models is to split the historical data into training, validation, and test datasets. The specific consideration in doing so for time series data is twofold: to preserve the chronological order within datasets, and to ensure that there is no data leakage between the splits.

4. **Training**: During this phase, the model is fitted to the training dataset by adjusting its parameters. This can be supervised with predefined labels or actual outcomes, or unsupervised, as explained in *Chapter 2*. In the case of supervised training, the model parameters are adjusted using a process such as gradient descent to minimize the difference, using a loss function, between model prediction and actual outcome. For unsupervised training, the model is adjusted until a stopping criterion is met, such as the number of runs or the number of categorization classes.

5. **Validation**: As part of training iterations, model validation uses unseen validation datasets with techniques such as time-based cross-validation. This is to check that there is no overfitting and that the trained model can generalize to unseen data with acceptable accuracy. The model is evaluated for accuracy using metrics such as **mean absolute percentage error** (**MAPE**) or **mean absolute error** (**MAE**). As an iterative process, this stage includes hyperparameter tuning, where models with different settings are trained and validated to find the best model configuration. Techniques such as grid search or Bayesian optimization are used to search for the optimal hyperparameters.

> **Parameters and hyperparameters**
>
> Note the difference between parameters and hyperparameters. These terms are often confused. Model **parameters** are learned from the data as part of a training run, such as a neural network's weights and biases. **Hyperparameters** define the configuration of the model prior to model training, which, in the case of a neural network, can be the number of nodes and layers defining its architecture.

6. **Testing** – As a final step in model development, the model is evaluated against the unseen testing dataset and compared with different algorithms or types of models. Testing can also include other criteria beyond model accuracy, such as response time, and integration testing with the application code used with the model.

Model training, validation, and testing will be covered in detail in *Chapter 7*.

Model deployment and monitoring

Model deployment and monitoring involves the transition of time series analysis models from development to a live production environment, together with continuous oversight of their performance. This ongoing monitoring allows retraining and updating the model to adapt to changes in the data patterns or in the behavior of the underlying system being analyzed.

We will now detail further each of these steps:

1. **Deployment**: Models are deployed for production into a model-serving framework. This can be containerized with tools such as Kubernetes and Docker or deployed to a cloud-based solution such as Databricks Model Serving, Amazon SageMaker, Azure Machine Learning, or Google Vertex AI. Once deployed, the model can be used for batch inferencing, scheduled at recurring intervals, or real-time inferencing based on continuously streaming data sources or in response to API requests.

2. **Monitoring**: Once the model is deployed in production, monitoring is required to ensure that it remains fit for purpose and of value. With **data drift** (the change in the characteristics of the data over time) and **concept drift**, where the model's representation of reality worsens over time, model accuracy decreases. This can be detected with model monitoring, and alerts sent accordingly.

3. **Retraining**: When the monitoring alerts about a drift, and if the drift is significant enough, retraining the model is the next step. This can be manually launched or automated. If retraining does not yield a sufficiently accurate model, then we will have to go back to the model development cycle to find another model fit for purpose.

4. **Governance**: This includes several key considerations. We need to keep track of model versions and life cycle stages throughout the model's life cycle and associated processes. In addition, for auditability purposes, logs of training, deployment, and accuracy metrics are kept, and in some cases, requests to and responses from model inference are also saved. Additional considerations include access control to the model and ensuring it meets all legal and regulatory compliance requirements, including when dealing with personal or sensitive data.

In summary, ModelOps for a time series analysis project covers the end-to-end process of developing, deploying, and maintaining models, while overlapping with DataOps for its data requirements. ModelOps ensures continuous improvement, reproducibility, collaboration, and fitness for purpose with respect to business objectives. It also maintains the model's effectiveness and ensures that it keeps delivering value over time.

We will cover the practical considerations for ModelOps in *Chapter 7, Building and Testing Models*. The next phase is DevOps, which we will detail now.

DevOps

Next after ModelOps, DevOps is a set of practices and tools that smoothen the handover between **development (Dev)** and **operations (Ops)**. This is for both the model and related application code. By automating the building, testing, deployment, and monitoring of time series applications, DevOps ensures that they are reliable, scalable, and continuously deliver value to the business.

The DevOps practices can be broadly broken down into **continuous integration/continuous deployment (CI/CD)**, infrastructure management, and monitoring and governance.

CI/CD

CI/CD involves automating the integration and deployment of time series analysis models for seamless updates to production.

This includes the following steps:

1. **Code and model versioning and repository**: Code and model changes require tracking, with the possibility of rolling back to previous versions if needed. This means that the code and models need to be version-controlled and stored in a repository from where the different versions can be accessed.

2. **Testing**: It is crucial that there is no regression whenever changes are made to the time series model and associated code. One way to ensure this is through automated testing, with unit and integration testing, which can be kicked off either when production monitoring detects a degradation or when there are model or associated code changes in development.

3. **Deployment**: Once the time series model and code are ready in development, the next steps are deployment to staging and production. It is recommended to automate this deployment with CI/CD pipelines to minimize the risks of errors due to manual steps and make this a seamless, repeatable, and scalable process.

In summary, CI/CD pipelines ensure that new features, improvements, and bug fixes are consistently integrated, tested, and deployed while minimizing downtime and enhancing the efficiency of new code rollout.

Infrastructure management

Infrastructure as code (IaC) is a recommended approach to provisioning as it enables the infrastructure configurations to be version-controlled, self-documented, reproducible, and scalable. This is how compute, storage, and networking configurations can be set consistently. In a virtual environment such as a cloud environment, the infrastructure itself is, in a sense, version-controlled as it is software-defined in nature.

In addition to the previous core resources, security-specific configurations require provisioning for access controls, encryption, and firewalls for network security.

As demand for the application changes, the corresponding workload changes with a requirement for additional or fewer infrastructure resources. A scalable infrastructure management process ensures that the infrastructure is automatically scaled based on demand.

Monitoring, security, and governance

DevOps has similar requirements for monitoring, security, and governance to DataOps and ModelOps. The scope for DevOps encompasses everything that is deployed to the production environment, including models, code, and configurations. This is typically fulfilled via processes such as application, security, and compliance monitoring, logging and alerting, and incident management.

In summary, DevOps ensures that applications, including time series analysis, are highly available and scalable by automating their deployment, management, and scaling. The key here is to make the transition from *Dev* to *Ops* seamless by facilitating collaboration and using automation to ensure that a time series analysis project can evolve from a use case concept to its technical implementation to a fully operational system that drives significant business impact and value.

Now that we understand the end-to-end phases of a time series analysis project, the next section will provide practical examples and tools for implementing what we have learned so far in this chapter.

Implementation examples and tools

With the end-to-end phases defined, this section will examine two implementation examples: a notebook-based approach and an orchestrator-based approach.

> **Note**
>
> If you do not intend to build your own end-to-end environment, you can skip the practical part of this section and use a managed platform such as Databricks, as we will do in future chapters.

Let's start by setting up the environment required to run the examples.

Environment setup

We will be using Docker containers, as in *Chapter 3*, for the platform infrastructure. Refer to the *Using a container for deployment* section in *Chapter 3* for instructions on installing Docker.

> **Alternative to Docker**
>
> You can use Podman as an open source alternative to Docker. You can find more information here: `https://podman.io/`.

Before we can deploy the Docker containers, we will validate in the next section that there is no conflict with the network ports that will be used by the containers.

Network ports

The following network ports need to be available on your local machine or development environment:

- Apache Spark: `7077`, `8070`, and `8081`
- Jupyter Notebook: `4040`, `4041`, `4042`, and `8888`
- MLflow: `5001`
- Airflow: `8080`

You can check for the current use of these ports by existing applications with the following command, run from the command line or terminal:

```
% netstat -an | grep LISTEN
```

If you see the required ports in the list of ports already in use, you must either stop the application using that port or change the docker-compose file to use another port.

As an example, let's assume that the output of the preceding netstat command reveals that port 8080 is already in use on your local machine or development environment, and you are not able to stop the existing application using this port.

In this case, you will need to change port 8080 (meant for the Airflow web server) in the docker-compose.yaml file to another, unused port. Just search and replace 8080 on the left of the colon (:) to say 8090 if this port is free, as per the following example:

- From this:

```
ports:
  - '7077:7077'
  - '8080:8080'
```

- To this:

```
ports:
  - '7077:7077'
  - '8090:8080'
```

Keep note of the new port and use this instead of the existing one whenever you need to type the corresponding URL. In this example, port 8080 is changed to 8090, and the matching URL change for the Airflow web server is as follows:

- From this:

```
http://localhost:8080/
```

- To this:

```
http://localhost:8090/
```

> **Note**
>
> You will need to change the network port in all URLs in the following sections that you had to modify as per this section.

Environment startup

Once Docker is installed and running, and the network port configuration is validated, the following instructions guide you to set up and start the environment:

1. We first download the deployment script from the Git repository for this chapter, which is at the following URL:

    ```
    https://github.com/PacktPublishing/Time-Series-Analysis-with-
    Spark/tree/main/ch4
    ```

    We will be using the `git clone`-friendly URL, which is as follows:

    ```
    https://github.com/PacktPublishing/Time-Series-Analysis-with-
    Spark.git
    ```

    To do this, start a terminal or command line and run the following commands:

    ```
    git clone https://github.com/PacktPublishing/Time-Series-
    Analysis-with-Spark.git
    cd Time-Series-Analysis-with-Spark/ch4
    ```

    Note that the preceding is for a macOS or Linux/Unix-based system, and you will need to run the equivalent for Windows as per the following GitHub documentation:

    ```
    https://docs.github.com/en/repositories/creating-and-managing-
    repositories/cloning-a-repository?platform=windows&tool=cli
    ```

2. On macOS, you may see the following error when you run the preceding `git` command:

    ```
    xcrun: error: invalid active developer path (/Library/Developer/
    CommandLineTools), missing xcrun at: /Library/Developer/
    CommandLineTools/usr/bin/xcrun
    ```

    In this case, you will need to reinstall the command-line tools with the following command:

    ```
    xcode-select --install
    ```

3. We can now start the container build and startup. A makefile is provided to simplify the process of starting and stopping the containers. The following command builds the Docker images for the containers and then starts them:

    ```
    make up
    ```

> **Windows environment**
>
> If you are using a Windows environment, you can install a Windows version of `make`, as per the following documentation: `https://gnuwin32.sourceforge.net/packages/make.htm`

The make up command will give the following or equivalent output:

```
make prep && docker-compose up -d
sh prep-airflow.sh
[+] Running 9/9
  ✔  Container ts-spark-env-spark-master-1        Started
  ✔  Container ts-spark-env-postgres-1            Healthy
  ✔ Container ts-spark-env-mlflow-server-1      Started ✔
Container ts-spark-env-jupyter-1              Started ✔
Container ts-spark-env-airflow-init-1         Exited ✔ Container
ts-spark-env-spark-worker-1-1     Started ✔ Container
ts-spark-env-airflow-scheduler-1 Running ✔ Container
ts-spark-env-airflow-triggerer-1 Running ✔ Container ts-spark-
env-airflow-webserver-1 Running
```

4. You may see the following error when you run the preceding make up command:

```
open /Users/<USER_LOGIN>/.docker/buildx/current: permission
denied
make: *** [up] Error 1
```

In this case, you will need to change the permission for the Docker folder with the following command, replacing <USER_LOGIN> with your own user login:

```
chmod 755 /Users/<USER_LOGIN>/.docker/buildx/current
```

Then, rerun the make up command.

5. You may get an error if you have bash instead of sh in your environment and the script cannot locate the sh file. In this case, change the last line in makefile from "sh prep-airflow. sh" to "bash prep-airflow.sh" and then run the make up command again.

By the end of the process, as in *Chapter 3*, you will have a running Spark cluster and a separate node for Jupyter Notebook. In addition, we have deployed the following components here:

- **MLflow** – An open source platform, originally developed by Databricks, for managing the end-to-end machine learning life cycle. With features for experimentation and deployment, MLflow is designed to work with any machine learning library and programming language. This makes it flexible for various environments and use cases, which explains its broad adoption.

  You can find more information here: https://mlflow.org/.

- **Apache Airflow** – Created by Airbnb, Airflow is an open source platform for orchestrating data processing pipelines and computational workflows. With the ability to programmatically define, schedule, and monitor workflows at scale, Airflow is widely adopted, including by data engineers and data scientists, for diverse types of workflows.

  You can find more information here: `https://airflow.apache.org/`.

- **Postgres** – This is the relational database used in the backend by Airflow.

Let's now validate the environment that we have just deployed.

Accessing the UIs

We will now access the **user interfaces** (**UIs**) of the different components as a quick way to validate the deployment:

1. Follow the instructions in *Chapter 3* to validate the deployment of Jupyter Notebook and the Apache Spark cluster. Note that due to the Airflow web server using port `8080`, which is the same port we used in *Chapter 3* for Apache Spark, we have changed the Spark master node to the following local URL:

    ```
    http://localhost:8070/
    ```

2. MLflow is accessible at the following local URL:

    ```
    http://localhost:5001/
    ```

    This will open the web page as per *Figure 4.4*.

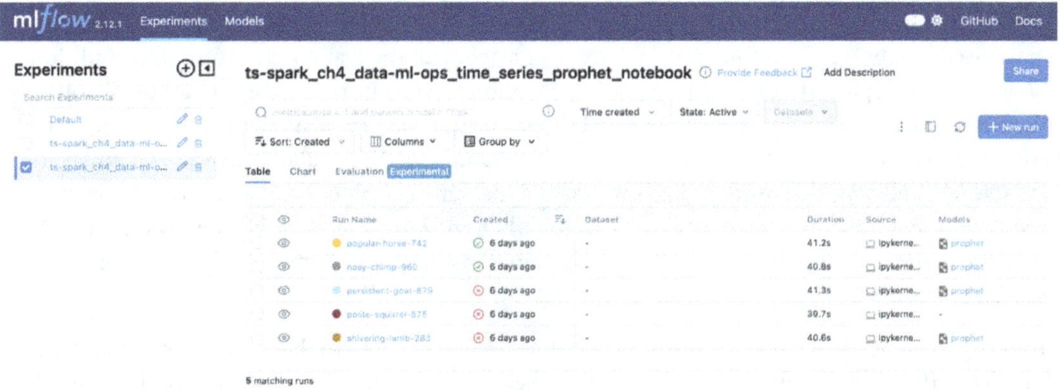

Figure 4.4: MLflow

3. The next UI, *Figure 4.5*, is for Airflow, accessible via the following local URL:

```
http://localhost:8080/
```

The default username and password are `airflow`, which is highly recommended to change.

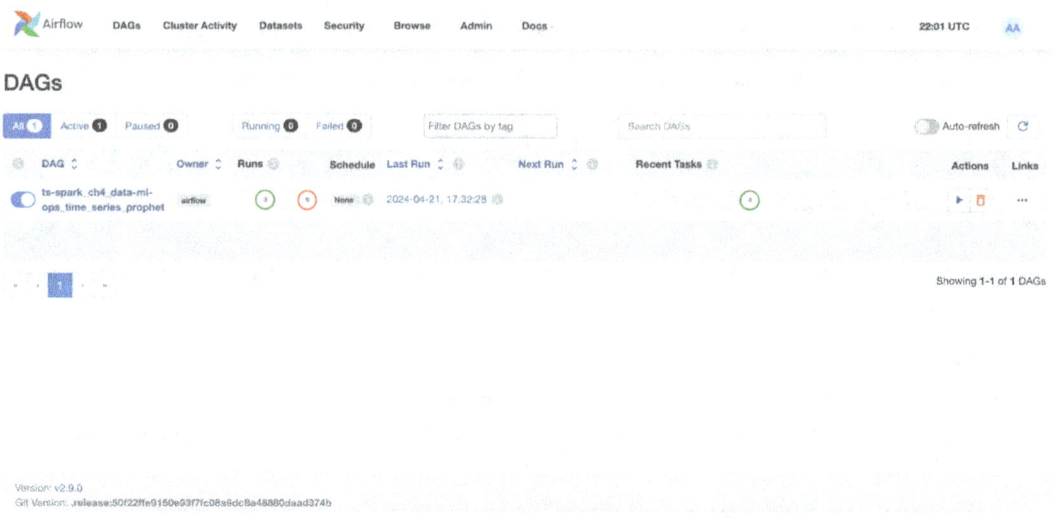

Figure 4.5: Airflow

We now have our environment set up, which we will use next.

Notebook approach

We have used notebooks from *Chapter 1*, where we started with the Databricks Community edition. In *Chapter 3*, we deployed our own notebook environment with Jupyter, which is an open source implementation. As we have seen by now, notebooks give us a feature-rich document-type interface where we can combine executable code, visualizations, and text. This makes notebooks popular for interactive and collaborative work in data science and machine learning. Notebooks can also be built for execution in a non-interactive way, which, together with the fact that they have already been used in the earlier data science and experimentation phases, makes them readily adaptable to an end-to-end notebook.

In this first example, we will use an all-in-one notebook based on the Prophet-based code introduced in *Chapter 1*. If you followed the instructions in the earlier *Environment setup* section, the example notebook should be accessible directly within the Jupyter Notebook UI, at the `work / notebooks` location on the left folder navigation panel, as shown in *Figure 4.6*, at the following URL: `http://localhost:8888/lab`.

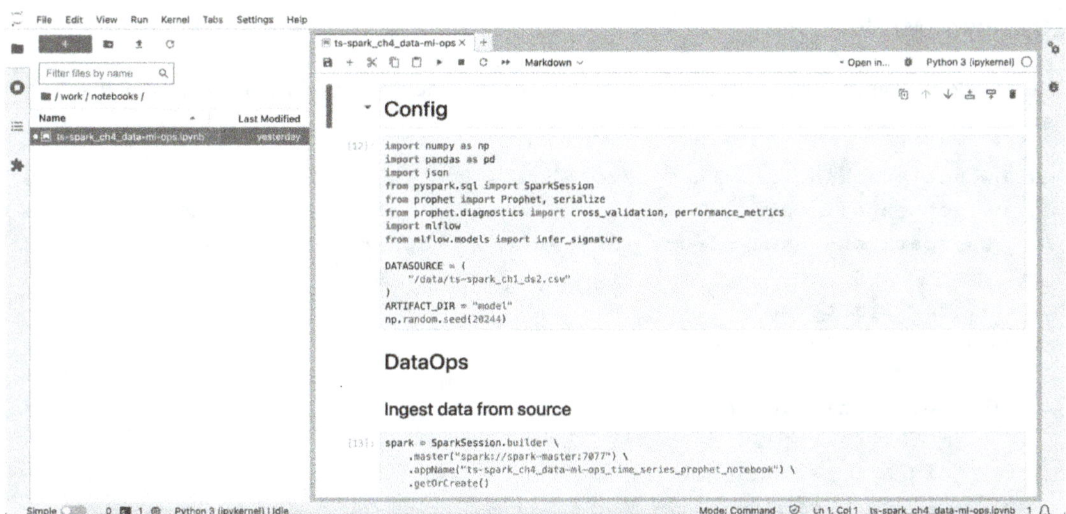

Figure 4.6: Notebook

The notebook is also downloadable from the following GitHub location:

```
https://github.com/PacktPublishing/Time-Series-Analysis-with-Spark/
raw/main/ch4/notebooks/ts-spark_ch4_data-ml-ops.ipynb
```

With a focus more on structure here than on the code itself, which does not change much from *Chapter 1*, we structured the notebook into the following sections:

- Config

- DataOps

- Ingest data from source

- Transform data

- ModelOps

- Train and log model

- Forecast with model

The notable addition to the code from *Chapter 1*, in addition to the structure explained previously, is the MLOps part, which we will detail next.

MLOps with MLflow

In this notebook example, we use MLflow as the tool to implement several MLOps requirements. The following code extract focuses on this specific part:

```
mlflow.set_tracking_uri("http://mlflow-server:5000")
mlflow.set_experiment(
    'ts-spark_ch4_data-ml-ops_time_series_prophet_notebook')

with mlflow.start_run():
    model = Prophet().fit(pdf)
...
    mlflow.prophet.log_model(
        model, artifact_path=ARTIFACT_DIR,
        signature=signature)
    mlflow.log_params(param)
    mlflow.log_metrics(cv_metrics)
```

The MLflow functionalities used in the preceding code are the following:

- `set_tracking_uri` – This sets the URI of the tracking server where MLflow will store model-related information. This centralizes model data and facilitates collaboration among team members. The tracking server can be a remote server or a local file path.

- `set_experiment` – This creates a new experiment or uses an existing one. An experiment is a logical grouping of runs (separate model training or trials), useful to organize and compare different trials.

- `start_run` – This starts a new MLflow run, which can be within a given experiment. As a representation of a single training or trial, `run` groups related artifacts such as parameters, metrics, and models.

- `prophet.log_model` – This function logs a Prophet model as an artifact in the current MLflow run.

- `log_params` – This logs key-value pairs of parameters used during the run. Parameters are model configurations.

- `log_metrics` – This logs key-value pairs of metrics evaluated during the run. Metrics are numerical values about the model's performance (e.g., Mean Squared Error, accuracy).

The outcome of this can then be accessed via the MLflow UI at the following URL: `http://localhost:5001/`.

This will open the UI to a similar page as per *Figure 4.4*, from where you can navigate on the left panel to the experiment named `ts-spark_ch4_data-ml-ops_time_series_prophet_notebook`. This experiment name seen in the UI comes from the code, which is highlighted in the preceding code.

The **Overview** tab for the experiment, shown in *Figure 4.7*, has information about the experiment such as the creator, creation date, status, source code creating the experiment, and model logged from the experiment. It also shows the model parameters and metrics as logged in the code.

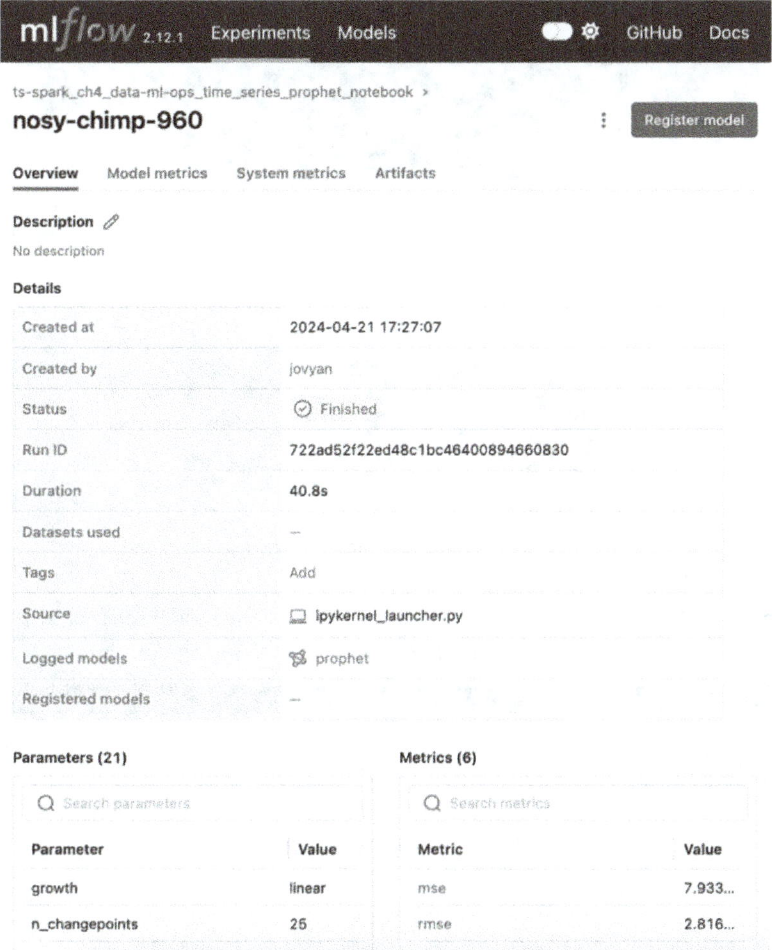

Figure 4.7: MLflow experiment overview

The **Model metrics** tab, shown in *Figure 4.8*, allows one to search and view the metrics graph.

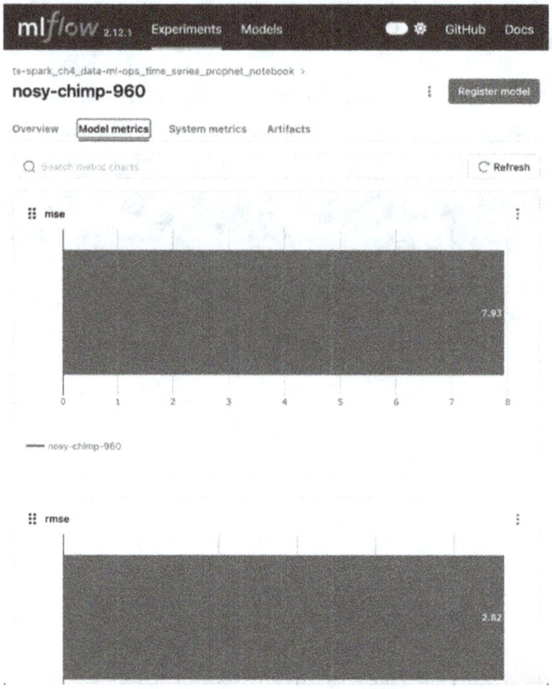

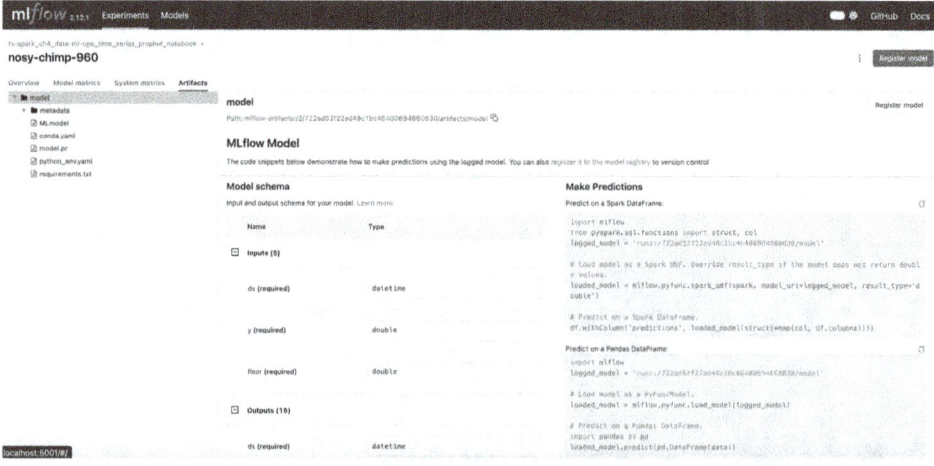

Figure 4.8: MLflow model metrics

The initial screen of the **Artifacts** tab, shown in *Figure 4.9*, shows the model schema, which we logged in the code as the signature. It also gives code examples of how to use the model.

Figure 4.9: MLflow model schema

The **MLmodel** section of the **Artifacts** tab, shown in *Figure 4.10*, shows the model artifact with its path.

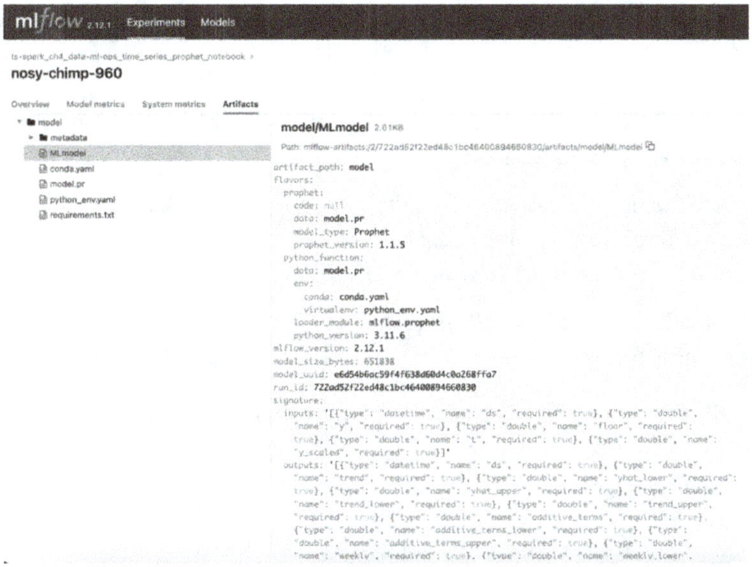

Figure 4.10: MLflow model artifact

This is as far as we will go with MLflow in this example. We will use MLflow in a similar way in the next example with an orchestrator and expand into further use of MLflow in *Chapter 9, Going to Production*. For now, we will be looking at other considerations with the notebook approach.

Multiple notebooks

The notebook example here is only a starting point that can be adapted and extended based on the requirements of your own use case, as well as the techniques that will be discussed in the following chapters. For more complex requirements, it is recommended to use separate notebooks for the following:

- Exploratory data analysis and data science

- Feature engineering

- Model development, selection, and deployment of the best model

- Production data pipeline, potentially including feature engineering as well

- Production model inferencing

- Monitoring

- Model retraining

While notebooks are great for their interactivity, collaborative ease, relative simplicity, and versatility, they have limitations, which we will cover in the next section.

Limitations

However good they are, notebooks for end-to-end time series analysis present several challenges. These are as follows:

- No scheduling and orchestration capabilities. This makes it hard to go beyond simple sequential workflows and develop complex workflows.

- Scalability issue. The notebook code runs in the notebook kernel, which is limited to the resource of the single machine where it is located. Note that this can be resolved by submitting the task from the notebook to run on the Apache Spark cluster, as we have done in our example.

- Lack of error handling. If the code in a notebook cell fails, the whole workflow execution stops. It is, of course, possible to write error-handling code, but this adds additional coding effort.

To answer these challenges, we will be considering another approach next, using an orchestrator.

Orchestrator approach

Before diving into the approach, let's first understand what an orchestrator means. Airflow, which we will use here, was mentioned earlier as an example.

An **orchestrator** plays a central role in managing workflows, including data engineering and processing. A workflow or pipeline is a set of computing tasks executed together in a certain order, in parallel or sequentially, usually with dependency on the outcome of the preceding task or tasks. In addition to scheduling the workflows, an orchestrator usually has features to author them before and monitor their execution post-scheduling.

Benefits of an orchestrator

Using an orchestrator provides the following benefits over the limitations of the notebook-only approach:

- Scheduling the tasks within the workflows, considering their dependencies and parallel or sequential execution requirements. This also includes conditional logic for task execution.

- Scalable and distributed task execution.

- Monitoring and logging workflow execution, including performance and errors. This is crucial for production environments.

- Error handling and alerting with possibilities to retry, skip to the next task, or fail the entire pipeline. This is also a key requirement for production environments.

- Integration with other systems and tools. This is required to build end-to-end workflows, covering DataOps, ModelOps, and DevOps, which usually means working with different specialized tools.

Now that we have seen the benefits and have the environment set up with Airflow as the orchestrator, let's get into the practice.

Authoring the workflow

The first step is to create the workflow or **direct acyclic graph (DAG)** as it is also called.

If you followed the instructions in the earlier *Environment setup* section, the example DAG is already loaded and accessible directly within the Airflow UI, as shown in *Figure 4.5*, at the following URL: `http://localhost:8080/`. At this point, you can jump to the next section to run the DAG or continue here for details on the DAG code.

The DAG definition is in a Python code file in the `dags` folder and is also downloadable from the following GitHub location:

`https://github.com/PacktPublishing/Time-Series-Analysis-with-Spark/raw/main/ch4/dags/ts-spark_ch4_airflow-dag.py`

The core of the code is very similar to what we saw in the previous notebook example. This section focuses on integrating with Airflow and defining the DAG's tasks, which are the individual steps of the DAG.

Task definition – Python code

When the orchestrator runs the tasks, it calls the following corresponding Python functions as the underlying code that needs to be executed. Note the function parameters that are passed in and the return values. These are aligned with the task's definition, which we will see next:

1. `ingest_data` – for task `t1`. Note that `spark.read` will run on the Spark cluster:

```python
def ingest_data():
    sdf = spark.read.csv(
        DATASOURCE, header=True, inferSchema=True)
    pdf = sdf.select("date", "daily_min_temperature").toPandas()
    return pdf
```

2. `transform_data` – for task `t2`:

```python
def transform_data(pdf, **kwargs):
    pdf.columns = ["ds", "y"]
    pdf["y"] = pd.to_numeric(pdf["y"], errors="coerce")
    pdf.drop(index=pdf.index[-2:], inplace=True)
    pdf.dropna()

    return pdf
```

3. `train_and_log_model` – for task `t3`. Note that the MLflow functions, such as `mlflow.set_experiment` and `mlflow.prophet.log_model`, make calls to the MLflow server. A partial extract of the code is shown here:

```python
def train_and_log_model(pdf, **kwargs):
    mlflow.set_experiment(
```

```
        'ts-spark_ch4_data-ml-ops_time_series_prophet')
    ...
        mlflow.prophet.log_model(
            model, artifact_path=ARTIFACT_DIR,
            signature=signature)
    ...
        return model_uri
```

4. `forecast` – for task `t4`. Note that `mlflow.prophet.load_model` loads the model from the MLflow server. This is done in this way here only to show how to retrieve the model from an MLflow server. It is not strictly required here as we could have kept the reference to the model locally:

```
def forecast(model_uri, **kwargs):
    _model = mlflow.prophet.load_model(model_uri)

    forecast = _model.predict(
        _model.make_future_dataframe(30))
    forecast[
        ['ds', 'yhat', 'yhat_lower','yhat_upper']
    ].to_csv('/data/ts-spark_ch4_prophet-forecast.csv')

    return '/data/ts-spark_ch4_prophet-forecast.csv'
```

These tasks are referenced by the DAG, which we will define next.

DAG definition

Overarching the preceding task definitions, we have the high-level Airflow DAG, which is defined as per the following:

```
dag = DAG(
    'ts-spark_ch4_data-ml-ops_time_series_prophet',
    default_args=default_args,
    description='ts-spark_ch4 - Data/MLOps pipeline example - Time
series forecasting with Prophet',
    schedule_interval=None
)
```

This points to `default_args`, which contains the following DAG parameters.

```
default_args = {
    'owner': 'airflow',
    'depends_on_past': False,
    'start_date': datetime(2024, 1, 1),
```

```
    'email_on_failure': False,
    'email_on_retry': False,
    'retries': 1,
    'retry_delay': timedelta(minutes=1),
}
```

Further information on these is available in the following Airflow documentation:

```
https://airflow.apache.org/docs/apache-airflow/stable/_api/airflow/
models/baseoperator/index.html#airflow.models.baseoperator.BaseOperator
```

We have not set `schedule_interval` as we want to trigger the DAG manually from the Airflow UI.

DAG tasks

The DAG tasks are defined as per the following. Note the reference to `dag` and to the underlying Python function defined previously. The use of `PythonOperator` means that the tasks will be calling Python functions:

1. `t1`:

```
t1 = PythonOperator(
    task_id='ingest_data',
    python_callable=ingest_data,
    dag=dag,
)
```

2. `t2`:

```
t2 = PythonOperator(
    task_id='transform_data',
    python_callable=transform_data,
    op_kwargs={'pdf': t1.output},
    provide_context=True,
    dag=dag,
)
```

Notable for task `t2` is how the output from task `t1`, `t1.output`, is passed as input, `pdf`, to task `t2`.

3. `t3`:

```
t3 = PythonOperator(
    task_id='train_and_log_model',
    python_callable=train_and_log_model,
    op_kwargs={'pdf': t2.output},
```

```
        provide_context=True,
        dag=dag,
    )
```

The output from task t2, t2.output, is passed as input, pdf, to task t3.

4. t4:

```
    t4 = PythonOperator(
        task_id='forecast',
        python_callable=forecast,
        op_kwargs={'model_uri': t3.output},
        provide_context=True,
        dag=dag,
    )
```

The output from task t3, t3.output, is passed as input, model_uri, to task t4.

These tasks are then configured with the following code to be orchestrated sequentially by Airflow:

```
# Task dependencies
t1 >> t2 >> t3 >> t4
```

This concludes the workflow definition as a DAG in Airflow. The example here is only a starting point, with a simple sequential workflow that can be adapted and extended based on your specific requirements and the additional time series analysis tasks that will be discussed in the following chapters.

> **Orchestrating notebooks**
>
> Note that it is also possible to combine the orchestrator and notebook approach by calling notebooks from Airflow tasks using the `PapermillOperator` operator. You can find more information on this operator here: `https://airflow.apache.org/docs/apache-airflow-providers-papermill/stable/operators.html`.

Once the DAG is written and placed in Airflow's dags folder, it will be automatically picked up by Airflow, checked for syntax errors in the Python definition file, and then listed in the list of DAGs available to run, which we will cover next.

Running the workflow

The workflow can be launched by clicking on the run button (>) on the right of the DAG, as seen in *Figure 4.5* of the *Accessing the UIs* section. By clicking on the DAG name on the left panel, the details and graph of the DAG can be viewed in the Airflow UI, as shown in *Figure 4.11*.

Figure 4.11: Airflow DAG

To view information on a specific run and task of the DAG, select the run on the left, and then the task from the graph. This will provide the option to view the execution log of the task.

Another interesting piece of information is the execution time of the different tasks, which can be viewed from the **Gantt** tab on the same screen.

We are only exploring the surface of Airflow here, which is a feature-rich tool beyond the scope of this book. Refer to the Airflow documentation for more information.

As was mentioned earlier, some of the code runs on the Apache Spark cluster. This can be visualized from the Spark master node, as per *Figure 3.6* in *Chapter 3*. The URL is the following: `http://localhost:8070/`. The Spark UI will show a running application if it is still running. This application is the Spark code launched from the Airflow tasks.

As for MLflow, you can view the outcome in the MLflow UI at the following URL: `http://localhost:5001/`.

From the MLflow UI page, similar to *Figure 4.4*, you can navigate on the left panel to the experiment named `ts-spark_ch4_data-ml-ops_time_series_prophet`. This experiment name seen in the UI comes from the code, which is highlighted in the code for `train_and_log_model` previously.

`This concludes the second approach discussed in this chapter. We will build on this orchestrator example using the concepts we learn in the upcoming chapters.

Environment shutdown

We can now stop the container environment. The makefile provided simplifies the process with the following command:

```
make down
```

This will give the following or equivalent output:

```
docker-compose down
[+] Running 10/10
  ✔ Container ts-spark-env-spark-worker-1-1  Removed
  ✔ Container ts-spark-env-mlflow-server-1   Removed
  ✔ Container ts-spark-env-airflow-scheduler-1Removed
  ✔ Container ts-spark-env-airflow-webserver-1Removed ✔
ontainer ts-spark-env-jupyter-1            Removed ✔ Container
ts-spark-env-airflow-triggerer-1Removed ✔ Container
ts-spark-env-airflow-init-1       Removed ✔ Container
ts-spark-env-postgres-1           Removed ✔ Container
ts-spark-env-spark-master-1       Removed ✔ Network ts-spark-env_
default                 Removed
```

If you do not intend to use it further, you can go ahead and delete the Docker containers created with the `Delete` action, as explained here: `https://docs.docker.com/desktop/use-desktop/container/#container-actions`.

Summary

In this chapter, we detailed the important phases of a time series analysis project, starting with the choice of a use case corresponding to a business requirement. The use case was then mapped to the technical solution, with DataOps, ModelOps, and DevOps components. We finally looked at two approaches for implementation, including examples of baseline implementations with an all-in-one notebook and with an orchestrator, which will be further extended in the rest of this book.

In the following chapter, we will do just that, focusing on DataOps with data preparation.

Join our community on Discord

Join our community's Discord space for discussions with the authors and other readers:

`https://packt.link/ds`

5

Data Preparation

So far, we have covered the foundations of time series and Apache Spark and the full lifecycle of a time series analysis project. In this chapter, we delve into the critical steps of organizing, cleaning, and transforming time series data for effective analysis. It covers techniques for handling missing values, dealing with outliers, and structuring data to suit Spark's distributed computing model. This information is invaluable as it equips you with the skills to ensure data quality and compatibility with Spark, laying a robust foundation for accurate and efficient time series analysis. Proper data preparation enhances the reliability of subsequent analytical processes, making this chapter an essential prerequisite to derive meaningful insights from time-dependent datasets using Spark.

We're going to cover the following main topics in this chapter:

- Data ingestion and persistence

- Data quality checks and cleaning

- Transformations

Technical requirements

Hands-on coding is predominant in this chapter, covering the common data preparation steps of a time series analysis project. The code for this chapter can be found in the `ch5` folder of the book's GitHub repository at this URL:

```
https://github.com/PacktPublishing/Time-Series-Analysis-with-Spark/
tree/main/ch5
```

> **Note**
>
> The code will be used with the Databricks Community Edition, as per the approach explained in *Chapter 1* and this chapter.

Data ingestion and persistence

In this first section, we will cover the methods of getting time series data from sources and persisting the dataset to storage.

Ingestion

Ingestion is the process by which data is retrieved from a source system for further processing and analysis. This process can be executed in batches to ingest a large amount of data as a one-off on demand or scheduled to run automatically at regular intervals, such as every night. Alternatively, if the data is available from the source system on a continual basis and is required as such, the other ingestion method is structured streaming.

> **Note**
>
> We can technically code the ingestion process as structured streaming and configure it to run at triggered intervals. This gives the flexibility to adjust to changing business requirements on data freshness without having to redevelop the ingestion process.

In this chapter, we will focus on batch ingestion, the most common method today. We will also briefly discuss structured streaming, which is quickly gaining adoption and has even overtaken batch ingestion in some organizations.

Batch ingestion

Batch ingestion is usually done from file storage or from a database.

From file storage

As we saw in the hands-on sections of the previous chapters, reading from a file is a frequently used batch ingestion method. This is done as follows with Apache Spark, using `spark.read()`:

```
df = spark.read.csv("file_path", header=True, sep=";",
inferSchema=True)
```

With this example, we are reading a CSV-formatted file from a `file_path` storage location. The header is present in this file as the first line. The different columns are separated with a `;` character. We want Spark to find out the data columns and types present in the file, as specified with `inferSchema`.

This example is based on the code in `ts-spark_ch5_1.dbc`, which we can import from the GitHub location for *Chapter 5*, mentioned in the *Technical requirements* section, into Databricks Community Edition, as per the approach explained in *Chapter 1*.

The code URL is `https://github.com/PacktPublishing/Time-Series-Analysis-with-Spark/raw/main/ch5/ts-spark_ch5_1.dbc`.

The ingested data can then be further processed and analyzed, as shown in *Figure 5.1*, based on the code example provided for this chapter.

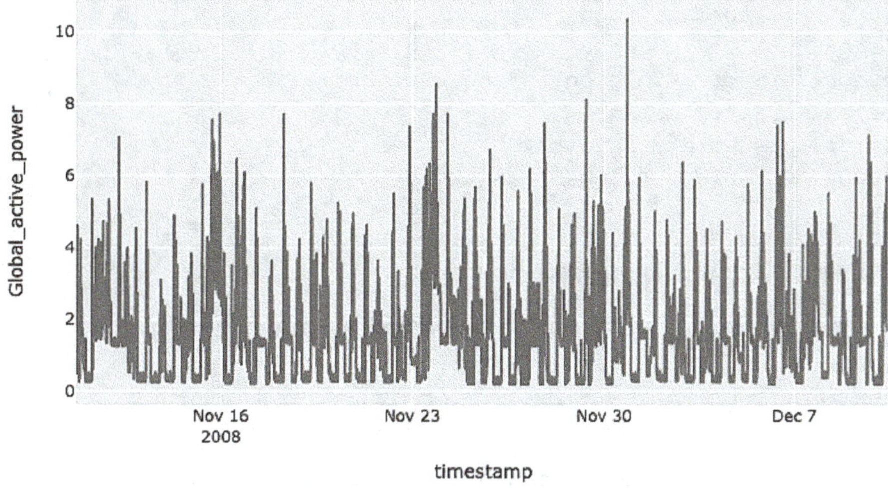

Figure 5.1: Viewing the ingested data

When reading files, it is also possible to read multiple files from a storage folder by proving the folder location instead of a specific file location. This is a common ingestion pattern for files. Another frequently used feature is to provide a filter (`pathGlobFilter`) to only include filenames matching a pattern.

There are many other options for the `spark.read` command, depending on the source being read. The following Apache Spark documentation on data sources details these options:

`https://spark.apache.org/docs/latest/sql-data-sources.html`

From a database

Another frequently used type of source is a relational database. An example for reading from PostgreSQL follows:

```
df = spark.read \
    .format("jdbc") \
    .option("url", "jdbc:postgresql:dbserver") \
    .option("dbtable", "schema.tablename") \
    .option("user", "username") \
    .option("password", "password") \
    .load()
```

This is further detailed in the following documentation: `https://spark.apache.org/docs/latest/sql-data-sources-jdbc.html`

Data from specialized time series databases, such as QuestDB, can be ingested in a similar way, as shown here:

```
df = spark.read.format("jdbc") \
    .option("url", "jdbc:postgresql://localhost:8812/questdb") \
    .option("driver", "org.postgresql.Driver") \
    .option("user", "admin") \
    .option("password", "quest") \
    .option("dbtable", "timeseries_table") \
    .load()
```

This is further detailed in the following documentation:

```
https://questdb.io/blog/integrate-apache-spark-questdb-time-series-
analytics/
```

> **Note**
>
> You will need to include the JDBC driver for the particular database on the Spark classpath. The previously referenced documentation explains this.

Structured Streaming

In the case of event-driven or near-real-time processing with Apache Spark, time series data can be ingested from streaming sources such as Apache Kafka, Amazon Kinesis, Google Cloud Pub/Sub, and Azure Event Hubs. This typically involves setting up Spark Structured Streaming with the corresponding connectors for the source.

The following example shows how to ingest data from Apache Kafka using Spark:

```
df = spark \
    .readStream \
    .format("kafka") \
    .option("kafka.bootstrap.servers", "host1:port1,host2:port2") \
    .option("subscribe", "topic1") \
    .load()
```

The Apache Spark documentation provides further details on reading from streaming sources:

```
https://spark.apache.org/docs/latest/structured-streaming-programming-
guide.html#input-sources
```

Once the data has been ingested, the next step is to persist it to storage for further processing, as we will see next.

Persistence

Data is typically persisted to files on disk or to databases. With Apache Spark, a proven solution for files is Delta Lake, an open source storage protocol.

> **Note**
>
> Apache Iceberg is another common open source storage protocol.

Delta provides ACID transactions to Apache Spark and big data workloads, effectively combining the best of file and database storage, in what is called a **lakehouse** (merge of the terms *data lake* and *data warehouse*). Built on top of the Parquet file format, Delta provides capabilities such as schema enforcement, data versioning, and time travel.

Here's an example of how you can persist time series data in Delta storage format using Apache Spark in Python:

```
df.write.format("delta").mode("overwrite").option("path", delta_table_
path).saveAsTable(table_name)
```

With this example, we are writing in Delta format to a `delta_table_path` storage location. The `overwrite` mode means that existing data at this location will be overwritten. With Delta format, the data is written as a table that is given the name specified in `table_name`.

This example is based on the code in `ts-spark_ch5_1.dbc`, which we imported in the earlier section on batch ingestion.

There are many other options for the `spark.write` command, depending on the destination being written to. The following Apache Spark documentation on saving details these options:

```
https://spark.apache.org/docs/latest/sql-data-sources-load-save-
functions.html#saving-to-persistent-tables
```

When the data is persisted in Delta format, in addition to the data, metadata is also stored together to disk. This can be retrieved with the following code:

```
# Load the Delta table as a DeltaTable object
delta_table = DeltaTable.forPath(spark, delta_table_path)


# Details on the Delta table
print("Delta table details:")
delta_table.detail().display()
```

> **Note**
>
> In the code example, we did not have to install Delta as it is already installed when using the Databricks Community Edition. You will need to install the Delta packages if you are using another Apache Spark environment where Delta is not pre-installed. You can find the instructions here: `https://docs.delta.io/latest/quick-start.html`.

Figure 5.2 shows some of the metadata such as location and creation date.

	format	id	name	description	location	createdAt	lastModified	partitionColu...	clusteringColumns
1	delta	› 66beb4b4-72...	null	null	dbfs:/tmp/delta_table/ts-spark_ch6	2024-05-26T17:10:45.027...	2024-05-26T22:14:12.0...	› []	› []

Figure 5.2: Metadata for the Delta table

Once data has been persisted, it can be read from storage as needed at a later stage for querying and analysis. The `spark.read` command can be used here as well, as per the following example:

```
spark.read.load(delta_table_path).display()
```

The Delta table storage location, `delta_table_path`, is passed to the `load` command, which retrieves the stored table from the disk storage.

As mentioned earlier, Spark can also write to a database, among other destinations. The following example shows how to write to a PostgreSQL database.

```
jdbcDF.write \
    .format("jdbc") \
    .option("url", "jdbc:postgresql:dbserver") \
    .option("dbtable", "schema.tablename") \
    .option("user", "username") \
    .option("password", "password") \
    .save()
```

This is further detailed in the following documentation: `https://spark.apache.org/docs/latest/sql-data-sources-jdbc.html`

> **Note**
>
> You will need to include the JDBC driver for the particular database on the Spark classpath. The previously referenced documentation explains this.

As seen in this section, persistence allows longer-term storage and retrieval. Delta also stores different versions of the data whenever it changes, which we will investigate next.

Versioning

Data versioning is one of the key features provided by Delta Lake, allowing you to keep track of changes made to your data over time. This storage of different versions is done in an optimal way to minimize storage footprint.

With a record of different versions, Delta enables a functionality called **time travel**. With this, you can query data at specific versions or timestamps, revert to previous versions, and perform time travel queries. This is also useful from a reproducibility point of view, whereby we can go back to the specific version of data used previously, even if it has since changed, to audit, review, and redo an analysis.

The code provided in this chapter has an example of using versioning and time travel. The following extract shows how to read a specific version of the Delta table. `version_as_of` is an integer representing the version number:

```
df_ = spark.read.format("delta").option("versionAsOf", version_as_of).
load(delta_table_path)
```

It is also possible to read a specific version based on the timestamp, as per the following code extract, where `timestamp_as_of` represents the timestamp of the version of interest:

```
df_ = spark.read.format("delta").option("timestampAsOf", timestamp_as_
of).load(delta_table_path)
```

As changes are made to the Delta table, the metadata about the different versions is stored in a Delta table history log. The history can be read with the `history` command, as follows:

```
print(f"Delta table history - after modification:")
delta_table.history().display()
```

An example of output from the history is shown in *Figure 5.3*.

	version	timestamp	userId	userName	operation	operationParameters
1	16	2024-05-26T22:15:18Z	1619420825461316	yonira2@yahoo.fr	RESTORE	▸ {"version": "14", "timestamp": null}
2	15	2024-05-26T22:14:29Z	1619420825461316	yonira2@yahoo.fr	CREATE OR REPLACE TABLE AS SELECT	▸ {"partitionBy": "[]", "clusterBy": "[]", "description": null, "isManaged": "false", '
3	14	2024-05-26T22:14:12Z	1619420825461316	yonira2@yahoo.fr	CREATE OR REPLACE TABLE AS SELECT	▸ {"partitionBy": "[]", "clusterBy": "[]", "description": null, "isManaged": "false", '
4	13	2024-05-26T18:27:49Z	1619420825461316	yonira2@yahoo.fr	RESTORE	▸ {"version": "11", "timestamp": null}
5	12	2024-05-26T18:25:27Z	1619420825461316	yonira2@yahoo.fr	UPDATE	▸ {"predicate": "[\"((timestamp#56876 >= 2008-11-10 18:00:00) AND (timesta 18:15:00))\"]"}
6	11	2024-05-26T18:25:10Z	1619420825461316	yonira2@yahoo.fr	RESTORE	▸ {"version": "9", "timestamp": null}
7	10	2024-05-26T18:24:21Z	1619420825461316	yonira2@yahoo.fr	CREATE OR REPLACE TABLE AS SELECT	▸ {"partitionBy": "[]", "clusterBy": "[]", "description": null, "isManaged": "false", '

Figure 5.3: Delta table versions

Finally, it is possible to restore the Delta table back to a previous version with the `restoreToVersion` command, overwriting the latest version, as per the following:

```
delta_table.restoreToVersion(latest_version)
```

You can also find more information on time travel here:

```
https://delta.io/blog/2023-02-01-delta-lake-time-travel/
```

This concludes the section on ingestion and persistence. We will now move on to verify and clean the data.

Data quality checks, cleaning, and transformation

Once the data has been ingested from source systems to a storage location from which we can access it, we will need to ensure that it is of usable quality and, if not, do the necessary cleaning and transformation.

Data quality checks

The outcome of any analysis done with the data can be only as good as the data, making data quality checks an important next step.

Consistency, accuracy, and completeness

Data quality checks for consistency, accuracy, and completeness are essential to ensure the reliability of your data. With its powerful tools for data processing and analysis, Apache Spark is suitable for implementing these checks. The following are examples of how you can perform data quality checks for consistency, accuracy, and completeness using Apache Spark in Python.

Consistency check

In the following consistency test example, we are counting the number of records for each date:

```python
# Example consistency check: Check if a column has consistent values

consistency_check_result = df.groupBy("Date").count().orderBy("count")

print(f"Data consistency result:")
consistency_check_result.display()
```

As per *Figure 5.4*, this simple check shows that some dates do not consistently have the same number of records, which can indicate missing values for some dates.

```
Data consistency result:
```

Table ∨   +

	Date	count
1	2008-11-10	371
2	2008-12-10	648
3	2008-11-12	1438
4	2008-11-23	1439
5	2008-11-14	1440
6	2008-11-27	1440

↓   31 rows | 2.01 seconds runtime

Figure 5.4: Consistency check results

Accuracy check

In the accuracy test example, we want to verify the accuracy of Global_active_power, as follows:

```python
# Example accuracy check:
# Check if values in a column meet certain criteria
accuracy_check_expression = "Global_active_power < 0 OR Global_active_
power > 10"

# Check
accuracy_check_result = df.filter(accuracy_check_expression)
accuracy_check_result_count = accuracy_check_result.count()

if accuracy_check_result_count == 0:
    print(f"Data meets accuracy check - !({accuracy_check_
expression}).")
else:
    print(f"Data fails accuracy check - {accuracy_check_expression} -
count {accuracy_check_result_count}:")
    accuracy_check_result.display()
```

As per *Figure 5.5*, this check shows that in two cases, `Global_active_power` is outside of the accuracy criteria that we have defined for this check. This indicates that either these values are wrong or that they are correct but are now going beyond the previously known ranges that we have used to define the criteria. We must update the criteria in this latter case.

```
Data fails accuracy check – Global_active_power < 0 OR Global_active_power > 10 – count 2:
```

	Date	Time	Global_active_power	Global_reactive_power	Voltage
1	2008-11-30	20:17:00	10.074	0.06	231.41
2	2008-11-30	20:19:00	10.348	0.084	231.6

↓ 2 rows | 1.70 seconds runtime

Figure 5.5: Accuracy check results

Completeness check

In the completeness test example, we want to verify whether `Global_active_power` has null values:

```python
# Example completeness check: Check for null values in a column
completeness_check_expression = "Global_active_power is NULL"


# Check
completeness_check_result = df.filter(
    completeness_check_expression)
completeness_check_result_count = completeness_check_result.count()

if completeness_check_result_count == 0:
    print(f"Data meets completeness check - !({completeness_check_
expression})")
else:
    print(f"Data fails completeness check - {completeness_check_
expression} - count {completeness_check_result_count}:")
    completeness_check_result.display()
```

> **Note**
>
> The consistency check example presented earlier can also be used for completeness.

These examples show basic data quality checks for consistency, accuracy, and completeness using Apache Spark. These checks can be extended and integrated into your data pipelines for more comprehensive data quality assurance.

Data quality framework

To better manage the suite of tests, it is recommended that a framework such as *Great Expectations* be used for data quality checks. You can find more information here: `https://github.com/ great-expectations/great_expectations`

We will cover another framework approach with the integration of data quality in the Delta Live Tables pipeline, and monitoring and alerting in *Chapter 5*.

Once the data quality has been tested, the next step is to clean the data.

Data cleaning

The previous step of data quality checks indicates the issues with the data that need to be corrected, which we will now address.

Missing values

Apache Spark offers various methods to handle missing values in time series data. The following examples show how you can clean time series data for missing values using Apache Spark in Python.

Forward filling

The forward filling method to handle missing values replaces the missing values with the previous known value, with the values sorted in chronological order based on their timestamp. In the following code example, missing values for `Global_active_power` are replaced in this way. The `Window. rowsBetween` function in the following case goes from the first record to the current one. The `last` function then finds the last non-null value within that window. As the window slides over all the records, all the missing values are replaced with the last known value:

```python
from pyspark.sql import functions as F
from pyspark.sql import Window

# Example: Handling missing values by forward filling
# "timestamp" column is ordered chronologically
df = spark.sql(
    f"select timestamp, Global_active_power from {table_name} order by timestamp"
)

window = Window.rowsBetween(float('-inf'),0)

filled_df = df.withColumn(
    "filled_Global_active_power",
    F.last(df['Global_active_power'],
```

```
        ignorenulls=True).over(window))


# Display updated values
filled_df.filter(
    "timestamp BETWEEN '2008-11-10 17:58:00' AND'2008-11-10 18:17:00'"
).display()
```

The result of forward filling can be seen in *Figure 5.6*, where the filled values are shown in the `filled_Global_active_power` column.

	timestamp	Global_active_power	filled_Global_active_power
1	2008-11-10T17:58:00Z	4.016	4.016
2	2008-11-10T17:59:00Z	4.012	4.012
3	2008-11-10T18:00:00Z	null	4.012
4	2008-11-10T18:01:00Z	null	4.012
5	2008-11-10T18:02:00Z	null	4.012
6	2008-11-10T18:03:00Z	null	4.012

20 rows | 2.10 seconds runtime

Figure 5.6: Forward filling

Forward filling works well when the last known value is a good indication of the next value, such as for a slow-changing value. It is not a good method when the value can change suddenly or when there is seasonality.

Backward filling

The backward filling method to handle missing values replaces the missing values with the next known value, with the values sorted in chronological order based on their timestamp. In the following code example, missing values for `Global_active_power` are replaced in this way. The `Window.rowsBetween` function in the following case goes from the current one to the last record. The `first` function then finds the next non-null value within that window. As the window slides over all the records, all the missing values are replaced with the next known value:

```
from pyspark.sql import functions as F
from pyspark.sql import Window


# Example: Handling missing values by backward filling
# "timestamp" column is ordered chronologically
df = spark.sql(
    f"select timestamp, Global_active_power from {table_name} order by
timestamp"
```

```
)

window = Window.rowsBetween(0,float('inf'))

filled_df = df.withColumn(
    "filled_Global_active_power",
    F.first(df['Global_active_power'],
            ignorenulls=True).over(window))

# Display updated values
filled_df.filter(
    "timestamp BETWEEN '2008-11-10 17:58:00' AND'2008-11-10 18:17:00'"
).display()
```

The result of backward filling can be seen in *Figure 5.7*, where the filled values are shown in the `filled_Global_active_power` column.

	timestamp	Global_active_power	filled_Global_active_power
1	2008-11-10T17:58:00Z	4.016	4.016
2	2008-11-10T17:59:00Z	4.012	4.012
3	2008-11-10T18:00:00Z	null	0.522
4	2008-11-10T18:01:00Z	null	0.522
5	2008-11-10T18:02:00Z	null	0.522
6	2008-11-10T18:03:00Z	null	0.522
7	2008-11-10T18:04:00Z	null	0.522
8	2008-11-10T18:05:00Z	null	0.522
9	2008-11-10T18:06:00Z	null	0.522
10	2008-11-10T18:07:00Z	null	0.522
11	2008-11-10T18:08:00Z	null	0.522
12	2008-11-10T18:09:00Z	null	0.522
13	2008-11-10T18:10:00Z	null	0.522
14	2008-11-10T18:11:00Z	null	0.522
15	2008-11-10T18:12:00Z	null	0.522
16	2008-11-10T18:13:00Z	null	0.522
17	2008-11-10T18:14:00Z	null	0.522
18	2008-11-10T18:15:00Z	null	0.522
19	2008-11-10T18:16:00Z	0.522	0.522
20	2008-11-10T18:17:00Z	0.508	0.508

20 rows | 46.37 seconds runtime

Figure 5.7: Backward filling

Backward filling works well when the next known value can reasonably indicate the previous value, such as with slow-changing data or when collecting data retrospectively with gaps in the past. However, it is not suitable for analyzing causality or leading indicators.

Interpolation

The interpolation method to handle missing values replaces the missing values with a combination, such as the average, of the previous and next non-missing values, with the values sorted in chronological order based on their timestamp.

> **Note**
>
> There are several different interpolation calculation methods, including linear, polynomial, and spline interpolation. The average method used here is a simple form of linear interpolation.

In the following code example, missing values for `Global_active_power` are replaced in this way. The `Window.rowsBetween` function, used twice, in the following case, goes from the first record to the current one for `windowF`, and from the current one to the last record for `windowB`. The `last` function then finds the previous non-null value within `windowF`, while the `first` function finds the next non-null value within `windowB`. These two non-null values are averaged. As the window slides over all the records, all the missing values are replaced by the averaged value:

```
from pyspark.sql import Window

# Example: Handling missing values by backward filling
# "timestamp" column is ordered chronologically
df = spark.sql(
    f"select timestamp, Global_active_power from {table_name} order by
timestamp"
)

windowF = Window.rowsBetween(float('-inf'),0)
windowB = Window.rowsBetween(0,float('inf'))

filled_df = df.withColumn(
    "filled_Global_active_power", (F.last(
        df['Global_active_power'], ignorenulls=True
    ).over(windowF) + F.first(
        df['Global_active_power'], ignorenulls=True
    ).over(windowB))/2)

# Display updated values
filled_df.filter(
    "timestamp BETWEEN '2008-11-10 17:58:00' AND'2008-11-10 18:17:00'"
).display()
```

The result of interpolation can be seen in *Figure 5.8*, where the filled values are shown in the `filled_Global_active_power` column.

	timestamp	Global_active_power	filled_Global_active_power
1	2008-11-10T17:58:00Z	4.016	4.016
2	2008-11-10T17:59:00Z	4.012	4.012
3	2008-11-10T18:00:00Z	null	2.267
4	2008-11-10T18:01:00Z	null	2.267
5	2008-11-10T18:02:00Z	null	2.267
6	2008-11-10T18:03:00Z	null	2.267
7	2008-11-10T18:04:00Z	null	2.267
8	2008-11-10T18:05:00Z	null	2.267
9	2008-11-10T18:06:00Z	null	2.267
10	2008-11-10T18:07:00Z	null	2.267
11	2008-11-10T18:08:00Z	null	2.267
12	2008-11-10T18:09:00Z	null	2.267
13	2008-11-10T18:10:00Z	null	2.267
14	2008-11-10T18:11:00Z	null	2.267
15	2008-11-10T18:12:00Z	null	2.267
16	2008-11-10T18:13:00Z	null	2.267
17	2008-11-10T18:14:00Z	null	2.267
18	2008-11-10T18:15:00Z	null	2.267
19	2008-11-10T18:16:00Z	0.522	0.522
20	2008-11-10T18:17:00Z	0.508	0.508

20 rows | 45.76 seconds runtime

Figure 5.8: Interpolation

Interpolation works well for slow-changing values, when there is a predictable cyclical pattern, or when there is a small gap in data. It is not a good method when the value can change suddenly, is discrete, or when there is a large gap in data.

Of the three methods shown for handling missing values, the appropriate method to use is based on the characteristics of your time series data and the requirements of your analysis.

> **Data leakage**
>
> Note that the backward filling and interpolation methods can leak future data across the boundaries of training, validation, and test data splits. Use these methods within the splits, and not across, or use forward filling if this is going to be an issue.

Duplicates

The presence of duplicate values in time series data can skew analysis and lead to incorrect results. Apache Spark has functions to efficiently remove duplicate values. In the following example, we clean time series data for duplicate values using Apache Spark in Python.

The `dropDuplicates` function removes duplicates by comparing all columns by default and only considers a row to be a duplicate if all the columns match those of one or more other rows. This will not work if we have multiple rows with, say, the same `timestamp` column value but different values in one or more other columns. In this case, we can pass a subset of one or more columns as a parameter to be used to identify the duplicates, as opposed to using all the columns.

In the most common cases, we want to have one and only one row of values for each timestamp and consider the other rows with the same timestamp to be duplicates. Passing the timestamp as the subset parameter to `dropDuplicates` will remove all the other rows having the same timestamp value, as we will see in the following code example:

```python
# Example: Remove duplicate rows based on all columns
print(f"With duplicates - count: {df.count()}")
cleaned_df = df.dropDuplicates()
print(f"Without duplicates - count: {cleaned_df.count()}")


# Example: Remove duplicate rows based on selected columns
# Assuming "timestamp" is the column to identify duplicates
cleaned_df = df.dropDuplicates(["timestamp"])
print(f"Without duplicates timestamp - count: {cleaned_df.count()}")
```

Depending on your dataset and use case, you can choose the appropriate method based on the columns that uniquely identify duplicates in your time series data.

Outliers

The detection and handling of outliers in time series data is crucial to ensure the accuracy of analysis and modeling. Apache Spark provides various functions to detect and handle outliers efficiently. The following example shows how to clean time series data for outliers using Apache Spark in Python.

The z-score method used is based on how far the data point is from the mean relative to the standard deviation, `stddev`. The parametrizable threshold value, `z_score_threshold`, then specifies beyond which z-score value the data point is considered an outlier. A high threshold will allow more data points in, while a low threshold will flag more outliers:

```python
from pyspark.sql import functions as F


# Example: Detect outliers using z-score
# Compute z-score for each value in the "value" column
```

```python
mean_value = df.select(F.mean(
    "Global_active_power")).collect()[0][0]
stddev_value = df.select(F.stddev(
    "Global_active_power")).collect()[0][0]
z_score_threshold = 5  # Adjust the threshold as needed

df_with_z_score = df.withColumn("z_score", (F.col(
    "Global_active_power") - mean_value) / stddev_value)

# Filter out rows where z-score exceeds the threshold
outliers = df_with_z_score.filter(~F.col("z_score").between(
    -z_score_threshold, z_score_threshold))
cleaned_df = df_with_z_score.filter(F.col("z_score").between(
    -z_score_threshold, z_score_threshold))

# Mark as outliers
df_with_outlier = df_with_z_score.withColumn(
    "_outlier",
    F.when(
        (F.col("z_score") < -z_score_threshold) |
        (F.col("z_score") > z_score_threshold), 1
    ).otherwise(0))

print(f"With outliers - count: {df.count()}")
print(f"Global_active_power - mean: {mean_value}, stddev_value:
{stddev_value}, z_score_threshold: {z_score_threshold}")
print(f"Without outliers - count: {cleaned_df.count()}")
print(f"Outliers - count: {outliers.count()}")
print("Outliers:")
outliers.display()
```

Figure 5.9 shows the outcome of the outlier detection based on the z-score chosen.

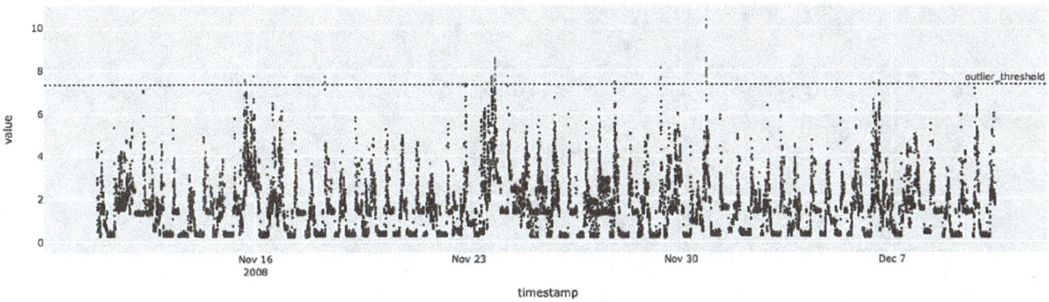

Figure 5.9: Outlier detection

Beyond this example, the choice of z-score threshold and outlier detection techniques is based on the data characteristics and requirements of the use case.

> **Note**
>
> Outliers can be indicative of one or more anomalies in the source system that generated the measurement, or data processing or transmission issues post source system. The identification of outliers flags the requirement to further investigate the source system and the data transmission chain to find the root cause.

After cleaning the data based on the issues identified with the data quality checks, other transformations, which we will look at next, are required to get the data into the right shape for the analytics algorithm to work.

Transformations

In this section, we will look at examples of normalizing and standardizing, and touch briefly on stationary transformation.

Normalizing

Normalizing time series data ensures that features are on a similar scale, which can improve the performance of machine learning algorithms while facilitating analysis. Apache Spark provides various functions for normalization. The following example shows how to normalize time series data using Apache Spark in Python.

The min-max normalization technique is used to scale the data points relative to the min-max range. The `min` and `max` values are calculated first. This brings the value to the range of 0 for the minimum value and 1 for the maximum value:

```python
from pyspark.sql import functions as F


# Define the columns to normalize (e.g., "value" column)
columns_to_normalize = ["Global_active_power"]


# Compute the minimum and maximum values for each column to normalize
min_max_values = df.select(
    [F.min(F.col(column)).alias(f"min_{column}")
     for column in columns_to_normalize] +
    [F.max(F.col(column)).alias(f"max_{column}")
     for column in columns_to_normalize]
).collect()[0]


# Normalize the data using min-max normalization
```

```python
for column in columns_to_normalize:
    min_value = min_max_values[f"min_{column}"]
    max_value = min_max_values[f"max_{column}"]
    df = df.withColumn(
        f"normalized_{column}",
        (F.col(column) - min_value) / (max_value - min_value))

print(f"Normalized - {columns_to_normalize}:")
df.display()
```

Figure 5.10 shows the outcome of normalizing the example time series data.

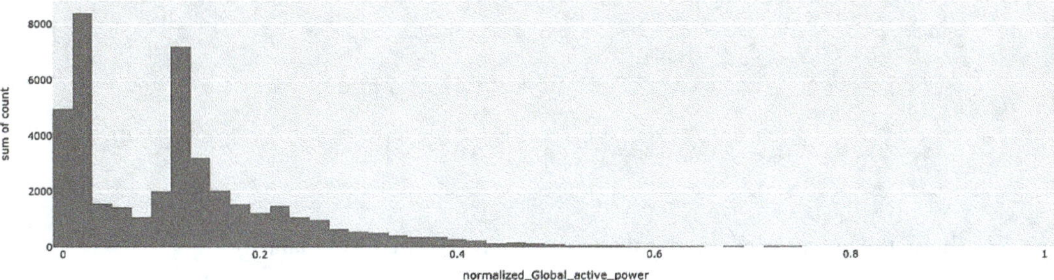

Figure 5.10: Normalizing

Depending on the specific requirements and data characteristics, the normalization method can be adjusted with the use of other techniques such as z-score normalization and decimal scaling, in addition to the min-max technique used in the example.

Standardizing

Standardizing time series data ensures that features are on a similar scale, which can improve the performance of machine learning algorithms while facilitating analysis. This method transforms the data such that it has a mean of 0 and a standard deviation of 1. Apache Spark provides various functions for standardization. The following example shows how to standardize time series data using Apache Spark in Python.

This example uses `log` values to account for the skewness of the data. First, `mean` and `stddev` are calculated. These values are then used in the formula to standardize:

```python
from pyspark.sql import functions as F

# Define the columns to standardize (e.g., "value" column)
columns_to_standardize = ["Global_active_power"]

# Compute the mean and standard deviation for each column to
# standardize
```

```
mean_stddev_values = df.select(
    [F.mean(F.log(F.col(column))).alias(f"mean_{column}")
     for column in columns_to_standardize] +
    [F.stddev(F.log(F.col(column))).alias(f"stddev_{column}")
     for column in columns_to_standardize]
).collect()[0]


# Standardize the data using z-score standardization
for column in columns_to_standardize:
    mean_value = mean_stddev_values[f"mean_{column}"]
    stddev_value = mean_stddev_values[f"stddev_{column}"]
    df = df.withColumn(
        f"standardized_{column}",
        (F.log(F.col(column)) - mean_value) / stddev_value
    )
print(f"Standardized - {columns_to_standardize}:")
df.display()
```

Figure 5.11 shows the outcome of standardizing the example time series data.

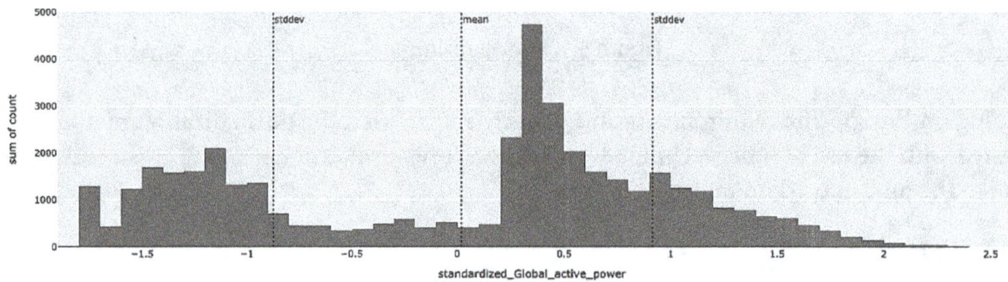

Figure 5.11: Standardizing

The standardization method can be adjusted depending on the specific requirements and data characteristics.

Stationary

In *Chapter 1*, we discussed the requirement of stationary time series for some analysis methods. Making time series data stationery involves removing trends and seasonality, which we will cover in the following chapter.

This concludes the section on testing for data quality and then cleaning and transforming time series data. We will cover the scalability considerations in data preparation when we discuss feature engineering in *Chapter 8*.

Summary

In conclusion, this chapter focused on the critical steps of organizing, cleaning, and transforming time series data for effective analysis. We have covered data preparation techniques using Apache Spark for ingestion, persistence, data quality checks, cleaning, and transformations. We looked at code examples for, among others, handling missing values and duplicates, addressing outliers, and normalizing data. This has set the stage for an accurate and efficient analytical process using Apache Spark. Proper data preparation significantly enhances the reliability of subsequent analytical processes, which is what we will progress toward in the next chapter.

6

Exploratory Data Analysis

After loading and preparing data (covered in the previous chapter), we will now go through exploratory data analysis to uncover patterns and insights in time series data. We will use statistical analysis techniques, including those specific to temporal patterns. The outcomes of these steps are crucial for identifying trends and seasonality, informing subsequent modeling decisions. Robust exploratory data analysis using Apache Spark ensures a comprehensive grasp of the dataset's characteristics, enhancing the accuracy and relevance of subsequent time series models and analyses.

In this chapter, we're going to cover the following main topics:

- Statistical analysis

- Resampling, decomposition, and stationarity

- Correlation analysis

Technical requirements

The hands-on coding predominant in this chapter covers the frequently used data exploration techniques for a time series analysis project. The code for this chapter can be found in the ch6 folder of the book's GitHub repository at this URL: https://github.com/PacktPublishing/Time-Series-Analysis-with-Spark/tree/main/ch6.

> **Note**
>
> We will use Spark DataFrames in the code examples and convert them to pandas DataFrames for libraries supporting pandas. This shows how to interchangeably use both. The use of pandas will be mentioned when this is the case.

Statistical analysis

This section starts with the statistical analysis of time series data and covers data profiling to gather these statistics, distribution analysis, and visualizations.

The examples in this chapter are based on the code in `ts-spark_ch6_1.dbc`, which we can import from the GitHub location for *Chapter 6*, mentioned in the *Technical requirements* section, into Databricks Community Edition, as per the approach explained in *Chapter 1*.

The code URL is as follows: `https://github.com/PacktPublishing/Time-Series-Analysis-with-Spark/raw/main/ch6/ts-spark_ch6_1.dbc`

We will start the hands-on examples with the household energy consumption dataset, which we also used in *Chapter 2* and *Chapter 5*. After loading the dataset with `spark.read`, as per the following code extract, we cache the DataFrame in memory with `df.cache()` to accelerate subsequent processing. Due to lazy evaluation, the caching will happen on the next action and not immediately. As we want the caching to happen, we have added an `df.count()` action to force this. We then create a `timestamp` column combining the `Date` and `Time` columns. As the numerical columns have been loaded as strings, we must convert them to the numerical `double` data type to be able to do calculations. Note that we have coded the operations on the `df` DataFrame in separate lines for readability. We could alternatively chain the multiple operations in a single line:

```python
…
# Code in cell 5
df = spark.read.csv(
    "file:///" + SparkFiles.get(DATASET_FILE),
    header=True, sep=";", inferSchema=True)
df.cache()
df.count()

…
# Code in cell 7
df = df.withColumn('Time', F.date_format('Time', 'HH:mm:ss'))
# Create timestamp column
df = df.withColumn('timestamp', F.concat(df.Date, F.lit(" "),
df.Time))
df = df.withColumn(
    'timestamp',
    F.to_timestamp(df.timestamp, 'yyyy-MM-dd HH:mm:ss'))
# Fix data types
df = df \
    .withColumn('Global_active_power',
    df.Global_active_power.cast('double')) \

…
print("Schema:")
df.printSchema()
```

The schema is inferred by the `spark.read` option `inferSchema`. The data types before conversion, displayed with `printSchema()`, are shown in *Figure 6.1*.

```
Inferred schema:
root
 |-- Date: date (nullable = true)
 |-- Time: timestamp (nullable = true)
 |-- Global_active_power: string (nullable = true)
 |-- Global_reactive_power: string (nullable = true)
 |-- Voltage: string (nullable = true)
 |-- Global_intensity: string (nullable = true)
 |-- Sub_metering_1: string (nullable = true)
 |-- Sub_metering_2: string (nullable = true)
 |-- Sub_metering_3: double (nullable = true)
```

Figure 6.1: Inferred schema with data types

The updated schema is as per *Figure 6.2*, showing the converted data types.

```
Schema:
root
 |-- Date: date (nullable = true)
 |-- Time: string (nullable = true)
 |-- Global_active_power: double (nullable = true)
 |-- Global_reactive_power: double (nullable = true)
 |-- Voltage: double (nullable = true)
 |-- Global_intensity: double (nullable = true)
 |-- Sub_metering_1: double (nullable = true)
 |-- Sub_metering_2: double (nullable = true)
 |-- Sub_metering_3: double (nullable = true)
 |-- timestamp: timestamp (nullable = true)
```

Figure 6.2: Updated schema with converted data types

We are now ready to profile the data.

Data profiling

Data profiling involves analyzing the dataset's structure, quality, and statistical properties. This helps to identify anomalies, missing values, and outliers, ensuring data integrity. This process can also be comprehensive, including the analysis of trends, seasonal patterns, and correlations, guiding more accurate forecasting and modeling.

> **Note**
>
> Data profiling can also guide preprocessing steps such as normalization and transformation, covered in *Chapter 5*.

Apache Spark provides the convenient `summary()` function, as per the following code, for summary statistics:

```
#### Summary Statistics
# Code in cell 10
df.summary().display()
```

This generates the following outcome:

	summary	Time	Global_active_power	Global_reactive_power	Voltage	Global_intensity	Sub_metering_1	Sub_metering_2
1	count	42779	42776	42776	42776	42776	42776	42776
2	mean	null	1.454234430521762	0.0983391153918067	241.44194244436048	6.09856461567243	1.2780764914905554	1.0239386571909481
3	stddev	null	1.1780282540019587	0.09222277157899714	3.199648514091844	4.966548325001971	6.466406071700989	5.219501011405793
4	min	00:00:00	0.194	0.0	228.32	0.8	0.0	0.0
5	25%	null	0.396	0.052	239.27	1.8	0.0	0.0
6	50%	null	1.362	0.072	241.64	5.6	0.0	0.0
7	75%	null	1.932	0.136	243.75	8.0	0.0	0.0
8	max	23:59:00	10.348	0.818	250.92	44.6	54.0	76.0

Figure 6.3: Summary statistics

While these summary statistics are useful, they are usually not sufficient. A data profiling tool such as YData Profiling, which we will look at next, provides more extensive analysis and reporting.

The following code extract shows how to launch a Profile Report with YData. Notable here is the use of a Pandas DataFrame, `pdf`, and of the time series mode (`tsmode` parameter), with the `sortby` parameter to sort by timestamp. We also want correlations to be included in the report. After the report is generated, it is converted to HTML for display with the `to_html()` function.

```
# Code in cell 12
...
profile = ProfileReport(
    pdf,
    title='Time Series Data Profiling',
    tsmode=True,
    sortby='timestamp',
    infer_dtypes=False,
    interactions=None,
```

```
    missing_diagrams=None,
    correlations={
        "auto": {"calculate": False},
        "pearson": {"calculate": True},
        "spearman": {"calculate": True}})


# Save the profiling report to an HTML file
profile.to_file("time_series_data_profiling_report.html")


# Show the profiling report in the notebook
report_html = profile.to_html()
displayHTML(report_html)
```

The generated report contains an **Overview** section, as per *Figure 6.4,* with an indication, among other things, of the number of variables (columns), observations (rows), and missing values and duplicate counts.

Overview

Dataset statistics		Variable types	
Number of variables	10	DateTime	3
Number of observations	42779	TimeSeries	7
Missing cells	21		
Missing cells (%)	< 0.1%		
Duplicate rows	0		
Duplicate rows (%)	0.0%		
Total size in memory	3.6 MiB		
Average record size in memory	88.0 B		

Figure 6.4: Data profile report – Overview

Scrolling down from **Overview**, we can see column-specific statistics, as shown in *Figure 6.5*, such as the minimum, maximum, mean, number of zeros, and number of distinct values.

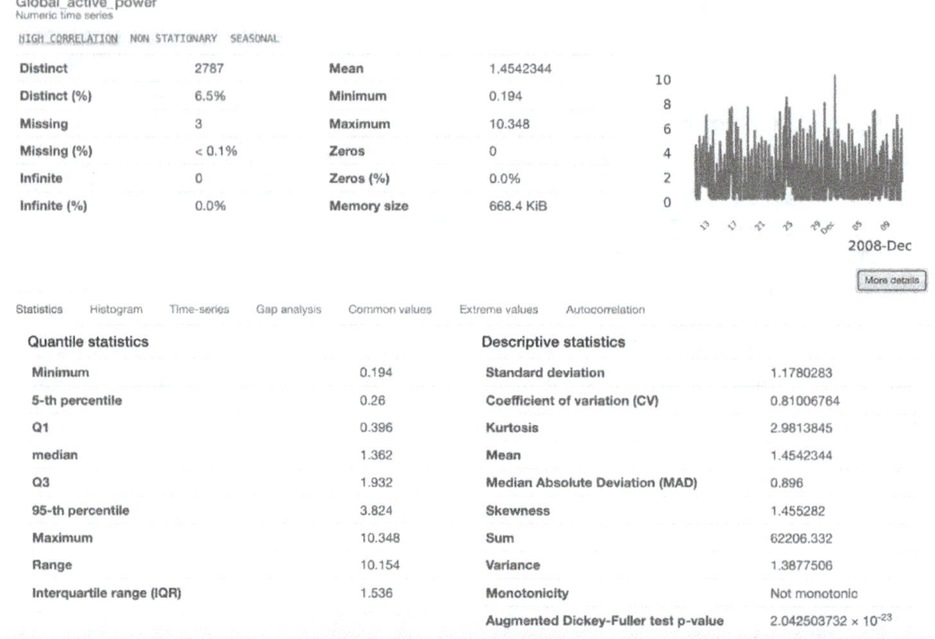

Figure 6.5: Data profile report – Details

This section has further sub-sections, such as **Histogram**, showing the distribution of values, and **Gap analysis**, as per *Figure 6.6*, with indications of data gaps for the column.

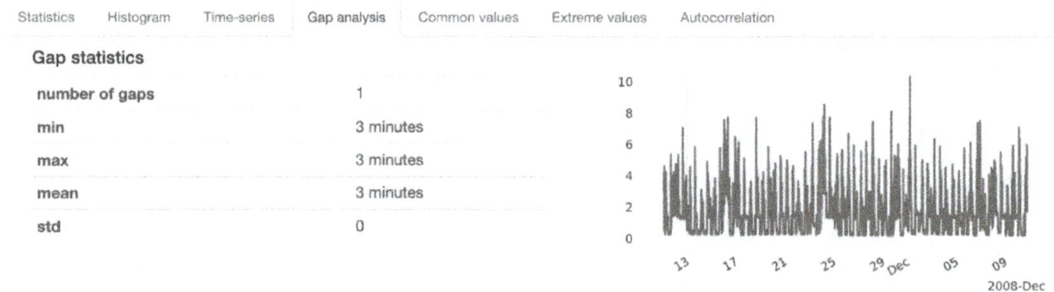

Figure 6.6: Data profile report – Gap analysis

With the time series mode specified earlier, we also get a basic **Time Series** part of the report, shown in *Figure 6.7*

Figure 6.7: Data profile report – Time Series

Other sections of the report cover **Alerts**, shown in *Figure 6.8*, with outcomes of tests run on the dataset, including time-series-specific ones, and a **Reproduction** section with details on the profiling run.

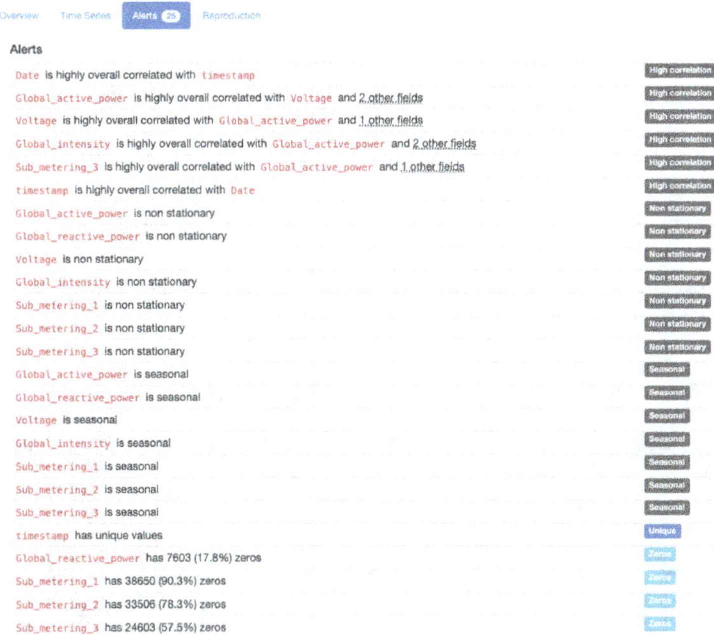

Figure 6.8: Data profile report – Time Series

This section provided an example of how to perform data profiling on time series data using YData Profiling and Apache Spark. Further information on YData Profiling can be found here: `https://github.com/ydataai/ydata-profiling`.

We will now drill down further in our understanding of the data, by analyzing the gaps in the dataset.

Gap analysis

In the previous section, we mentioned gap analysis for gaps in value for a specific column. Another consideration for time series data is gaps in the timeline itself, as in the following example with the household energy consumption dataset, where we are expecting values every minute.

In this case, we first calculate the time difference between consecutive timestamps using `diff()`, as in the following code, with a pandas DataFrame, `pdf`. If this is greater than `1 minute`, we can flag the timestamp as having a prior gap:

```python
# test for gaps
# Code in cell 15
# test for gaps
pdf['gap_val'] = pdf['timestamp'].sort_values().diff()
pdf['gap'] = pdf['gap_val'] > ps.to_timedelta('1 minute')
pdf[pdf.gap]
```

As *Figure 6.9* shows, we found 3 gaps of 2 minutes each in this example.

	Date	Time	Global_active_power	Global_reactive_power	Voltage	Global_intensity	Sub_metering_1	Sub_metering_2	Sub_metering_3	timestamp	gap_val	gap
916	2008-11-11	09:06:00	2.334	0.000	239.45	9.8	0.0	0.0	17.0	2008-11-11 09:06:00	0 days 00:02:00	True
16894	2008-11-22	11:25:00	0.346	0.054	241.23	1.6	0.0	0.0	0.0	2008-11-22 11:25:00	0 days 00:02:00	True
28755	2008-11-30	17:07:00	0.816	0.116	238.95	3.4	0.0	0.0	0.0	2008-11-30 17:07:00	0 days 00:02:00	True

Figure 6.9: Gap analysis

Depending on the size of the gap and the nature of the dataset, we can adopt one of the following approaches:

- Ignore the gap

- Aggregate, for example, use the mean value at a higher interval

- Use one of the missing-value handling techniques we saw in *Chapter 5*, such as forward filling

Regular or irregular time series

The gap analysis presented here assumes a regular time series. The approach is slightly different in detecting gaps in the timeline of irregular time series. The previous example of checking for the absence of values at every minute interval is not applicable for an irregular time series. We will have to look at the distribution of the count of values over the timeline of the irregular time series and make reasonable assumptions about how regularly we expect values in the irregular time series. For instance, if we are considering the energy consumption of a household, the time series may be irregular at minute intervals, but based on historical data, we expect energy use every hour or daily. In this case, not having a data point on a given hour or day can be indicative of a gap. Once we have identified a gap, we can use the same approaches as discussed for regular time series, that is, forward filling or similar imputation, aggregation at higher intervals, or just ignoring the gap.

We discussed here the specific problem of gaps in the time series. We mentioned that, to identify gaps, we can look at the distribution of the data, which will be covered next.

Distribution analysis

Distribution analysis of time series provides an understanding of the underlying patterns and characteristics of the data, such as skewness, kurtosis, and outliers. This helps detect deviations from normal distribution, trends, and seasonal patterns, and visualize the variability of the time series. This understanding then feeds into choosing the appropriate statistical models and forecasting methods. This is required as models are built on assumptions of the distribution of the time series. Done correctly, distribution analysis ensures that model assumptions are met. This also improves the accuracy and reliability of the predictions.

In this section, we will examine a few examples of distribution analysis, starting with the profiling output of *Figure 6.5*, which shows a kurtosis of 2.98 and a skewness of 1.46. Let's explain what this means by first defining these terms.

Kurtosis indicates how peaked or flat a distribution is compared to a normal distribution. A value greater than 2, as in our example in *Figure 6.5*, indicates the distribution is too peaked. Less than -2 means too flat.

Skewness indicates how centered and symmetric the distribution is compared to a normal distribution. A value between -1 and 1 is considered near normal, between -2 and 2, as in the example in *Figure 6.5*, is acceptable, and below -2 or above 2 is not normal.

When both kurtosis and skewness are zero, we have a perfectly normal distribution, which is quite unlikely to be seen with real data.

Let's now do some further distribution analysis with the following code extract. We want to understand the frequency distribution of `Global_active_power`, the distribution by day of the week, `dayOfWeek`, and the hour of the day. We will use the Seaborn (`sns`) visualization library for the plots, with the pandas DataFrame, `pdf`, passed as a parameter:

```
#### Distribution Analysis
# Code in cell 17

…

# Extract day and hour
df = df.withColumn("dayOfWeek", F.dayofweek(F.col("timestamp")))
df = df.withColumn("hour", F.hour(F.col("timestamp")))

…

# Distribution analysis using Seaborn and Matplotlib

…

sns.histplot(pdf['Global_active_power'], kde=True, bins=30)
plt.title(
    'Distribution of Global_active_power in Time Series Data'
)

…

# Boxplot to visualize the distribution per dayOfWeek

…

sns.boxplot(x='dayOfWeek', y='Global_active_power', data=pdf)
plt.title(
    'Daily Distribution of Global_active_power in Time Series Data'
)

…

# Boxplot to visualize the distribution per hour

…

sns.boxplot(x='hour', y='Global_active_power', data=pdf)
plt.title(
    'Hourly Distribution of Global_active_power in Time Series Data'
)

…
```

We can see the frequency of occurrence of the different values of `Global_active_power` in *Figure 6.10*, with the skewness to the left.

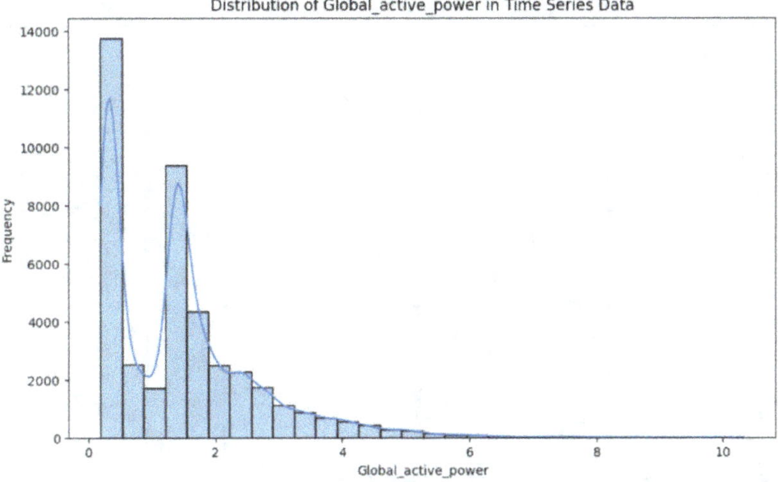

Figure 6.10: Distribution by frequency

If we look at the distribution by day of the week, as in *Figure 6.11*, power consumption during the weekends is higher, as can be expected for a household, with 1 on the *x* axis representing Sundays and 7 Saturdays. The distribution is also over a broader range of values these days.

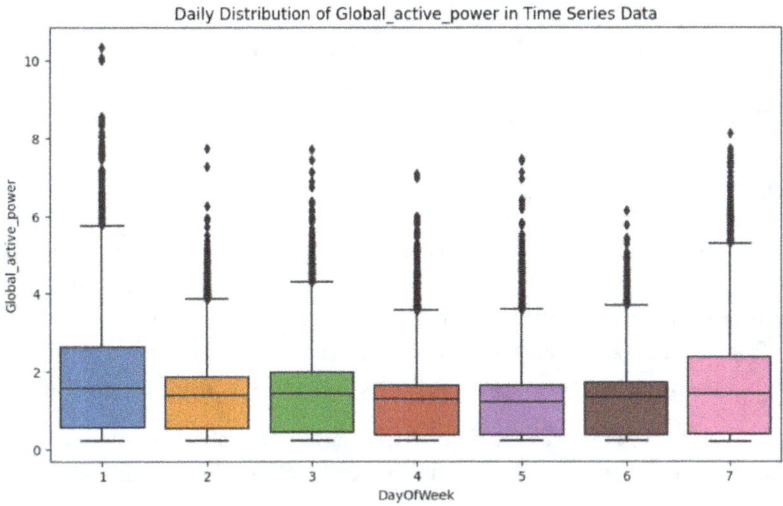

Figure 6.11: Distribution by day of the week

The distribution by hour of the day, as in *Figure 6.12*, shows higher power consumption during the morning and evening, again as can be expected for a household.

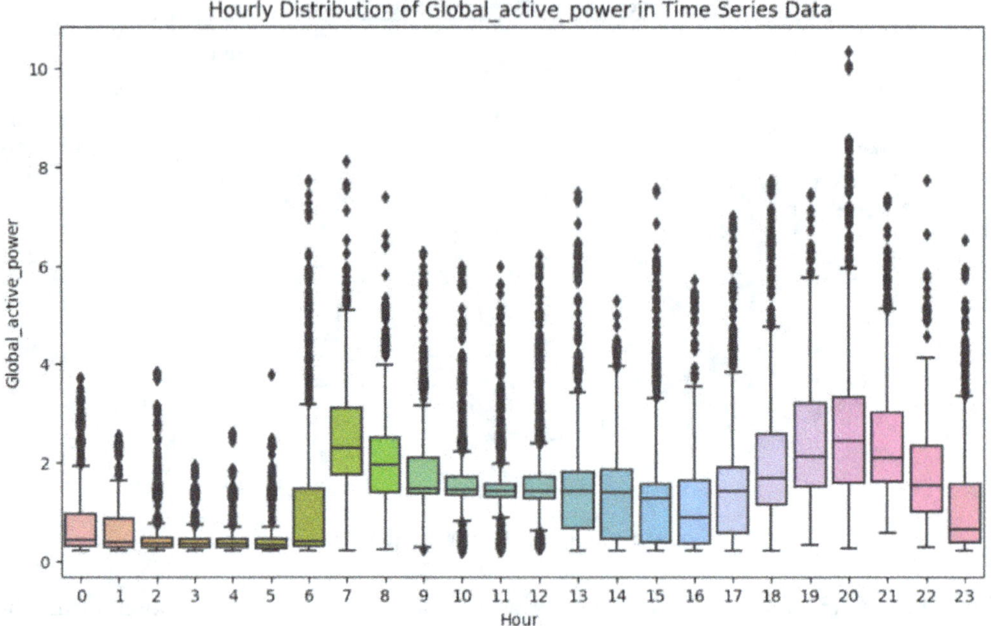

Figure 6.12: Distribution by hour of the day

You will also notice in the distribution plots the values that are flagged as outliers, lying beyond the whiskers. These are at a 1.5 **inter-quartile range** (**IQR**) above the third quartile. You can use other thresholds for outliers, as in *Chapter 5*, where we used a cutoff on the z-score value.

Visualizations

As we have seen so far in this book and, more specifically, this chapter, visualizations play an important role in time series analysis. By providing us with an intuitive and immediate understanding of the data's underlying patterns, they help to identify seasonal variations, trends, and anomalies that might not otherwise be seen from raw data alone. Furthermore, visualizations facilitate the detection of correlations, cycles, and structural changes over time, contributing to better forecasting and decision-making.

Fundamentally, (and this is not only true for time series analysis) visualizations aid in communicating complex insights to stakeholders and, in doing so, improve their ability to understand and act accordingly.

Building on the techniques for statistical analysis seen in this chapter, we will now move on to other important techniques to consider while analyzing time series—resampling, decomposition, and stationarity.

Resampling, decomposition, and stationarity

This section details additional techniques used in time series analysis, introduced in *Chapter 1*. We will see code examples of how to implement these techniques.

Resampling and aggregation

Resampling and aggregation are used in time series analysis to transform and analyze data at different time scales. **Resampling** is changing the frequency of the time series, such as converting hourly data to daily data, which can reveal trends and patterns at different time frequencies. **Aggregation**, on the other hand, is the summarizing of data over specified intervals and is used in conjunction with resampling to calculate the resampled value. This can reduce noise, handle missing values, and convert an irregular time series to a regular series.

The following code extract shows the resampling at different intervals, together with the aggregation. The original dataset has data every minute. With `resample('h').mean()` applied to the pandas DataFrame, `pdf`, we resample this value to the mean over the hour:

```
#### Resampling and Aggregation
# Code in cell 22
...
# Resample data to hourly, daily and weekly frequency and aggregate by
# mean
hourly_resampled = pdf.resample('h').mean()
hourly_resampled_s = pdf.resample('h').std()
daily_resampled = pdf.resample('d').mean()
daily_resampled_s = pdf.resample('d').std()
weekly_resampled = pdf.resample('w').mean()
weekly_resampled_s = pdf.resample('w').std()
...
```

Figure 6.13 shows the outcome of the hourly resampling.

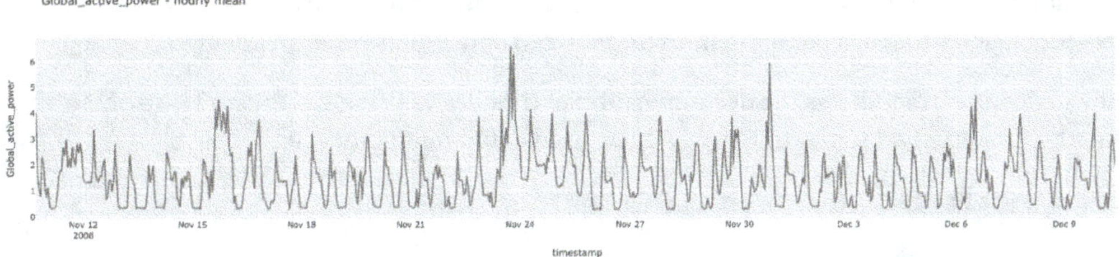

Figure 6.13: Resampled hourly

Figure 6.14 shows the outcome of the daily resampling.

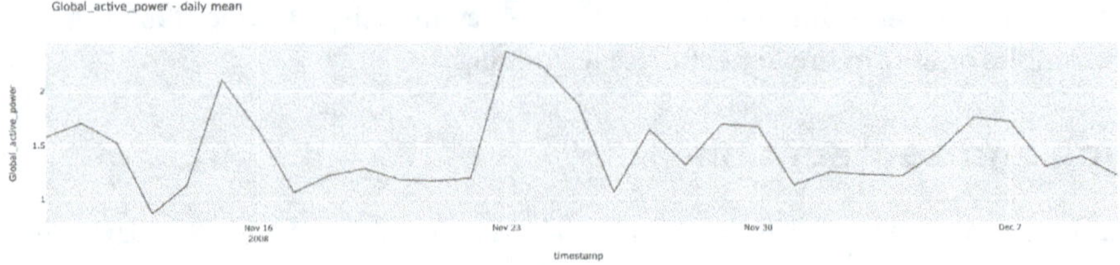

Figure 6.14: Resampled daily

Figure 6.15 shows the outcome of the weekly resampling.

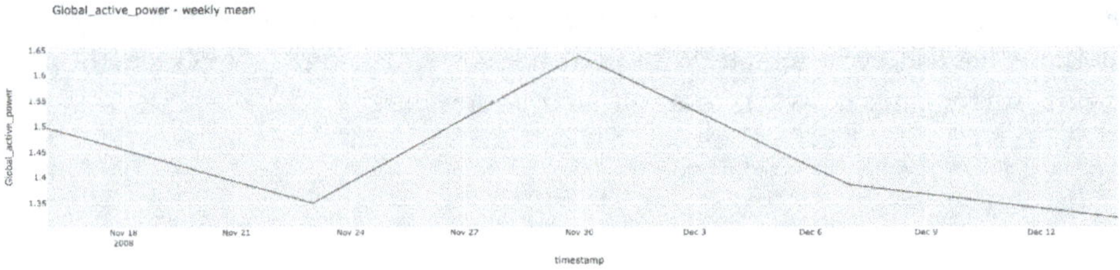

Figure 6.15: Resampled weekly

With these examples, we have resampled and aggregated time series data using Apache Spark. We will next expand on the time series decomposition of the resampled time series.

Decomposition

As introduced in *Chapter 1*, decomposition breaks down the time series into its fundamental components: trend, seasonality, and residuals. This separation helps uncover underlying patterns within the data more clearly. The trend shows long-term movement, while seasonal components show repeating patterns. Residuals highlight any deviation from the trend and seasonal components. This decomposition allows for each component to be analyzed and addressed individually.

The following code extract shows the decomposition of time series using `seasonal_decompose` from the `statsmodels` library. In *Chapter 1*, we used a different library, `Prophet`.

```
# Code in cell 30
...
from statsmodels.tsa.seasonal import seasonal_decompose

# Perform seasonal decomposition
hourly_result = seasonal_decompose(
```

```
    hourly_resampled['Global_active_power'])
daily_result = seasonal_decompose(
    daily_resampled['Global_active_power'])
...
```

Figure 6.16 shows the components of the hourly resampled time series. The seasonal component shows a pattern, with each repeating pattern corresponding to a day, and the ups in power consumption every morning and evening are visible.

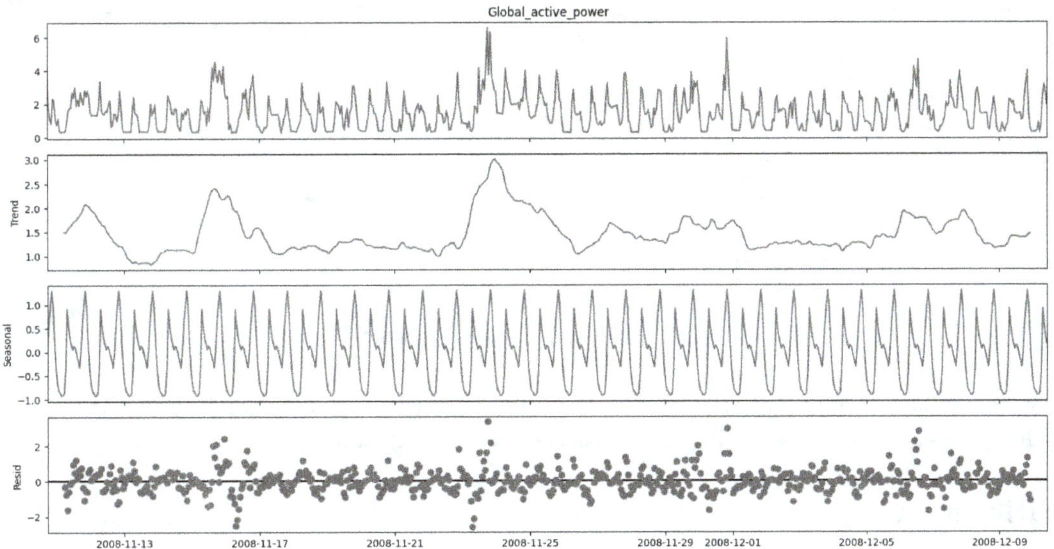

Figure 6.16: Decomposition of hourly data

Figure 6.17 shows the components of the daily resampled time series. The seasonal component shows a pattern, with each repeating pattern corresponding to a week, and the ups in power consumption every weekend are visible.

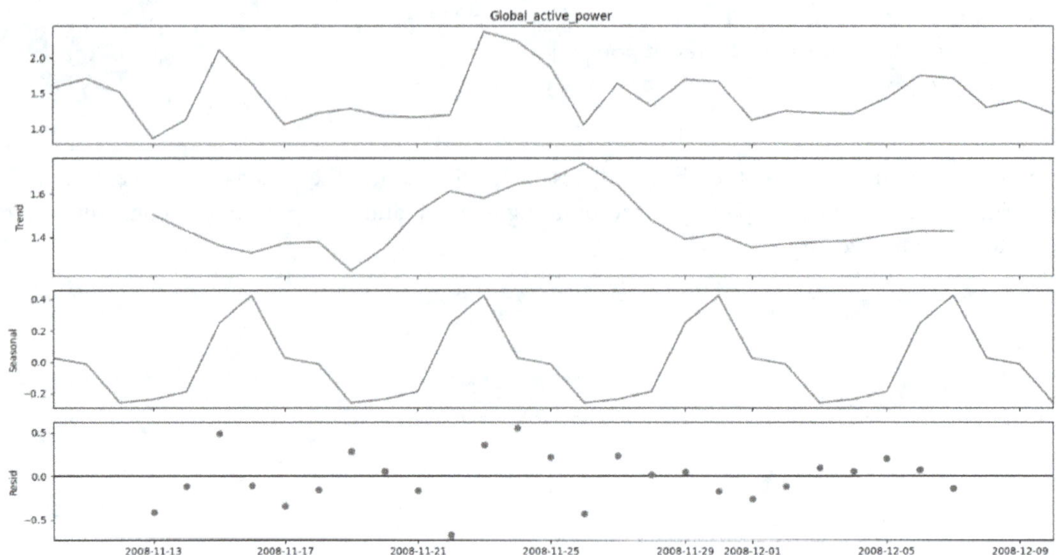

Figure 6.17: Decomposition of daily data

Now that we have performed time series decomposition using Apache Spark and `statsmodels` for time series at different resampling intervals, let's discuss the next technique.

Stationarity

Another key concept related to time series data, introduced in *Chapter 1*, stationarity concerns the statistical properties of the series, such as mean, variance, and autocorrelation remaining constant over time. This is an assumption on which time series models, such as **AutoRegressive Integrated Moving Average (ARIMA)** are built. A series must be identified and converted to stationary before using such models. In general, stationary time series facilitate analysis and improve model accuracy.

The first step in handling non-stationarity is to check the time series, which we will look at next.

Check

The **Augmented Dickey-Fuller (ADF)** test and the **Kwiatkowski-Phillips-Schmidt-Shin (KPSS)** test are commonly used statistical tests to check for stationarity. Without going into the details of these tests, we can say they calculate a value, which is called the p-value. A value of $p < 0.05$ for ADF means that the series is stationary. Additionally, we can check for stationarity by visual inspection of the time series plot and **autocorrelation function (ACF)** plots, and by comparing summary statistics over different time periods. Mean, variance, and autocorrelation remaining constant across time suggest stationarity. Significant changes indicate non-stationarity.

The following example code checks for stationarity using the ADF test, `adfuller`, from the `statsmodels` library. We will use the hourly resampled data in this example.

```
#### Stationarity
# Code in cell 33
...
from statsmodels.tsa.stattools import adfuller


# Perform Augmented Dickey-Fuller test
result = adfuller(hourly_resampled)


# if Test statistic < Critical Value and p-value < 0.05
#    reject the Null hypothesis, time series does not have a unit root
#    series is stationary
...
```

In this case, the p-value, as shown in *Figure 6.18*, is less than 0.05, and we can conclude the time series is stationary from the ADF test.

```
ADF Statistic: -4.432630228536613
p-value: 0.00025975551240001214
Critical Values:
    1%: -3.4398214107097225
    5%: -2.8657196436385663
    10%: -2.5689957624690525
```

Figure 6.18: ADF test results – Power consumption dataset

Running the ADF test on the dataset for the annual mean temperature of Mauritius, used in *Chapter 1*, gives a p-value greater than 0.05, as shown in *Figure 6.19*. In this case, we can conclude that the time series is non-stationary.

```
ADF Statistic: -1.173048675260568
p-value: 0.6850807369173555
Critical Values:
    1%: -3.528889992207215
    5%: -2.9044395987933362
    10%: -2.589655654274312
```

Figure 6.19: ADF test results – Annual mean temperature dataset

As we now have a non-stationary series, we will next consider converting it to a stationary series using differencing.

Differencing

The following code extract shows the conversion of a non-stationary time series to a stationary one. We'll use differencing, a common method to remove trends and seasonality, which can make the time series stationary. By using a combination of the `Window` function and `lag` of 1, we can find the difference between an annual mean and the previous year's value.

```
###### Differencing
# Code in cell 41

...

from pyspark.sql.window import Window


# Calculate the difference (differencing)
window = Window.orderBy("year")
df2_ = df2.withColumn(
    "annual_mean_diff",
    F.col("annual_mean") - F.lag(
        F.col("annual_mean"), 1
    ).over(window))

...
```

We can see the original time series compared to the differenced time series in *Figure 6.20*. The removal of the trend is visible.

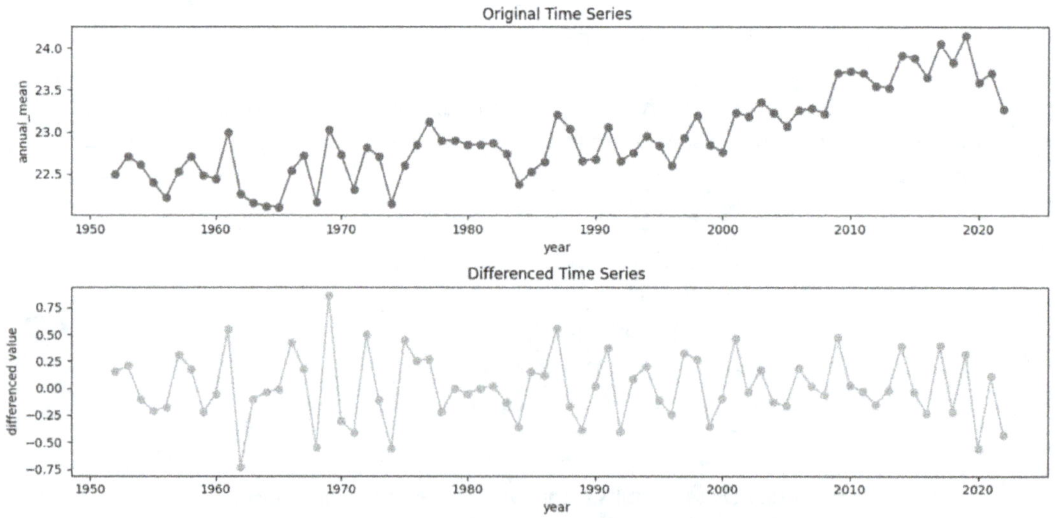

Figure 6.20: Differencing – Annual mean temperature dataset

Running the ADF test after differencing, gives a p-value less than 0.05, as shown in *Figure 6.21*. We can conclude that the difference in time series is stationary.

```
ADF Statistic: -3.8736850261650635
p-value: 0.0022372764341414245
Critical Values:
    1%: -3.540522678829176
    5%: -2.9094272025108254
    10%: -2.5923136524453696
```

Figure 6.21: ADF test results – Differenced annual mean temperature dataset

Building on our understanding of techniques for exploratory analysis learned in this section, we will now move on to the last section of this chapter, which is about correlation of time series data.

Correlation analysis

Correlation measures the relationship between two variables. This relationship can be causal, whether one is the result of the other. This section will explore the different types of correlation applicable to time series.

Autocorrelation

The **AutoCorrelation Function** (ACF) measures the relationship between a time series and its past values. High autocorrelation indicates that past values have a strong influence on future values. This information can then be used to build predictive models, for instance, in selecting the right parameters for models such as ARIMA, thereby enhancing the robustness of the analysis. Understanding autocorrelation also helps in identifying seasonal effects and cycles.

The **Partial AutoCorrelation Function** (PACF) similarly measures the relationship between a variable and its past values, but contrary to the ACF, with the PACF we discount the effect of values of the time series at all shorter lags.

Check

The following code shows how you can check for autocorrelation and partial autocorrelation using Apache Spark and `plot_acf` and `plt_pacf` from the `statsmodels` library.

```
#### Autocorrelation
# Code in cell 45
from statsmodels.graphics.tsaplots import plot_acf, plot_pacf


# Plot Autocorrelation Function (ACF)
plt.figure(figsize=(12, 6))
```

```
plot_acf(hourly_resampled['Global_active_power'], lags=3*24)
plt.title('Autocorrelation Function (ACF)')
plt.show()

# Plot Partial Autocorrelation Function (PACF)
plt.figure(figsize=(12, 6))
plot_pacf(hourly_resampled['Global_active_power'], lags=3*24)
plt.title('Partial Autocorrelation Function (PACF)')
plt.show()
...
```

The resulting ACF and PACF plots are shown in *Figure 6.22*.

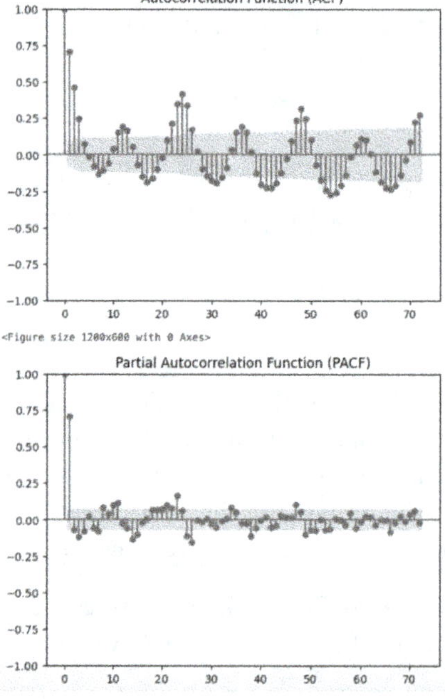

Figure 6.22: ACF and PACF plots

The outcomes of ACF and PACF indicate the nature of the time series and guide the selection of the appropriate models and parameters for forecasting. Let's now make sense of these plots and how we can use their outcome.

Interpretation of ACF

We will consider the peaks and the decay from the ACF plot to interpret the outcome, using the upper graph in *Figure 6.22* as an example.

Peaks in the autocorrelation plot outside the confidence interval indicate notable autocorrelations. Regular intervals point to seasonality. From the example, we can see autocorrelation at lags 1, 2, and 3 and seasonality at lags 12 and 24, which correspond to a 12- and 24-hour interval.

A slow decay in the autocorrelation plot suggests that the series is non-stationary with a trend. In this case, we can convert the series to stationary by differencing it, as discussed in the previous section on *Differencing*. This, however, is not the case in our example in *Figure 6.22*, as there is no slow decay.

The outcome of the ACF can be used to define the **moving average (MA)** parameter q of an ARIMA model. Major peaks at lags 1, 2 and 3 in our example, means q=1, q=2, and q=3.

Interpretation of PACF

We will consider the peaks and the cut-off from the PACF plot to interpret the outcome, using the lower graph in *Figure 6.22* as an example.

Peaks in the partial autocorrelation plot outside the confidence interval indicate notable partial autocorrelations. In the example, this is seen at lags 1, 12, and 24.

An immediate cut-off after some lags indicates an **autoregressive (AR)** component. In the example, this is after lag 1.

The outcome of the PACF can be used to define the AR parameter p of an ARIMA model. Major peaks at lag 1 in our example, means p=1.

Model parameters

Based on the interpretation of the ACF and PACF plots in *Figure 6.22*, we can consider the following candidate ARIMA(p, d, q) models, where p is the PACF cut-off point, d is the order of differencing, and q is the ACF autocorrelation lag:

- ARIMA(1, 0, 1)
- ARIMA(1, 0, 2)
- ARIMA(1, 0, 3)

We will discuss model selection and parameters in detail in the next chapter. The depth of our discussion here is just enough to conclude the discussion on ACF and PACF. Let's move on to other lag analysis methods.

Lag analysis

In addition to ACF and PACF plots seen previously, we will explore another lag analysis method in this section.

We'll start by calculating the different lag values of interest, as per the following code extract, using the `Window` and `lag` functions we have seen previously.

```
#### Lag Analysis
# Code in cell 49

...

window = Window.orderBy("timestamp")


# Create lagged features
hourly_df = hourly_df.withColumn(
    "lag1", F.lag(F.col("Global_active_power"), 1).over(window))
hourly_df = hourly_df.withColumn(
    "lag2", F.lag(F.col("Global_active_power"), 2).over(window))
hourly_df = hourly_df.withColumn(
    "lag12", F.lag(F.col("Global_active_power"), 12).over(window))
hourly_df = hourly_df.withColumn(
    "lag24", F.lag(F.col("Global_active_power"), 24).over(window))

...
```

This creates the lag columns, as shown in *Figure 6.23*.

	timestamp	Global_active_power	lag1	lag2	lag12	lag24
1	2008-11-10T17:00:00Z	4.056181818181819	null	null	null	null
2	2008-11-10T18:00:00Z	1.6607666666666667	4.056181818181819	null	null	null
3	2008-11-10T19:00:00Z	1.1009666666666669	1.6607666666666667	4.056181818181819	null	null
4	2008-11-10T20:00:00Z	0.7837999999999999	1.1009666666666669	1.6607666666666667	null	null
5	2008-11-10T21:00:00Z	2.3224	0.7837999999999999	1.1009666666666669	null	null
6	2008-11-10T22:00:00Z	2.0828333333333333	2.3224	0.7837999999999999	null	null
7	2008-11-10T23:00:00Z	1.048	2.0828333333333333	2.3224	null	null
8	2008-11-11T00:00:00Z	0.7471	1.048	2.0828333333333333	null	null
9	2008-11-11T01:00:00Z	1.1287333333333334	0.7471	1.048	null	null
10	2008-11-11T02:00:00Z	0.359	1.1287333333333334	0.7471	null	null
11	2008-11-11T03:00:00Z	0.3082333333333333	0.359	1.1287333333333334	null	null
12	2008-11-11T04:00:00Z	0.3397	0.3082333333333333	0.359	null	null
13	2008-11-11T05:00:00Z	0.32449999999999996	0.3397	0.3082333333333333	4.056181818181819	null
14	2008-11-11T06:00:00Z	0.36489999999999995	0.32449999999999996	0.3397	1.6607666666666667	null
15	2008-11-11T07:00:00Z	0.8057666666666666	0.36489999999999995	0.32449999999999996	1.1009666666666669	null
16	2008-11-11T08:00:00Z	1.5471666666666666	0.8057666666666666	0.36489999999999995	0.7837999999999999	null
17	2008-11-11T09:00:00Z	1.7733999999999999	1.5471666666666666	0.8057666666666666	2.3224	null
18	2008-11-11T10:00:00Z	1.7636	1.7733999999999999	1.5471666666666666	2.0828333333333333	null
19	2008-11-11T11:00:00Z	2.6970866666666667	1.7636	1.7733999999999999	1.048	null
20	2008-11-11T12:00:00Z	2.3492	2.6970666666666667	1.7636	0.7471	null
21	2008-11-11T13:00:00Z	3.0147666666666666	2.3492	2.6970666666666667	1.1287333333333334	null
22	2008-11-11T14:00:00Z	1.8891333333333333	3.0147666666666666	2.3492	0.359	null
23	2008-11-11T15:00:00Z	2.2617666666666665	1.8891333333333333	3.0147666666666666	0.3082333333333333	null
24	2008-11-11T16:00:00Z	1.8957000000000002	2.2617666666666665	1.8891333333333333	0.3397	null
25	2008-11-11T17:00:00Z	2.7046666666666668	1.8957000000000002	2.2617666666666665	0.32449999999999996	4.056181818181819
26	2008-11-11T18:00:00Z	2.1882666666666664	2.7046666666666668	1.8957000000000002	0.36489999999999995	1.6607666666666667

Figure 6.23: Lag values

We then calculate the correlation of the current values with their lag values, as in the following code, using the `stat.corr()` function.

```
# Code in cell 50

...

# Calculate autocorrelation for lag 1
```

```
df_lag1 = hourly_df.dropna(subset=["lag1"])
autocorr_lag1 = df_lag1.stat.corr("Global_active_power", "lag1")
...
# Calculate autocorrelation for lag 24
df_lag24 = hourly_df.dropna(subset=["lag24"])
autocorr_lag24 = df_lag24.stat.corr("Global_active_power", "lag24")
...
```

Figure 6.24 shows the autocorrelation values, significant at lag 1, 2, and 24, as we saw on the ACF plot previously.

```
Autocorrelation for lag 1: 0.7081649636155366
Autocorrelation for lag 2: 0.4661329447026447
Autocorrelation for lag 12: 0.19477674447190363
Autocorrelation for lag 24: 0.4320312708180719
```

Figure 6.24: Autocorrelation at different lag values

Finally, by plotting the current and lag values together, we can see in *Figure 6.25* how they compare to each other. We can visually confirm here the greater correlation at lag 1, 2, and 24.

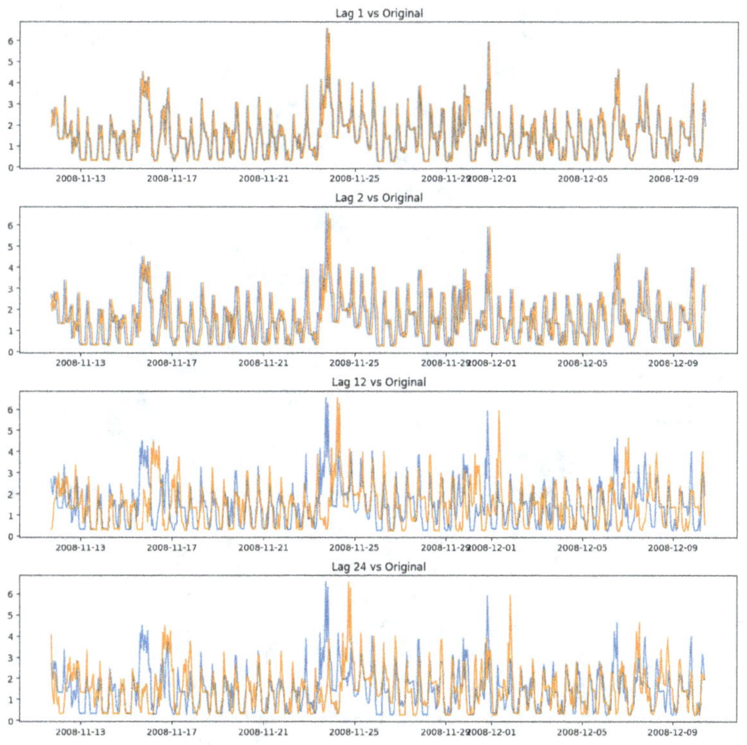

Figure 6.25: Comparison of current and lag values

This concludes the section on autocorrelation, where we looked at ACF and PACF, and how to calculate lagged features and their correlation using Apache Spark. While the lag analysis methods in this section have been used for autocorrelation, they can also be used for cross-correlation, which we will cover next, as another type of correlation, this time between different time series.

Cross-correlation

Cross-correlation measures the relationship between two different time series. One series may influence or predict the other over different time lags, in what is called a **lead-lag relationship**. Cross-correlation is used for multivariate time series modeling and causality analysis.

Going back to the profiling report we saw earlier, we can see a graph of the correlation of the different columns of the example dataset included in the report, as in *Figure 6.26*.

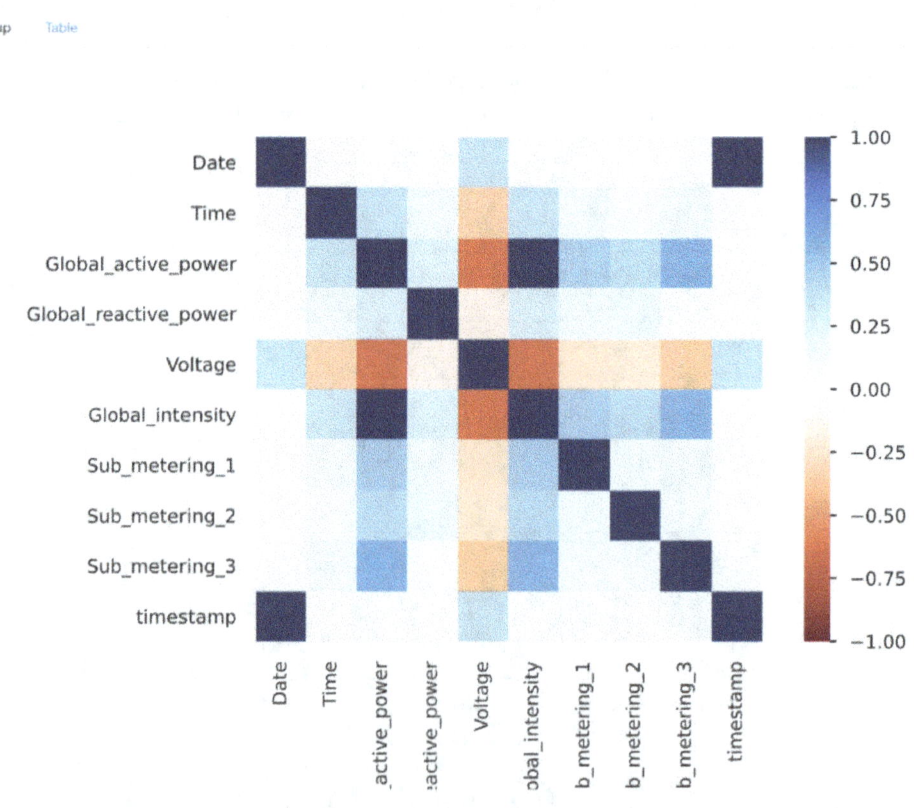

Figure 6.26: Cross-correlation heatmap

We can calculate the cross-correlation directly with the following code.

```
#### Cross-correlation
# Code in cell 53

...

# Compute cross-correlation between value1 and value2
cross_corr = hourly_df.stat.corr("Global_active_power", "Voltage")

...
```

The cross-correlation calculation yields the value in *Figure 6.26*. As this correlation is at the same lag, it does not have predictive value, in the sense that we are not using the past to predict the future. However, this pair of attributes is still worth further analysis at different lags, due to the significant cross-correlation.

```
Cross-correlation between Global_active_power and Voltage: -0.655325736768359
```

Figure 6.27: Cross-correlation value

> **Note**
>
> We know that P=IV, where P is electrical power, I is current, and V is voltage, indicates how power and voltage are related. Hence, these two time series are not independent of each other. Even if there is no further insight into the P and V relationship, we will continue this analysis as an example of cross-correlation analysis.

As cross-correlation at the same lag does not help much for prediction, we will now look at using different lag values with the following code. This uses the cross-correlation `ccf()` function, which calculates the cross-correlation at different lag values.

```
# Code in cell 54

...

from statsmodels.tsa.stattools import ccf

hourly_ = hourly_resampled.iloc[:36]

# Calculate cross-correlation function
ccf_values = ccf(hourly_['Global_active_power'], hourly_['Voltage'])

# Plot cross-correlation function
plt.figure(figsize=(12, 6))
plt.stem(range(len(ccf_values)),
         ccf_values, use_line_collection=True, markerfmt="-")
plt.title('Cross-Correlation Function (CCF)')

...
```

This generates the plot in *Figure 6.27*, which shows the correlation of the two attributes at different lags.

Figure 6.28: Cross-correlation function

To conclude, this section showed how to perform cross-correlation analysis by creating lagged features, and calculating and visualizing cross-correlation.

Summary

In this chapter, we used exploratory data analysis to uncover patterns and insights in time series data. Starting with statistical analysis techniques, where we profiled the data and analyzed its distribution, we then resampled and decomposed the series into its components. To understand the nature of the time series, we also checked for stationarity, autocorrelation, and cross-correlation. By this point, we have gathered enough information on time series to guide us into the next step of building predictive models for time series.

In the next chapter, we will dive into the core topic of this book, which is developing and testing models for time series analysis.

Join our community on Discord

Join our community's Discord space for discussions with the authors and other readers:

```
https://packt.link/ds
```

7

Building and Testing Models

Having covered the data preparation and exploratory data analysis stages of time series analysis, we will now direct our focus to constructing predictive models for time series data. We will cover the diverse types of models and how to decide which one to choose. We will also learn how to train, tune, and evaluate models.

The concepts covered in this chapter will act as a practical guide to model development, providing essential building blocks for effective time series models and facilitating accurate predictions and insightful analyses. We will factor in common execution constraints faced in real-life projects and conclude with a comparison of the outcome of the different models to solve a forecasting problem.

We are going to cover the following main topics:

- Model selection

- Development and testing

- Model comparison

Technical requirements

The code for this chapter, which will be covered in the *Development and testing* section, can be found in the ch7 folder of the book's GitHub repository at this URL:

```
https://github.com/PacktPublishing/Time-Series-Analysis-with-Spark/
tree/main/ch7.
```

Model selection

The first step before developing a time series analysis model is to select which model to use. As discussed in *Chapter 1*, one of the key challenges of time series analysis is using the right model. This choice impacts, among other things, the accuracy, reliability, efficiency, and scalability of the analysis. This, in turn, ensures that the analysis leads to better-informed decisions and more effective outcomes while being scientifically robust and practically useful.

There are different types of models, each with its own characteristics.

Types of models

Time series analysis models can be categorized into statistical, classical Machine Learning (ML), and Deep Learning (DL) models:

- **Statistical models** for time series analysis are based on statistical theories with assumptions about the characteristics of the time series, such as linearity and stationarity. Examples of classical models include **Autoregressive Moving Average (ARIMA)**, **Seasonal Autoregressive Integrated Moving Average Exogenous (SARIMAX)**, **Exponential Smoothing (ETS)**, **Generalized Autoregressive Conditional Heteroskedasticity (GARCH)**, and state-space models.

- **Classical Machine Learning models** for time series analysis use algorithms that can learn from data without explicit programming. These models can handle non-linear relationships. However, they often require more data for training compared to classical models. Examples of Machine Learning models include linear regression, **Support Vector Machines (SVMs)**, **k-Nearest Neighbors (kNN)**, random forests, and gradient boosting machines.

- **Deep Learning models** use neural networks with multiple layers to learn complex patterns in time series data. These models can handle non-linear relationships and long-term dependencies. They, however, require large datasets for training and significant computational resources. Examples of Deep Learning models include **Long Short-Term Memory (LSTM) Networks**, **Convolutional Neural Networks (CNNs)**, **Temporal Convolutional Networks (TCNs)**, transformers, and autoencoders.

> **Machine Learning and Deep Learning**
>
> Deep Learning is a subset of Machine Learning that uses deep neural networks. As is common practice, we are using the term classical Machine Learning here to refer to approaches and models that are not neural-network-based. The term Deep Learning is used for approaches and models using neural networks.

Each of the preceding categories and models has distinct characteristics and approaches that determine their applicability, which we will explore next.

Selection criteria

When to use which model is based on several criteria. We touched on this briefly in the section on using the right model in *Chapter 1* and when initially discussing model selection in *Chapter 4*. The applicability of a model to solve a time series analysis problem is dependent on factors such as the objectives of the analysis, the characteristics of the data, and the computation power and time available.

We will now dive deep into the details of these and other important factors for model selection.

Types of use cases

Time series analysis broadly falls into use cases for forecasting, classification, and anomaly detection, as discussed in *Chapter 2*. We will briefly recap these types of use cases here, highlighting the frequently used models. We will go into further detail in the rest of the chapter.

- **Forecasting**'s goal is to predict future values based on patterns learned by the model from past values. As presented in *Chapter 2*, forecasting can be single or multi-steps, based on a single (**univariate**) or multiple (**multivariate**) time series. Commonly used models such as ARIMA, SARIMA, and **Exponential Smoothing (ETS)** are chosen for their simplicity while giving strong performance in forecasting tasks. LSTM and Prophet, introduced in previous examples in the book, are preferred for more complex forecasting requirements where they can be more effective.

- **Pattern recognition** and **classification** are used to identify and understand patterns and classify time series accordingly. Commonly used models are based on decomposition methods, such as **Seasonal-Trend decomposition using LOESS (STL)** and **Multiple STL (MSTL)**, and Fourier analysis. We spent some time on decomposition in *Chapter 1* and *Chapter 6*. We briefly discussed Fourier analysis in *Chapter 2*, in addition to distance-based approaches, shapelets analysis, ensemble methods and Deep Learning.

- **Anomaly detection** aims to identify outliers or anomalies in the time series. As presented in *Chapter 2*, this detection can be based on univariate or multivariate series and point, collective, or contextual analysis. What is initially flagged as an anomaly can turn out to be a novelty, in the sense of a new non-problematic pattern. Commonly used models are based on their capabilities for residual analysis, such as ARIMA. Machine learning models are frequently used as well, such as Isolation Forest or, when there is a high percentage of anomalies, specialized methods such as **Seasonal Hybrid Extreme Studentized Deviate (SH-ESD)**. We saw a code example in *Chapter 2* of Isolation Forest for anomaly detection, in addition to discussing supervised, unsupervised, semi-supervised, and hybrid approaches.

Another model selection criterion, which we will look at next, is the statistical nature of the time series.

Nature of time series

The nature of the time series, that is, its statistical properties, influences the choice of model. Models are researched and developed to work well, if at all, based on specific assumptions about the nature of the time series, which then determines their applicability. We will focus in this section on applicability and skip definitions, assuming that, by now, you are familiar with the terms we will use in this section, based on the introduction in *Chapter 1* and code examples in *Chapter 6*:

- **Stationary** time series can be modeled with ARIMA, which assumes stationarity. An example of a stationary time series is the daily percentage returns of a stock over a 3-year period. Assuming no significant structural changes in the market, stock returns tend to fluctuate around a stable mean with consistent variance.

Non-stationary time series can be converted to stationary, for example, by differencing, as seen in *Chapter 6*. The differenced series can then be used with such models. Alternatively, use Prophet, or Machine Learning models for non-stationary series. An example of a non-stationary time series is the monthly unemployment rate, which possibly has a trend, and cyclical patterns related to economic conditions.

- **Seasonal** time series require models that handle seasonality, such as SARIMA, ETS, Prophet, or Machine Learning models. We have seen this in action with the coding example in *Chapter 2* to forecast temperature using Prophet.

- **Trends** in time series can impact the performance of certain models, such as ARIMA. In this case, similarly to stationarity, we can remove the trend component by differencing, as per the code example in *Chapter 6*. ARIMA can then be used. Alternatively, use models that can handle trends, such as trend models, ETS, Prophet, or Machine Learning.

- **Volatility** in time series can be handled with models such as **Generalized Autoregressive Conditional Heteroskedasticity (GARCH)**, **Stochastic Volatility GARCH (SV-GARCH)**, or Machine Learning. Common use cases for these models are forecasting and risk management in highly volatile financial markets and other domains.

- **Linearity** of the relationship in the data means that linear models such as ARIMA are suitable. An example of a linear time series is daily temperature, where today's temperature can be predicted by a linear combination of the temperatures from the previous two days plus some random error.

  In the case of non-linear patterns, Machine Learning models with neural networks are preferable. An example of a non-linear time series is if a stock price follows one relationship if below a certain threshold (say 100) and follows a different relationship if it's above that threshold.

The volume and frequency of data to analyze, discussed next, is another property of time series that influences model selection.

Volume and frequency of data

The volume and frequency of data impact the computational power required and the duration of the analysis. The combination of these factors determines the choice of model to use. We will discuss volume and frequency here, and the other two factors in the following section:

- **Small datasets** can be analyzed with statistical models such as ARIMA and ETS. These are simple models that work well with smaller datasets. An example of a small dataset is the daily sales for a store over the past few years.

- **Large datasets** are a good match for Machine Learning models such as gradient boosting and LSTM. This works in both ways: in terms of processing capability and scalability of ML models for large datasets, and the substantial amount of data needed for model training to avoid overfitting. ML models can learn complex patterns present in large datasets at the cost of more computational resources. Examples of large datasets are minute-by-minute stock prices or sensor data over, say, the past 5 years.

As we will see in *Chapter 8*, we can scale models to large datasets by using the distributed computing capabilities of Apache Spark:

- **Low-frequency** time series, such as daily, weekly, monthly, quarterly, or annual, are usually small in size. As discussed before about small datasets, ARIMA and ETS are usually good choices for such datasets.

- **High-frequency** time series are likely to have rapid changes, noise, volatility, and heteroskedasticity, which can be handled with models such as GARCH, often used for financial time series.

If the analysis is required at a lower frequency than the data arrival rate, the high-frequency series can be converted to low frequency by resampling and aggregation, as discussed in *Chapter 6*. Resampling decreases the size of the dataset while smoothing out the noise and volatility. This opens the possibility of using models suited for low-frequency time series, as discussed earlier.

> **Diminishing value of high-frequency data**
>
> We discussed frequency here as pertaining to the time interval between consecutive data points in the time series, also referred to as granularity. Another consideration for high-frequency data is the requirement that the analysis also be done at high frequency. This is due to the quickly diminishing value of high-frequency data over time. Consider how real-time stock tick changes are critical at the moment they occur but become less relevant just a few hours later. In this scenario, the model must be capable of performing extremely rapid computations, potentially in real time.

Higher volume and frequency of data require more computational resources, which we will cover next.

Computational constraints

Like any other project, time series analysis occurs within a budget. This means that the amount of resources available, including the computing power to execute the analysis process, is constrained. At the same time, we know that higher volume and frequency of data require more computational resources. We also must factor in how fast the analysis needs to be completed for the outcome to be useful. With these constraints in mind, let's investigate the choice of model:

- **Limited computation** resources mean that we may have to consider a combination of dataset size reduction, with resampling, and simpler models such as ARIMA or ETS. Machine learning models, while better at detecting complex patterns and with larger datasets, usually require more computation resources.

- **Fast analysis** requires using faster models for training and prediction. Models such as ARIMA or ETS are, again, good candidates for smaller datasets.

If fast analysis is required for a large dataset, options include the following:

- Scaling out using the distributed processing of Apache Spark clusters on large datasets, which we will cover in the next chapter.

- Resampling to convert to a smaller dataset size, with the use of simpler models such as ARIMA or ETS.

- Using Machine Learning models with the following caveats. The training and tuning stage will be slower for larger datasets. The prediction speed can be improved by using more computation resources, which of course comes at a higher cost. Note that training, tuning, and prediction speed can also be improved by using the distributed processing of Apache Spark, as we will see in the next chapter.

- **Cost of compute resources** is another important factor that may limit the use of compute-intensive models. While the simpler statistical models can run on cheaper standard resources, Deep Learning models may require more expensive GPUs on high-performance hardware.

After considering how computational requirements influence the choice of models, we will now consider how model accuracy, complexity, and interpretability determine which model to use.

Model accuracy, complexity, and interpretability

Some of the other factors that are considered for model selection are model accuracy, complexity, and interpretability:

- **Model accuracy** is wrongly seen as the determining factor for model selection in many cases. Accuracy has been presented at the end of the list of selection criteria on purpose to highlight the importance of considering other factors as well. The best model is not always the most accurate one. It is the one that delivers the most ROI for the use case.

  When high accuracy is needed, especially in forecasting, more complex models such as SARIMAX or Deep Learning may be necessary. Hyperparameter tuning is used as part of the development process to further improve accuracy, but this comes at the cost of additional computations.

- **Complexity** and **interpretability** usually conflict. The need for higher accuracy leads to the use of more complex models, which are then harder to interpret and often referred to as black boxes.

  If interpretability is crucial, prefer simpler models such as ARIMA or ETS, which have the added benefit of lower compute requirements. Tree-based models such as GBM or **Tree-Based Pipelines for Time Series** (**TSPi**) offer a good balance of accuracy and compute requirement, while simpler tree-based models offer interpretability.

If the data exhibits complex patterns and high accuracy is crucial, there may not be many options, and we may have to use complex models, with a trade-off on compute and interpretability.

Overview of model selection

To conclude on model selection, there are a few points worth noting:

- Statistical models such as ARIMA are based on assumptions about the nature of the time series, requiring statistical tests and possibly additional pre-processing to convert the series before using the model.

- Prophet and Machine Learning models are more broadly applicable but have additional complexity and compute requirements.

- The models mentioned in this section are provided as examples applicable to the criteria discussed. Other models, from a growing list of publicly available models and approaches, can and should be tested. Finding the best model is an experimentation and iterative process, dependent on one's context.

As we have seen in this section on selection criteria, several factors influence the choice of models and determine which ones to invest more effort in. Which factors are most important depends on the project context and the use case. The best model to choose is the one resulting in the highest ROI, requiring a trade-off between the different factors discussed here.

At this point, with the models selected, we are ready to move on to the next development step, which is to train the model on our time series data.

Development and testing

In this section, we will compare forecasting performance across different categories of models: statistical, classical Machine Learning, and Deep Learning. We will use six different models: SARIMA, LightGBM, LSTM, NBEATS, NHITS, and NeuralProphet. These models are chosen for their wide and proven adoption and ease of access and use.

We will proceed with the following constraints:

- Use of the default model hyperparameters whenever possible for comparison and minimize tuning to a few cases, which will be explained

- The complete execution, from data loading to model training, testing, and forecasting, will be limited to under 15 minutes

- The computing resource used will also be constrained to the Databricks Community Edition compute as per *Figure 7.1*, with 15.3 GB of memory and 2 CPU cores

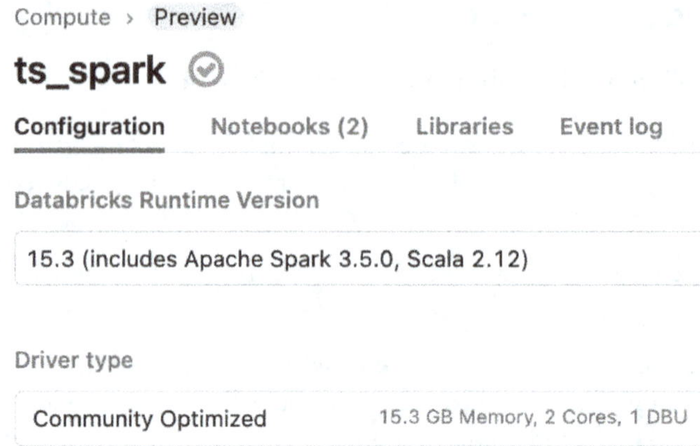

Figure 7.1: Databricks Community Edition compute resource

We all commonly face time and resource constraints in our real-life projects. This section also aims to give you the tools to work within these limits.

> **Single-threaded, multi-threaded, and clustering**
>
> We will use `Pandas` and `NumPy` in the code examples in this chapter. `Pandas` is single-threaded in terms of the use of a CPU core. `NumPy` is multi-threaded by default, so it makes use of multiple CPU cores in parallel. Both are bound to a single machine and do not leverage the multi-machine Spark clustering capability. We will address this limitation in *Chapter 8*, which covers scaling. As a lot of the existing code examples, you will find use `Pandas` and `NumPy`, it is important to start with these libraries as a foundation. We will then, in *Chapter 8*, cover how to convert the single-machine code to leverage Spark clustering capabilities.

The time series data that will be used for this section is an extended version of that used in *Chapter 2* for the energy consumption of a household. We will use the same time series for all the models we develop in the rest of this chapter. The dataset is in `ts-spark_ch7_ds1_25mb.csv` in the `ch7` folder. As this is a new dataset, we will go through the steps of exploring the data as part of the next section.

Data exploration

In this section, we want to check the stationarity, seasonality, and autocorrelation in the dataset. This is a crucial step in our understanding of the nature of the time series.

The code for this section is in `ts-spark_ch7_1e_sarima_comm.dbc`. We import the code into Databricks Community Edition, as per the approach explained in the *Hands-on: Loading and visualizing time series* section of *Chapter 1*.

The code URL is as follows:

```
https://github.com/PacktPublishing/Time-Series-Analysis-with-Spark/
raw/main/ch7/ts-spark_ch7_1e_sarima_comm.dbc
```

The first part of the code loads and prepares the data. We will not go into the details of this part here as we already covered data preparation in *Chapter 5*, and you can refer to the code in the notebook. The data exploration part is, however, pertinent to this chapter, so let's explore this further next, starting with the stationarity check.

Stationarity

We can check whether the energy consumption time series is stationary by running the **Augmented Dickey-Fuller (ADF)** test on the data with the following code:

```python
from statsmodels.tsa.stattools import adfuller


# Perform Augmented Dickey-Fuller test
result = adfuller(data_hr[-300:]['Global_active_power'])


# if Test statistic < Critical Value and p-value < 0.05
#    reject the Null hypothesis, time series does not have a unit root
#    series is stationary
# Extract and print the ADF test results
print('ADF Statistic:', result[0])
print('p-value:', result[1])
print('Critical Values:')
for key, value in result[4].items():
    print(f'    {key}: {value}')
```

This gives the following ADF statistics:

```
ADF Statistic: -6.615237252003429
p-value: 6.231223531550648e-09
Critical Values:
  1%: -3.4524113009049935
  5%: -2.8712554127251764
  10%: -2.571946570731871
```

As the ADF statistic is less than the critical values and the p-value is less than 0.05, we can conclude that the time series is stationary.

Seasonality

We can check on the seasonality with the following code:

```
from statsmodels.tsa.seasonal import seasonal_decompose

# Decompose the time series data into seasonal, trend, and residual
# components
results = seasonal_decompose(data_hr)

# Plot the last 300 data points of the seasonal component
results.seasonal[-300:].plot(figsize = (12,8));
```

This gives the seasonal decomposition in *Figure 7.2*.

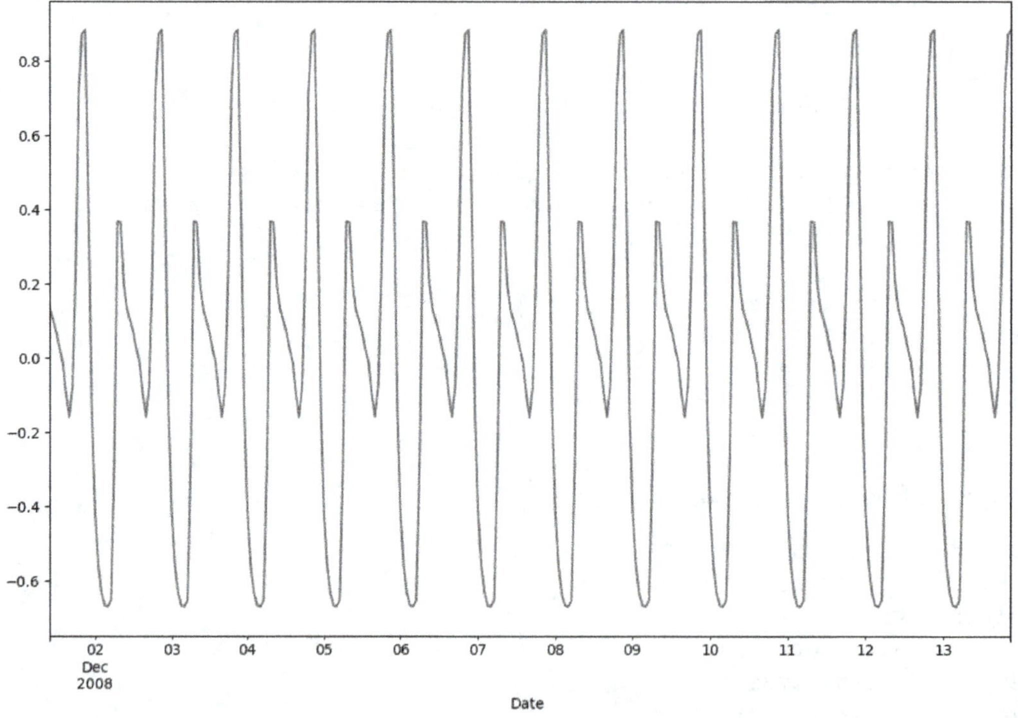

Figure 7.2: Seasonal decomposition

As the pattern repeats every 24 hours, we can conclude that the time series has a daily seasonality.

Autocorrelation

We can check on the autocorrelation and partial autocorrelation with the following code:

```python
import matplotlib.pyplot as plt
from statsmodels.graphics.tsaplots import plot_acf, plot_pacf

# Plot ACF to identify autocorrelation in 'data_hr' DataFrame
plot_acf(data_hr['Global_active_power'])

# Plot PACF to identify partial autocorrelation in 'data_hr' DataFrame
plot_pacf(data_hr['Global_active_power'])

# Display the ACF and PACF plots
plt.show()
```

This gives the autocorrelation plot in *Figure 7.3*.

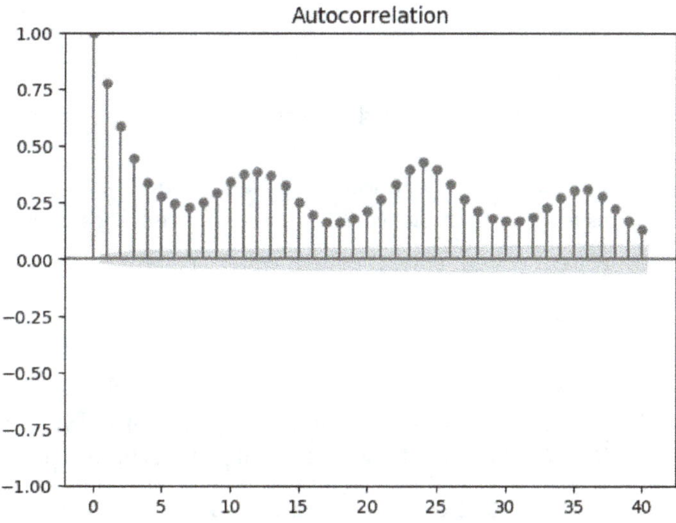

Figure 7.3: Autocorrelation (y axis) at different lags (x axis)

We can see the high autocorrelation at the lower lag values, including lag 1, and at lag 12, as well as the effect of seasonality at lag 24. This makes sense when we consider the following typical patterns of energy consumption in a household:

- Moments of active energy use, for example for cooking, washing, or use of the television, are likely to go over an hour (lag 1)

- The mornings and evenings (lag 12) are usually peaks in activity

- Daily routines mean that we have similar periods of activities every 24 hours (lag 24)

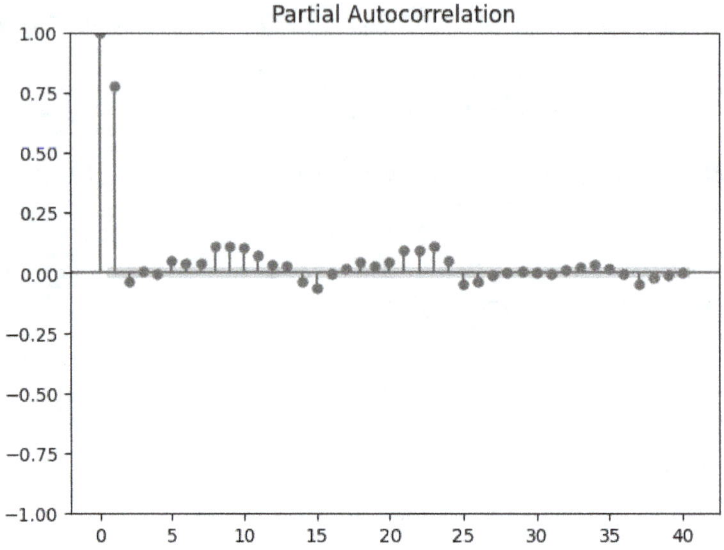

Figure 7.4: Partial autocorrelation

The PACF plot shows high partial autocorrelation at lag 1 and noticeable partial autocorrelation around lag 10 and lag 23. This is in line with the typical patterns of energy consumption in a household we mentioned.

Statistical model – SARIMA

The first model we will cover is SARIMA, which extends the ARIMA model by incorporating seasonal components. While ARIMA models address aspects such as autocorrelation, differencing for stationarity, and moving averages, SARIMA adds the handling of seasonal patterns in the data.

The code for this section is in `ts-spark_ch7_1e_sarima_comm.dbc`. We import the code into Databricks Community Edition, as per the approach explained in the *Hands-on: Loading and visualizing time series* section of *Chapter 1*.

The code URL is as follows:

```
https://github.com/PacktPublishing/Time-Series-Analysis-with-Spark/
raw/main/ch7/ts-spark_ch7_1e_sarima_comm.dbc
```

Development and tuning

For model development, we separated the last 48 hours of the dataset from the training data with the following code. This will be used for testing afterward. We use the rest for training:

```
# Split the data into training and testing sets
# The last 48 observations are used for testing,
# the rest for training
train = data_hr[:-48]
test = data_hr[-48:]
```

We will discuss two methods combining training and tuning to train the model and find the best parameters: `auto_arima` and `ParameterGrid`.

Auto ARIMA

With the auto ARIMA approach, we want to automatically find the model parameters that minimize the **Akaike Information Criterion (AIC)**. This criterion is a statistical measure evaluating the trade-off between model complexity and goodness of fit. A lower AIC indicates a better model. We will use the `pmdarima` library to demonstrate the auto ARIMA approach. As this is a compute-intensive operation, and we want to keep to the time (15 minutes) and resource (Databricks Community Edition) constraints explained previously, we will limit the dataset to the last 300 data points.

The code to use `pmdarima` is as follows:

```
import pmdarima as pm

# Create auto_arima model to automatically select the best ARIMA
parameters
model = pm.auto_arima(
    # Use the last 300 observations of the series for modeling:
    train[-300:]["Global_active_power"],
    # Enable seasonal differencing:
    seasonal=True,
    # Set the seasonal period to 24
    # (e.g., 24 hours for daily data):
    m=24,
    # Set the degree of non-seasonal differencing to 0
    # (assumes data is already stationary):
    d=0,
    # Set the degree of seasonal differencing to 1:
    D=1,
    # Set the maximum value of AR (p) terms to consider:
    max_p=3,
    # Set the maximum value of MA (q) terms to consider:
    max_q=3,
```

```python
    # Set the maximum value of seasonal AR (P) terms to consider:
    max_P=3,
    # Set the maximum value of seasonal MA (Q) terms to consider:
    max_Q=3,
    # Use AIC (Akaike Information Criterion) to select the best model:
    information_criterion='aic',
    # Print fit information to see the progression of
    # the model fitting:
    trace=True,
    # Ignore models that fail to converge:
    error_action='ignore',
    # Use stepwise algorithm for efficient search of the model space:
    stepwise=True,
    # Suppress convergence warnings:
    suppress_warnings=True
)


# Print the summary of the fitted model
print(model.summary())
```

The following code output shows the step-by-step search for the parameters minimizing the AIC. This will be the best set of model parameters to use with the ARIMA model to forecast this household's energy consumption:

```
Performing stepwise search to minimize aic
...
ARIMA(1,0,1)(2,1,0)[24] intercept : AIC=688.757, Time=9.37 sec
...
ARIMA(2,0,2)(2,1,0)[24] : AIC=681.750, Time=6.83 sec
...
ARIMA(1,0,1)(2,1,0)[24] : AIC=686.763, Time=6.02 sec
Best model: ARIMA(2,0,2)(2,1,0)[24]
```

Note that while this is the best set of model parameters, we may find, given the time and resource constraints, that we may be able to find a better model with a longer run of the algorithm.

ParameterGrid

With the `ParameterGrid` approach, we will sweep one by one through a list of parameter combinations to find the model parameters that minimize the AIC.

The code to use `ParameterGrid` is as follows:

```python
# Define parameter grid for SARIMAX model configuration
param_grid = {
    'order': [(0, 0, 0), (1, 0, 1), (2, 0, 0)],
    # Non-seasonal ARIMA orders

    'seasonal_order': [
        (0, 0, 0, 24),
        (2, 0, 1, 24),
        (2, 1, 1, 24)
    ],  # Seasonal ARIMA orders with period of 24
}

# Initialize variables to store the best AIC and
# corresponding parameters
best_aic = float("inf")
best_params = ["",""]

# Iterate over all combinations of parameters in the grid
for params in ParameterGrid(param_grid):
    print(
        f"order: {params['order']}, seasonal_order: {params['seasonal_
order']}"
    )
    try:
        # Initialize and fit SARIMAX model with current parameters
        model = SARIMAX(
            train['Global_active_power'],
            order=params['order'],
            seasonal_order=params['seasonal_order'])
        model_fit = model.fit(disp=False)
        print(f"aic: {model_fit.aic}")

        # Update best parameters if current model has lower AIC
        if model_fit.aic < best_aic:
            best_aic = model_fit.aic
            best_params = params
    except Exception as error:
        print("An error occurred:", error)
        continue
```

While both auto ARIMA and `ParamaeterGrid` are similar in terms of minimizing AIC, auto ARIMA is much simpler to use with only 1 line of code.

After the SARIMA model is trained, we will next test the model forecasting.

Testing and forecasting

We use the model to forecast the test dataset with the `predict` function, one period at a time, updating the model with the actual value after every time forecast. This iterative approach converts single-step forecasting in `forecast_step` into multi-step forecasting:

```python
def forecast_step():
    # Predicts the next period with confidence intervals
    forecast, conf_int = model.predict(
        n_periods=1, return_conf_int=True)

...


# Iterate over each observation in the test dataset
for obs in test['Global_active_power']:
    forecast, conf_int = forecast_step()  # Forecast next step
    forecasts.append(forecast)  # Append forecast to list

...

    # Update the model with the new observation
    model.update(obs)
```

We can then plot the forecast against the actual values in *Figures 7.5* and *7.6*.

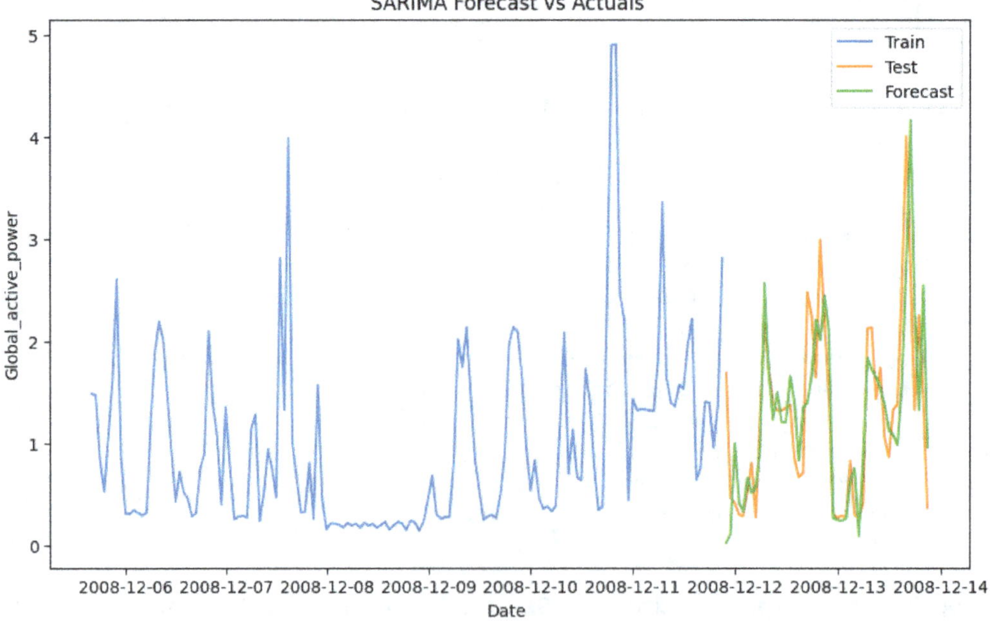

Figure 7.5: SARIMA Forecast vs Actuals (training and testing)

We zoom in on the testing period in *Figure 7.6* for a visual comparison of the forecast and actuals.

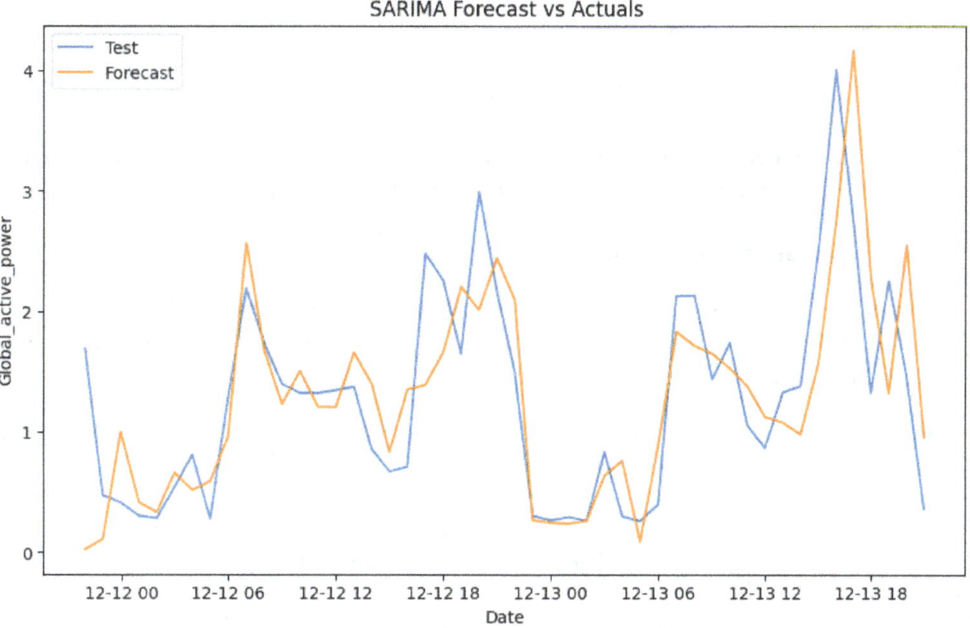

Figure 7.6: SARIMA Forecast vs Actuals (zoom on test data)

While visualizing the graphs gives us an idea of the forecasting capability of the model, we need quantifiable metrics on how good the model is. These metrics will also allow us to compare forecasting accuracy with other models.

There are several metrics available for time series forecasting. We will show the use of the following three in this chapter, to highlight how different metrics serve different objectives:

- **Mean Squared Error (MSE)** measures the average squared differences between the forecasted (F) and actual (A) values. It works well when we want to penalize large errors. However, it is sensitive to outliers because the squaring of errors gives importance to large discrepancies.

$$MSE = \frac{1}{n}\sum_{t=1}^{n} (F_t - A_t)^2$$

- **Symmetric Mean Absolute Percentage Error (SMAPE)** is the average of the absolute differences between forecasted (F) and actual (A) values. It is expressed as a percentage over half of the sum of absolute values of actual and forecasted values. SMAPE adjusts to the scale of the data, making it suitable for comparisons across different datasets. Due to its symmetric scaling, it is less sensitive to extreme values.

$$SMAPE = \frac{100\%}{n}\sum_{t=1}^{n} \frac{|F_t - A_t|}{(|A_t| + |F_t|)/2}$$

- **Weighted Absolute Percentage Error (WAPE)** is a normalized measure of error, weighing the absolute errors by the actual values. It works well when dealing with data of varying magnitudes but is sensitive to high-value errors.

$$WAPE = \frac{\sum_{t=1}^{n} |F_t - A_t|}{\sum_{t=1}^{n} |A_t|} \times 100\%$$

We will see two different approaches to metrics calculation: metrics calculation functions included in the model library, and a separate dedicated metrics calculation library.

Metric functions from the model library

In this approach, we want to use the functions for metrics calculations already included in the model library. We will use the `sklearn` and `pmdarima` libraries for the metric calculations to demonstrate this in the following code:

```python
from sklearn.metrics import mean_squared_error
from pmdarima.metrics import smape


# Calculate and print the mean squared error of the forecasts
print(f"Mean squared error: {mean_squared_error(test['Global_active_
power'], forecasts)}")
# Calculate and print the Symmetric Mean Absolute Percentage Error
# (SMAPE)
print(f"SMAPE: {smape(test['Global_active_power'], forecasts)}")
```

This gives the following results:

```
Mean squared error: 0.6131968222566936
SMAPE: 43.775868579535334
```

Separate metrics library

In this second approach for metrics calculation, we use the `SeqMetrics` library, as in the following code:

```python
from SeqMetrics import RegressionMetrics, plot_metrics


# Initialize the RegressionMetrics object with actual and
# predicted values
er = RegressionMetrics(
    test['Global_active_power'], forecasts)


# Calculate all available regression metrics
metrics = er.calculate_all()


# Plot the calculated metrics using a color scheme
```

```
plot_metrics(metrics, color="Blues")

# Display the Symmetric Mean Absolute Percentage Error (SMAPE)
print(f"Test SMAPE: {metrics['smape']}")

# Display the Weighted Absolute Percentage Error (WAPE)
print(f"Test WAPE: {metrics['wape']}")
```

This gives the following results:

```
Test SMAPE: 43.775868579535334
Test WAPE: 0.4202224470299464
```

This library also provides a nice visualization of all the metrics calculated, as in *Figures 7.7* and *7.8*.

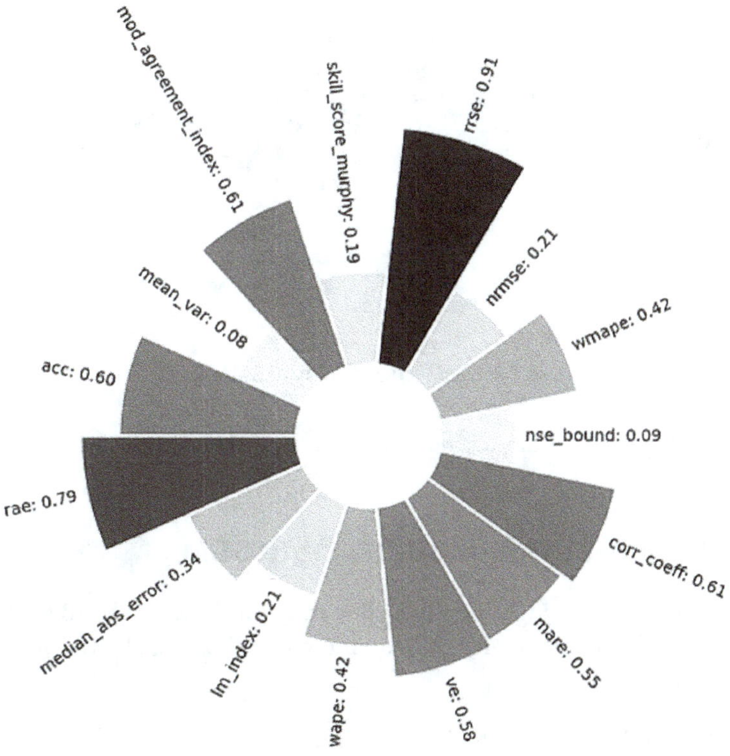

Figure 7.7: SeqMetrics display of WAPE

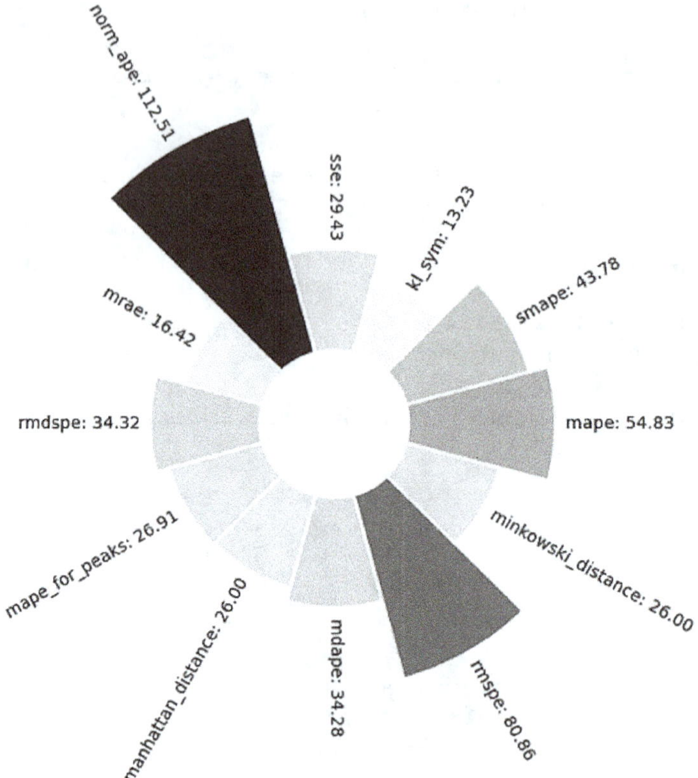

Figure 7.8: SeqMetrics display of SMAPE

After training and testing our first model, we can move on to the next model, which is a classical Machine Learning model.

Classical Machine Learning model – LightGBM

The second model we will cover is **Light Gradient Boosting Machine** (**LightGBM**), which is a free open source gradient boosting model. It is based on the tree learning algorithm, designed to be efficient and distributed.

The code for this section is in `ts-spark_ch7_1e_lgbm_comm.dbc`. We import the code into Databricks Community Edition, as per the approach explained in *Chapter 1*.

The code URL is as follows:

```
https://github.com/PacktPublishing/Time-Series-Analysis-with-Spark/
raw/main/ch7/ts-spark_ch7_1e_lgbm_comm.dbc
```

Development and tuning

For model development, we separated the last 48 hours of the dataset from the training data with the following code. This will be used for testing afterward. We use the rest for training:

```python
# Split the data into training and testing sets
# The last 48 observations are used for testing, the rest for training
train = data_hr[:-48]
test = data_hr[-48:]
```

We will use the `GridSearchCV` method to find the best parameters for the `LGBMRegressor` model. `TimeSeriesSplit` is used to split the training dataset for cross-validation, respecting the time series nature of the dataset:

```python
# Define the parameter grid for LightGBM
param_grid = {
    'num_leaves': [30, 50, 100],
    'learning_rate': [0.1, 0.01, 0.001],
    'n_estimators': [50, 100, 200]
}
# Initialize LightGBM regressor
lgbm = lgb.LGBMRegressor()

# Setup TimeSeriesSplit for cross-validation
tscv = TimeSeriesSplit(n_splits=10)

# Configure and run GridSearchCV
gsearch = GridSearchCV(
    estimator=lgbm,
    param_grid=param_grid,
    cv=tscv
)
gsearch.fit(X_train, y_train)

# Output the best parameters from Grid Search
print(f"Best Parameters: {gsearch.best_params_}")
```

We find the following best parameters:

```
Best Parameters: {'learning_rate': 0.1, 'n_estimators': 50, 'num_
leaves': 30}
```

Based on the training dataset, this will be the best set of parameters to use with the LightGBM model to forecast this household's energy consumption. We can then train the final model with these parameters:

```
final_model = lgb.LGBMRegressor(**best_params)
final_model.fit(X_train, y_train)
```

After the LightGBM model is trained, we will test the model forecasting next.

Testing and forecasting

We use the model to forecast the test dataset with the `predict` function. Note that in this case, we have not had the need to use iterative multi-step forecasting code. We have instead used the lag values as input features to the model:

```
# Predict on the test set
y_pred = final_model.predict(X_test)
```

We can then plot the forecast against the actual values in *Figures 7.8* and *7.9*.

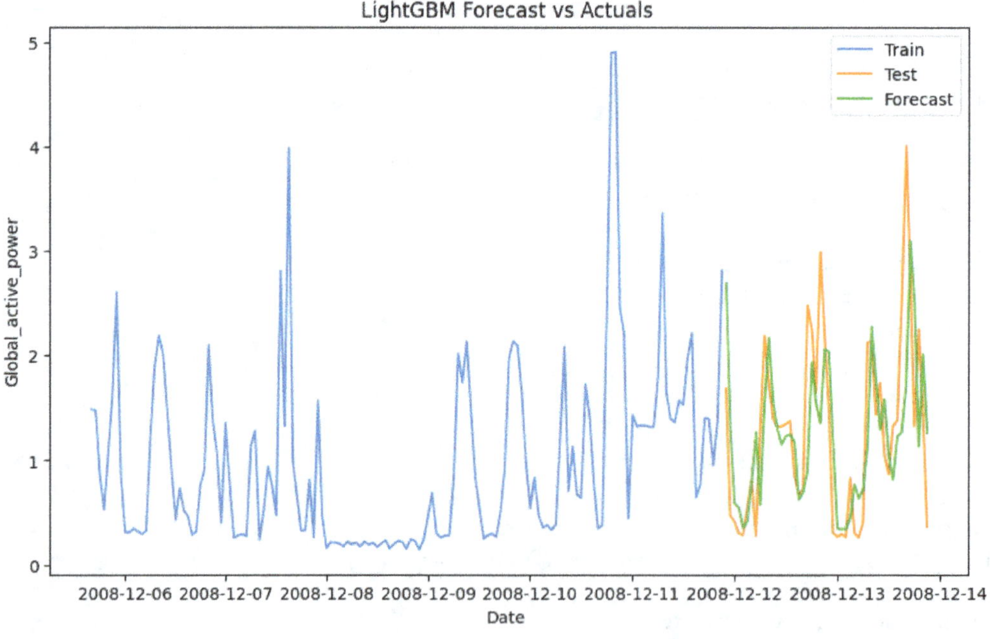

Figure 7.9: LightGBM Forecast vs Actuals (training and testing)

We zoom in on the testing period in *Figure 7.9* for a visual comparison of the forecast and actuals.

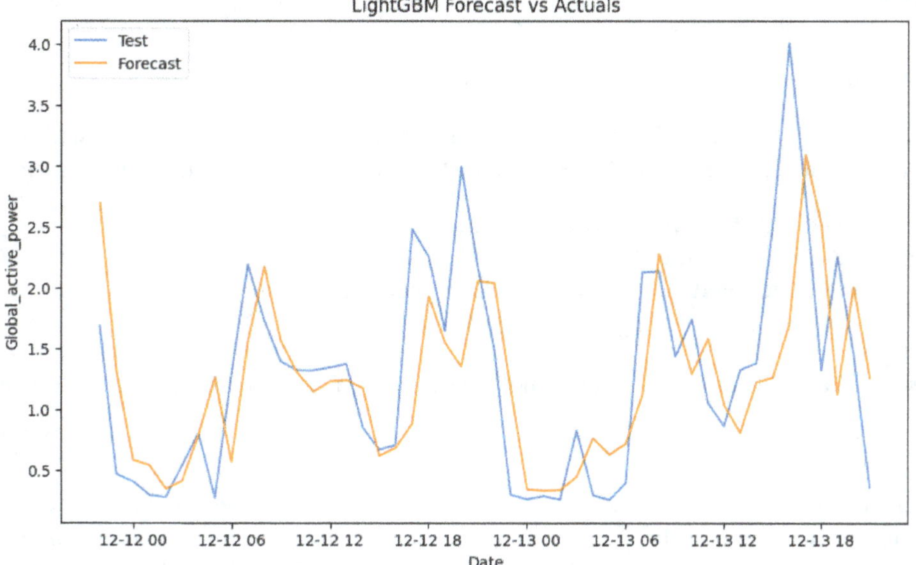

Figure 7.10: LightGBM Forecast vs Actuals (zoom on test data)

Based on the forecast and actuals, we can then measure the SMAPE and WAPE, getting the following values:

```
Test SMAPE: 41.457989848314384
Test WAPE: 0.38978585281926825
```

Now that we have trained and tested statistical and classical Machine Learning models, we can move on to a third type of model, which is a Deep Learning model.

Deep Learning model – NeuralProphet

The third model we will cover is NeuralProphet, which is a free open source Deep Learning model inspired by Prophet, which we used in previous chapters, and AR-Net. NeuralProphet is built on PyTorch.

The code for this section is in `ts-spark_ch7_1e_nprophet_comm.dbc`. We import the code into Databricks Community Edition, as per the approach explained in *Chapter 1*.

The code URL is as follows: `https://github.com/PacktPublishing/Time-Series-Analysis-with-Spark/raw/main/ch7/ts-spark_ch7_1e_nprophet_comm.dbc`

> **Note**
>
> Note that the notebook for this example requires Databricks compute DBR 13.3 LTS ML.

Development

We instantiate a `NeuralProphet` model, specifying with `n_lag` that we want to use the past 24 hours for the forecasting. We then train (the `fit` method) the model on the training dataset:

```python
# Initialize and fit the Prophet model
# model = NeuralProphet()
model = NeuralProphet(n_lags=24, quantiles=[0.05, 0.95])
metrics = model.fit(train_df)
```

With these two lines of code sufficient to train the model, we will next test the model forecasting.

Testing and forecasting

Before using the model to forecast the test dataset, we need to prepare the data for NeuralProphet, similar to how we did previously for Prophet. The required format is to have a `ds` column for the date/time and `y` for the forecasting target. We can then use the `predict` method. Note that in this case, we have not had the need to use iterative multi-step forecasting code. With the lag of 24 specified as a parameter in the previous code section, NeuralProphet uses a sliding window of the past 24 values to forecast the next values:

```python
# Convert the DataFrame index to datetime,
# removing timezone information
test_df['ds'] = test_df.index.to_pydatetime()
test_df['ds'] = test_df['ds'].apply(
    lambda x: x.replace(tzinfo=None))


# Rename the target variable for Prophet compatibility
test_df = test_df.rename(columns={'Global_active_power': 'y'})


# Use the trained model to make predictions on the test set
predictions_48h = model.predict(test_df)
```

We plot the forecast against the actual values in *Figures 7.12* and *7.13*.

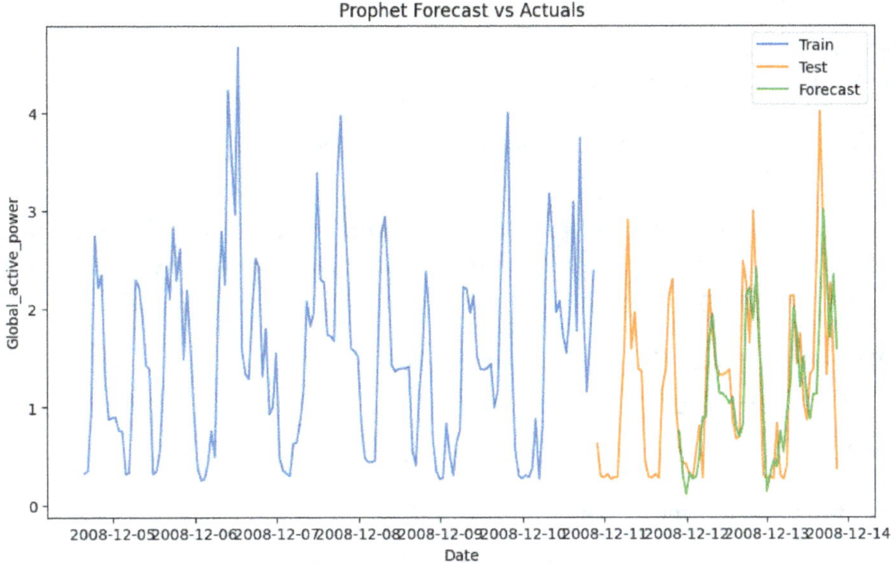

Figure 7.11: NeuralProphet Forecast vs Actuals (training and testing)

We zoom in on the testing period in *Figure 7.13* for a visual comparison of the forecast and actuals.

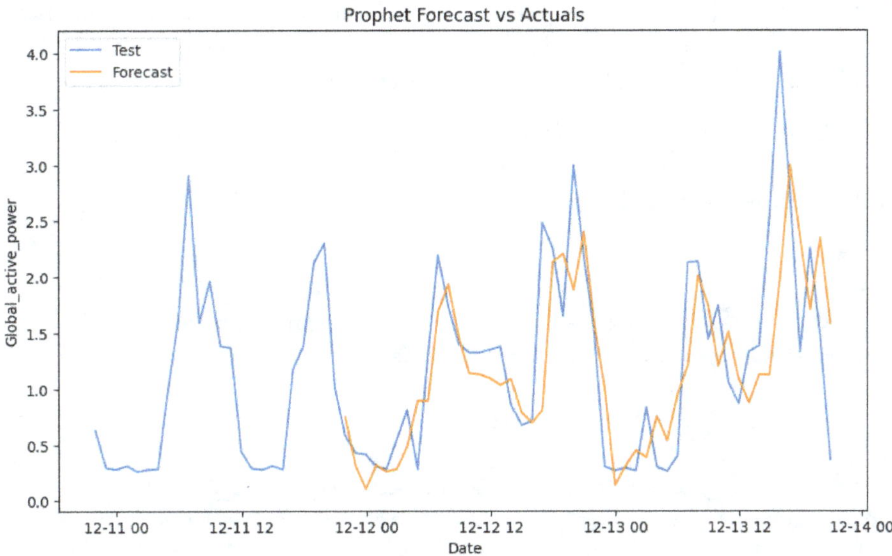

Figure 7.12: NeuralProphet Forecast vs Actuals (zoom on test data)

Based on the forecast and actuals, we can then measure the SMAPE and WAPE, getting the following values as a measurement of the accuracy of the model:

```
Test SMAPE: 41.193985580947896
Test WAPE: 0.35355667972102317
```

We will use these metrics to compare the different models we have used in this chapter, in the later *Model comparison* section.

So far, we have trained and tested each type of model: a statistical, a classical Machine Learning, and a Deep Learning model. Other examples of commonly used models for time series are provided in the book's GitHub repository:

- Prophet: `ts-spark_ch7_1e_prophet_comm.dbc`

- LSTM: `ts-spark_ch7_1e_lstm_comm1-cpu.dbc`

- NBEATS and NHITS: `ts-spark_ch7_1e_nbeats-nhits_comm.dbc`

We encourage you to explore these further.

Having a working model is great but is not sufficient. We also need to be able to explain the model we are working with. We will cover this next.

Explainability

Explainability is a key requirement in many cases, such as for financial and regulated industries. We will look at how to do this now using a widely used method called **Shapley Additive Explanations (SHAP)** to explain how the different features of the dataset contributed to the prediction.

We will use the `TreeExplainer` function of the `shap` library on the final model from the *Classical Machine Learning model – LightGBM* section to compute the SHAP values, which will give us the impact of each feature on the model output.

```
import shap

# Initialize a SHAP TreeExplainer with the trained model
explainer = shap.TreeExplainer(final_model)

# Select features for SHAP analysis
X = data_hr[[
    'Global_active_power_lag1', 'Global_active_power_lag2',
    'Global_active_power_lag3', 'Global_active_power_lag4',
    'Global_active_power_lag5', 'Global_active_power_lag12',
    'Global_active_power_lag24', 'Global_active_power_lag24x7'
]]
```

```
# Compute SHAP values for the selected features
shap_values = explainer(X)


# Generate and display a summary plot of the SHAP values
shap.summary_plot(shap_values, X)
```

We can then plot the feature importance in *Figure 7.10*. As expected from the data exploration we did in the earlier section, lag 1 and lag 24 are the features contributing the most to the forecasting.

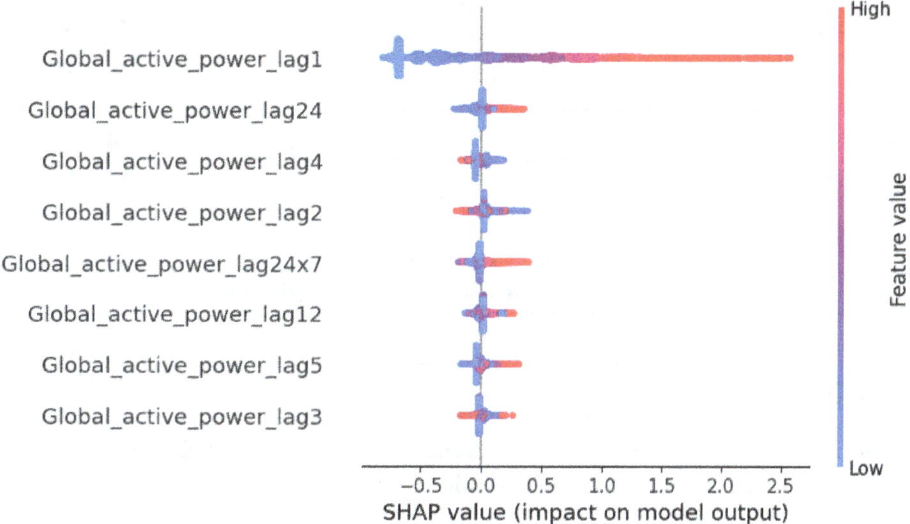

Figure 7.13: SHAP – feature importance

We can go further in the analysis by focusing on a specific forecast with the following code, where we want to explain the forecasting for the first value:

```
# Plot a SHAP waterfall plot for the first observation's SHAP values #
to visualize the contribution of each feature
shap.plots.waterfall(shap_values[0])
```

We can see in *Figure 7.11* the relative contributions of the features, again with pre-dominance of lag 1 and 24, and to a lesser extent lag 12. This is coherent with our analysis in the *Data exploration* section, where we established the pertinence of these lags in forecasting the energy consumption of a household.

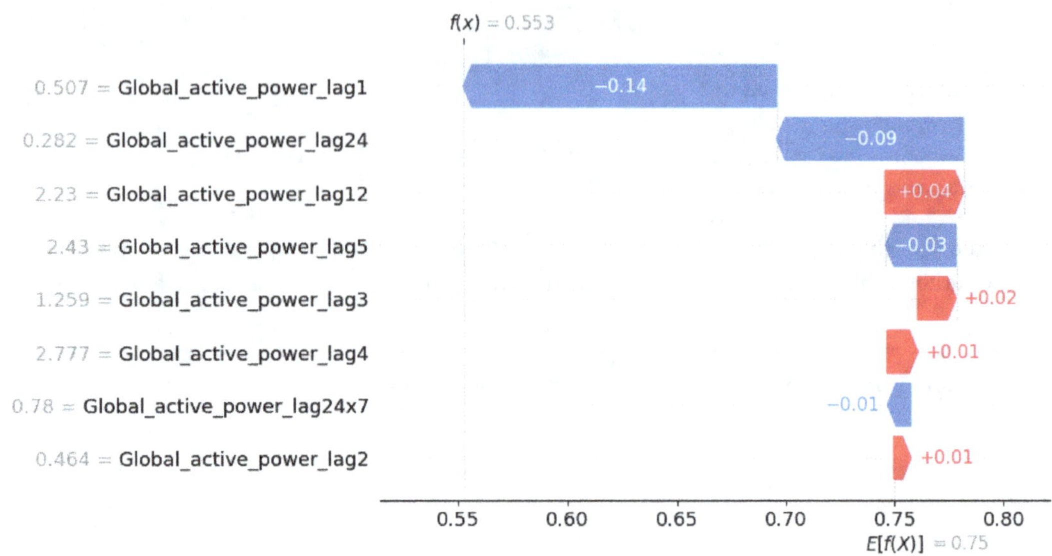

Figure 7.14: SHAP – feature importance (first observation)

Model comparison

Before concluding this chapter, we will compare all the models we have tested based on the metrics we measured and the code execution time. The results are shown in *Table 7.1*.

Model	Type	SMAPE	WAPE	Training	Tuning	Testing	Total incl. data prep.
NeuralProphet	DL/Mixed	41.19	0.35	60s	-	1s	90s
LightGBM	Classical ML	41.46	0.39	60s	Included	Included	137s
SARIMA	Statistical	43.78	0.42	Included	420s	180s	662s
Prophet	Statistical/Mixed	47.60	0.41	2s	-	1s	70s
NHITS	DL	54.43	0.47	35s	-	Included	433s
NBEATS	DL	54.91	0.48	35s	-	Included	433s
LSTM	DL	55.08	0.48	722s	-	4s	794s

Table 7.1: Model results comparison

Here are a few observations on the model accuracy:

- NeuralProphet and LightGBM gave the best forecasting accuracy with both the SMAPE and WAPE metrics. SARIMA was not very far behind.

- The Deep Learning models, NBEATS, NHITS, and LSTM, did not have good forecasting accuracy when used as single-input models. We encourage you to explore further how they can be improved with multiple inputs.

The following is in regard to execution time:

- In all the cases, we kept within the constraint of a total execution of 900s (15 minutes) with the 2 CPU cores on a single-node Databricks Community Edition cluster. This worked with the 25 MB dataset. We will see in *Chapter 8* how to scale for larger datasets.

- Prophet, NBEATS, and NHITS had the best execution time, with NeuralProphet and LightGBM coming after, still within 1 minute for training, tuning, and testing.

- SARIMA had a relatively high execution time, even if we limited the dataset to the last 300 observations. This was due to the Auto ARIMA algorithm searching for the best hyperparameter, and then the multi-step iterative forecasting code.

- LSTM had the longest execution time, which can be explained by the use of CPUs instead of GPUs, which are much faster for Deep Learning.

The overall conclusion from this model comparison is that NeuralProphet and LightGBM are the best choices for the dataset we used, with minimal tuning, and for the compute and execution time constraint that we set.

Summary

In this chapter, we have focused on the core topic of this book, which is the development of models for time series analysis, more specifically for forecasting. Starting with a review of the different types of models, we then looked at the important criteria guiding the choice of the right model to use. In the second part of the chapter, we put into practice the development and testing of several models, which we then compared on accuracy and execution time.

In the next chapter, we will expand on a topic where Apache Spark shines: scaling time series analysis to big data.

Get This Book's PDF Version and Exclusive Extras

Scan the QR code (or go to packtpub.com/unlock). Search for this book by name, confirm the edition, and then follow the steps on the page.

Note: Keep your invoice handly. Purchase made directly from packt don't require one.

Part 3: Scaling to Production and Beyond

In this last part, we will cover the considerations and practical examples of scaling and bringing to production the solutions covered in *Part 2*. We then conclude the book with techniques to go further with Apache Spark and time series analysis. This guides you to using Databricks and generative AI as part of your solutions.

This part has the following chapters:

- *Chapter 8, Going at Scale*

- *Chapter 9, Going to Production*

- *Chapter 10, Going Further with Apache Spark*

- *Chapter 11, Recent Developments in Time Series Analysis*

8

Going at Scale

After building and testing models in the previous chapter, we will now address the requirements and considerations for scaling time-series analysis in large and distributed computing environments. We will cover the different ways that Apache Spark can be used to scale the previous examples in *Chapter 7*, starting with feature engineering and moving on to hyperparameter tuning and single- and multi-model training. This information is crucial as we face the requirement to analyze large volumes of time-series data in a timely manner.

In this chapter, we're going to cover the following main topics:

- Why do we need to scale time-series analysis?
- Scaling out feature engineering
- Scaling out model training

Technical requirements

Before getting into the main topics, we will cover here the technical requirements for this chapter, which are as follows:

- **GitHub repository**: The code for this chapter can be found in the ch8 folder of the book's GitHub repository at this URL:

  ```
  https://github.com/PacktPublishing/Time-Series-Analysis-with-
  Spark/tree/main/ch8
  ```

- **Synthetic data**: We will use the Synthetic Data Vault tool, a Python library for creating synthetic tabular data. You can find more information on Synthetic Data Vault here: `https://docs.sdv.dev/sdv`.

- **Databricks platform**: The Databricks Community Edition, while free to use, is limited in resources. Similarly, the resources are likely to be limited when using a personal computer or laptop. With the requirement to demonstrate the scaling of computing power in this chapter, we will be using the non-Community version of the Databricks platform. As discussed in

Chapter 1, you can sign up for a 14-day free trial of Databricks, which will require you to first have an account with a cloud provider. Some cloud providers offer free credits at the start. This will provide you with more resources than on the Community Edition, for a limited time. Note that at the end of the trial period, the billing will switch to the credit card you provided at registration.

The Databricks compute configuration used is as per *Figure 8.1*. The worker and driver types shown here are based on AWS, which is different from what is available on Azure and GCP. Note that the UI can be subject to change, in which case refer to the latest Databricks documentation here:

```
https://docs.databricks.com/en/compute/configure.html
```

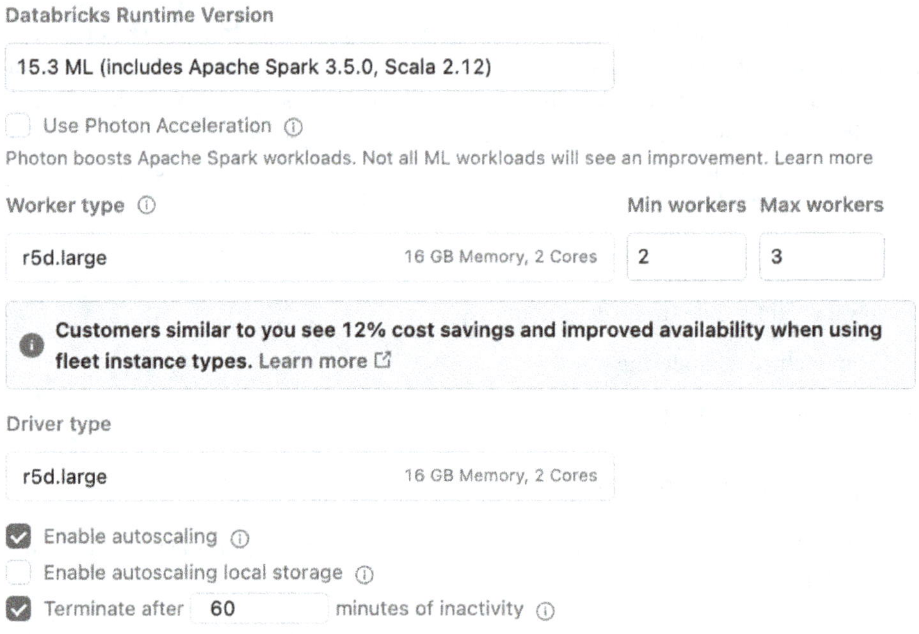

Databricks Runtime Version

15.3 ML (includes Apache Spark 3.5.0, Scala 2.12)

Use Photon Acceleration ⓘ

Photon boosts Apache Spark workloads. Not all ML workloads will see an improvement. Learn more

Worker type ⓘ		Min workers	Max workers
r5d.large	16 GB Memory, 2 Cores	2	3

ⓘ **Customers similar to you see 12% cost savings and improved availability when using fleet instance types.** Learn more ↗

Driver type

r5d.large	16 GB Memory, 2 Cores

☑ Enable autoscaling ⓘ

☐ Enable autoscaling local storage ⓘ

☑ Terminate after 60 minutes of inactivity ⓘ

Figure 8.1: Databricks compute configuration

Why do we need to scale time-series analysis?

The need to scale time-series analysis usually results from a requirement to perform the analysis faster or on a bigger dataset. In this chapter, we will look at decreasing the processing time achieved in *Chapter 7* while increasing the dataset size fivefold. This will be possible thanks to the scale of processing offered by Apache Spark.

Scaled-up dataset

To exercise Spark's scalability, we will need a more extensive dataset than we have used. While you may already have such a dataset, for the sake of this chapter, we will scale the household energy consumption dataset we used in *Chapter 7* and earlier chapters. The scaled dataset will be generated using the Synthetic Data Vault tool, mentioned in the *Technical requirements* section.

The code for this section is in `ts-spark_ch8_1.dbc`. We import the code into Databricks, similar to the approach explained for the Community Edition in the *Step-by-step: Loading and visualizing time series* section of *Chapter 1*.

In this code, we want to generate energy consumption data for four other families using one household's data to scale it fivefold.

We begin by capturing the metadata of `pdf_main`, which is the smaller reference dataset. The metadata is used as input to create a `GaussianCopulaSynthesizer` object named `synthesizer`, which represents a statistical model of the data. The synthesizer is, in turn, trained on the reference dataset (`pdf_main`) with the `fit` method. This model is finally used to generate synthetic data with the `sample` method.

The smaller reference dataset (`pdf_main`) is associated with customer identifier (`cust_id`) 1, and the synthetic datasets are associated with identifiers 2, 3, 4, and 5:

```python
# Initialize metadata object for the dataset
metadata = SingleTableMetadata()


# Automatically detect and set the metadata from the Pandas DataFrame
metadata.detect_from_dataframe(pdf_main)


# Initialize the Gaussian Copula Synthesizer with the dataset metadata
synthesizer = GaussianCopulaSynthesizer(metadata)


# Fit the synthesizer model to the Pandas DataFrame
synthesizer.fit(pdf_main)


...
# Define the number of customer datasets to generate:
num_customers = 5
# Count the number of rows in the original dataset:
sample_size = df_main.count()


i = 1
df_all = df_main.withColumn(
    'cust_id', F.lit(i)
) # Add a 'cust_id' column to the original dataset with a constant
# value of 1
```

```
...
    synthetic_data = spark.createDataFrame(
        synthesizer.sample(num_rows=sample_size)
) # Generate synthetic data matching the original dataset's size
...
```

Running the code in *Chapter 7* on this new, larger dataset is not going to be performant. We can scale up or out time-series analysis on larger datasets. We will explain both types of scaling next.

Scaling up

Scaling up is the simpler way to scale and does not require us to change the code we wrote in *Chapter 7*. We improve performance in this way by adding more memory (RAM) and using a more powerful CPU or even GPU. This works to a certain point before we reach scaling limits, prohibitive costs, or diminishing returns. In fact, due to system bottlenecks and overheads, scaling up does not result in linear performance improvement.

To scale further, we need to scale out.

Scaling out

Instead of making our one machine more powerful, scaling out involves adding more machines and parallelizing the processing. This requires a mechanism for the code to be distributed and executed in parallel, which is what Apache Spark provides.

In the upcoming sections, we will cover the following different ways that Apache Spark can be used to scale out time-series analysis:

- Feature engineering
- Model training

Feature engineering

Apache Spark can be used to scale out feature engineering with its distributed computing framework. This enables parallel processing of feature engineering tasks, which we will demonstrate in this section.

We will continue our discussion on data preparation in *Chapter 5* and improve the feature engineering done in *Chapter 7*. We will be using the pandas-based code examples from the *Development and testing* section of *Chapter 7* as a base for our discussion in this section. We will see in the following examples how non-Spark code is rewritten to be Spark compatible to avail the benefits of its scalability feature.

While there are many ways in which Spark can be used for feature engineering, we will focus on the following three related to improving *Chapter 7*'s code:

- Column transformations

- Resampling

- Lag values calculation

Let's begin with column transformations in the next section.

Column transformations

In the first code example, we will rewrite the column transformations code present in `ts-spark_ch7_1e_lgbm_comm.dbc`, which is used in the *Development and testing* section of *Chapter 7*. We will change the code to a Spark-enabled version by using the `pyspark.sql.functions` library. For this, we need to do the following:

1.   Replace the `Date` column with the concatenation (the `concat_ws` function) of the existing `Date` and `Time` columns.

2.   Convert (the `to_timestamp` function) the `Date` column into timestamp format.

3.   Replace selectively (with the `when` and `otherwise` condition) the incorrect values, ?, in `Global_active_power` to None.

4.   Replace (the `regexp_replace` function) , with . to be in the proper format for a `float` value.

The following code extract demonstrates the preceding steps:

```python
from pyspark.sql import functions as F

# Combine 'Date' and 'Time' into a single 'Date' column of timestamp
# type
df_all = df_all.withColumn(
    'Date',
    F.to_timestamp(
        F.concat_ws(' ', F.col('Date'), F.col('Time')),
        'd/M/yyyy HH:mm:ss')
)...
# Select only the 'cust_id', 'Date' and 'Global_active_power' columns
df_all = df_all.select(
    'cust_id', 'Date', 'Global_active_power'
)
# Replace '?' with None and convert 'Global_active_power' to float
df_all = df_all.withColumn(
    'Global_active_power',
```

```
    F.when(F.col('Global_active_power') == '?', None)
    .otherwise(F.regexp_replace(
        'Global_active_power', ',', '.').cast('float')
    )
)


# Sort the DataFrame based on 'cust_id' and 'Date'
df_all = df_all.orderBy('cust_id', 'Date')
```

After leveraging Spark to parallelize the column transformations, the next code improvement we will be covering is for resampling the time-series data.

Resampling

In the second code conversion example, we will rewrite the hourly resampling code present in ts-spark_ch7_1e_lgbm_comm.dbc, which is used in the *Development and testing* section of *Chapter 7*. We want to calculate the hourly mean of Global_active_power for each customer. For this, we need to do the following:

1. Convert the Date column to its date and hour components using the date_format function.

2. Resample to the hourly mean of Global_active_power (the agg and mean functions) for each customer (the groupBy function).

The following code demonstrates the preceding steps:

```
from pyspark.sql import functions as F


# Convert the 'Date' column to a string representing the
# start of the hour for each timestamp
data_hr = df_all.withColumn(
    'Date',
    F.date_format('Date', 'yyyy-MM-dd HH:00:00'))


# Group the data by 'cust_id' and the hourly 'Date',
# then calculate the mean 'Global_active_power' for each group
data_hr = data_hr.groupBy(
    'cust_id', 'Date').agg(
    F.mean('Global_active_power').alias('Global_active_power')
)
```

Now that we have used Spark to parallelize the resampling, the next code improvement we will be covering is for calculating the lag values of the time-series data.

Calculating lag values

In the third example of scaling feature engineering with Apache Spark, we will rewrite the lag calculation code present in `ts-spark_ch7_1e_lgbm_comm.dbc`, which is used in the *Development and testing* section of *Chapter 7*. We want to calculate different lag values for each customer. For this, we need to do the following:

1. Define a sliding date window over which to calculate the lags for each of the customers (the `partitionBy` function). We have the dates ordered (the `orderBy` function) for each customer.

2. Calculate the different lags over the sliding window (the `lag` and `over` functions).

3. Note that as the lag calculation is based on previous values, some of the lag values at the beginning of the dataset will not have enough prior values for calculation and will be empty. We remove the rows with these empty lag values using the `dropna` function.

The following code demonstrates the preceding steps:

```python
from pyspark.sql.window import Window
from pyspark.sql import functions as F

# Define a window specification partitioned by -
# 'cust_id' and ordered by the 'Date' column
windowSpec = Window.partitionBy("cust_id").orderBy("Date")

# Add lagged features to the DataFrame to incorporate
#  past values as features for forecasting
# Apply the lag function to create the lagged column,
#  separately for each 'cust_id'
# Lag by 1, 2, 3, 4, 5, 12, 24, 168 hours (24 hours * 7 days)
lags = [1, 2, 3, 4, 5, 12, 24, 24*7]
for l in lags:
    data_hr = data_hr.withColumn(
        'Global_active_power_lag' + str(l),
        F.lag(F.col('Global_active_power'), l).over(windowSpec))

# Remove rows with NaN values that were introduced by
#  shifting (lagging) operations
data_hr = data_hr.dropna()
```

By using Spark functions instead of pandas, we will enable Spark to parallelize the lag calculations for large datasets.

Now that we have covered the different ways of leveraging Apache Spark to improve the feature engineering part of *Chapter 7*'s code, we will dive deep into the scaling out of model training.

Model training

In this section, we will cover the following different ways that Apache Spark can be used for model training at scale:

- Hyperparameter tuning

- Single model training in parallel

- Multiple models training in parallel

These approaches enable efficient model training when we have large datasets or many models to train.

Hyperparameter tuning can be an expensive computation when the same model is trained repeatedly with many different hyperparameters. We want to be able to leverage Spark to find the best hyperparameters efficiently.

Similarly, training a single model on a large dataset can take a long time. In other cases, we may have many models to train for distinct time-series datasets. We want to speed these up by parallelizing the training on Spark clusters.

We will go into the details of these approaches next, starting with hyperparameter tuning in the next section.

Hyperparameter tuning

As discussed in *Chapter 4*, hyperparameter tuning in machine learning is the process of finding the best set of configurations for a machine learning algorithm. This search for optimal hyperparameters can be parallelized using libraries such as GridSearchCV, Hyperopt, and Optuna, which provide the framework, in conjunction with Apache Spark, for the backend processing parallelism.

We discussed Spark's processing parallelism in *Chapter 3*. Here we will focus more specifically on the use of Optuna in conjunction with Apache Spark for hyperparameter tuning.

If you recall, in *Chapter 7*, we used GridSearchCV on a single node to tune the hyperparameters of the LightGBM model. We will improve on this in the code example in this section by parallelizing the process. We will use Optuna with Spark to find the best hyperparameters for the LightGBM model we explored in *Chapter 7*.

Optuna is an open source hyperparameter optimization framework that is used to automate hyperparameter searches. You can find more information on Optuna here: `https://optuna.org/`.

We will begin the tuning process by defining an `objective` function (which we will later optimize using Optuna). This `objective` function does the following:

1. Define the search space in `params` with the range of hyperparameter values.

2. Initialize the LightGBM `LGBMRegressor` model with the parameters specific to the trial.

3. Train (`fit`) the model on the training dataset.

4. Use the model to predict the validation dataset.

5. Calculate the model evaluation metric (`mean_absolute_percentage_error`).

6. Return the evaluation metric.

The following code demonstrates the preceding steps:

```python
import lightgbm as lgb
from sklearn.metrics import mean_absolute_percentage_error
import optuna


def objective(trial):
    # Define the hyperparameter configuration space
    params = {
        # Specify the learning task and
        #  the corresponding learning objective:
        "objective": "regression",
        # Evaluation metric for the model performance:
        "metric": "rmse",
        # Number of boosted trees to fit:
        "n_estimators": trial.suggest_int("n_estimators", 50, 200),
        # Learning rate for gradient descent:
        "learning_rate": trial.suggest_float(
            "learning_rate", 0.001, 0.1, log=True),
        # Maximum tree leaves for base learners:
        "num_leaves": trial.suggest_int("num_leaves", 30, 100),
    }

    # Initialize the LightGBM model with the trial's parameters:
    model = lgb.LGBMRegressor(**params)
    # Train the model with the training dataset:
    model.fit(X_train, y_train)
    # Generate predictions for the validation dataset:
    y_pred = model.predict(X_test)
    # Calculate the Mean Absolute Percentage Error (MAPE)
    #  for model evaluation:
    mape = mean_absolute_percentage_error(y_test, y_pred)

    # Return the MAPE as the objective to minimize
    return mape
```

Once the objective function is defined, the next steps are as follows:

1. Register Spark (the `register_spark` function) as the backend.

2. Create a study (the `create_study` function), which is a collection of trials, to minimize the evaluation metric.

3. Run the study on the Spark `parallel_backend` to optimize the `objective` function over `n_trials`.

The following code demonstrates the preceding steps:

```python
from joblibspark import register_spark
# This line registers Apache Spark as the backend for
# parallel computing with Joblib, enabling distributed
# computing capabilities for Joblib-based parallel tasks.
register_spark()
...

# Create a new study object with the goal of minimizing the objective
# function
study2 = optuna.create_study(direction='minimize')
# Set Apache Spark as the backend for parallel execution of -
# trials with unlimited jobs
with joblib.parallel_backend("spark", n_jobs=-1):
    # Optimize the study by evaluating the -
    #   objective function over 10 trials:
    study2.optimize(objective, n_trials=10)
```

We have at this point the result of the optimization. We can now display the evaluation metric (`trial.value`) and parameters (`trial.params`) for `best_trial`:

```python
# Retrieve the best trial from the optimization study
trial = study2.best_trial


# Print the best trial's objective function value,
#   typically accuracy or loss
print(f"Best trial accuracy: {trial.value}")
print("Best trial params: ")


# Iterate through the best trial's hyperparameters and print them
for key, value in trial.params.items():
    print(f"    {key}: {value}")
```

The outcome of the hyperparameter tuning, shown in *Figure 8.2*, is the best hyperparameters found within the search space specified, as well as the related model accuracy.

```
Best trial accuracy: 0.4363694187190601
Best trial params:
    learning_rate: 0.0113361915849721
    num_leaves: 553
    subsample: 0.3607318111709123
    colsample_bytree: 0.37739691446973755
    min_data_in_leaf: 35
```

Figure 8.2: Hyperparameter tuning – best trials

In addition to the scaling of the hyperparameter tuning stage, which we have seen in this section, Spark clusters can also be used to parallelize the next step, that is, fitting the model to the training data. We will cover this next.

Single model in parallel

Ensemble methods such as Random Forest and gradient boosting machines can benefit from task parallelism during the model training stage. Each tree in a Random Forest can be trained independently, making it possible to parallelize across multiple processors. Similarly in the case of Gradient Boosting models such as LightGBM and XGBoost, the tree's construction can be parallelized, even though the boosting itself is sequential,

In *Chapter 7*'s example in the *Classical machine learning model* section, we used LightGBM. This model was not Spark enabled. Here, as we want to demonstrate training parallelism with a Spark-enabled Gradient Boosting model, we will use `SparkXGBRegressor` instead.

As a first step, we will build a vector of the features using `VectorAssembler`, as shown in the following code:

```python
from pyspark.ml.feature import VectorAssembler

# Define a list to hold the names of the lag feature columns
inputCols = []
# Loop through the list of lag intervals to create feature column
# names
for l in lags:
    inputCols.append('Global_active_power_lag' + str(l))

# Initialize VectorAssembler with the
# created feature column names and specify the output column name
assembler = VectorAssembler(
    inputCols=inputCols, outputCol="features")
```

We then create the `SparkXGBRegressor` model object, setting `num_workers` to all available workers, and specifying the target column with `label_col`:

```python
from xgboost.spark import SparkXGBRegressor


# Initialize the SparkXGBRegressor for the regression task.
# `num_workers` is set to the default parallelism level of -
#   the Spark context to utilize all available cores.
# `label_col` specifies the target variable column name for
# prediction.
# `missing` is set to 0.0 to handle missing values in the dataset.
xgb_model = SparkXGBRegressor(
    num_workers=sc.defaultParallelism,
    label_col="Global_active_power", missing=0.0
)
```

As we have seen so far, hyperparameter tuning is an important step in finding the best model. In the following code example, we will use `ParamGridBuilder` to specify the range of parameters that are specific to the model and that we want to evaluate.

We then pass the parameters to `CrossValidator` together with `RegressionEvaluator`. We will use the root mean square error (`rmse`) as the evaluation metric. This is the default metric for `RegressionEvaluator`, making it suitable for our example here:

```python
from pyspark.ml.tuning import CrossValidator, ParamGridBuilder
from pyspark.ml.evaluation import RegressionEvaluator


# Initialize the parameter grid for hyperparameter tuning
# - max_depth: specifies the maximum depth of the trees in the model
# - n_estimators: defines the number of trees in the ensemble
paramGrid = ParamGridBuilder()\
    .addGrid(xgb_model.max_depth, [5, 10])\
    .addGrid(xgb_model.n_estimators, [30, 100])\
    .build()


# Initialize the regression evaluator for model evaluation
# - metricName: specifies the metric to use for evaluation,
#     here RMSE (Root Mean Squared Error)
# - labelCol: the name of the label column
# - predictionCol: the name of the prediction column
evaluator = RegressionEvaluator(
    metricName="rmse",
    LabelCol = xgb_model.getLabelCol(),
    PredictionCol = xgb_model.getPredictionCol()
)
```

```
# Initialize the CrossValidator for hyperparameter tuning
# - estimator: the model to be tuned
# - evaluator: the evaluator to be used for model evaluation
# - estimatorParamMaps: the grid of parameters to be used for tuning
cv = CrossValidator(
    estimator = xgb_model, evaluator = evaluator,
    estimatorParamMaps = paramGrid)
```

At this point, we are ready to build a pipeline (`Pipeline`) to train (`fit`) the model. We will do this by combining in sequence the `VectorAssembler` (`assembler`) and `CrossValidator` (`cv`) stages:

```
from pyspark.ml import Pipeline
# Initialize a Pipeline object with two stages:
# a feature assembler and a cross-validator for model tuning
pipeline = Pipeline(stages = [assembler, cv])
```

In this example, we want to demonstrate parallelism for a single model corresponding to a single customer, so we will limit (the `filter` function) the training data to `cust_id` 1. We then take all the records (the `head` function) for training except the last 48 hours as these will be used for testing. This results in the `train_hr` DataFrame with the hourly training data:

```
# Filter the dataset for customer with cust_id equal to 1
train_hr = data_hr.filter('cust_id == 1')

# Create a Spark DataFrame excluding the last 48 records for training
train_hr = spark.createDataFrame(
    train_hr.head(train_hr.count() - 48)
)
# Fit the pipeline model to the training data
pipelineModel = pipeline.fit(train_hr)
```

Similarly, for testing, we will filter in `cust_id` 1 and, in this case, use the last 48 hours. We can then apply (`transform`) the model (`pipelineModel`) to the test data (`test_hr`) to get the prediction of energy consumption for these 48 hours:

```
# Filter the dataset for customer with cust_id equal to 1 for testing
test_hr = data_hr.filter('cust_id == 1')
# Create a Spark DataFrame including the last 48 records for testing
test_hr = spark.createDataFrame(train_hr.tail(48))
...
# Apply the trained pipeline model to the test data to generate
# predictions
predictions = pipelineModel.transform(test_hr)
```

Once we have the model's predictions on the test data, we can use `RegressionEvaluator` (the `evaluator` object) to calculate (the `evaluate` function) the RMSE:

```
# Evaluate the model's performance using
# Root Mean Squared Error (RMSE) metric
rmse = evaluator.evaluate(predictions)
```

For comparison, we also calculate the **Symmetric Mean Absolute Percentage Error (SMAPE)** and **Weighted Average Percentage Error (WAPE)** similarly to how we have done in the *Classical machine learning model* section of *Chapter 7*. The results are shown in *Figure 8.3*.

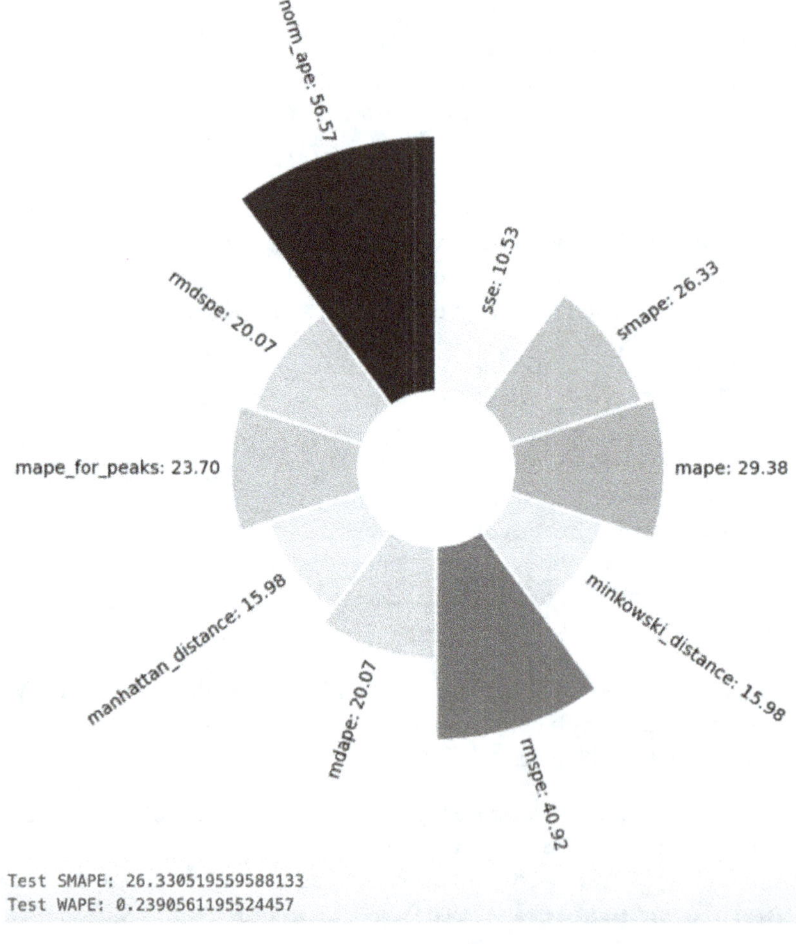

Figure 8.3: XGBoost evaluation metrics

We plot the forecast against the actual values in *Figures 8.4* and *8.5*.

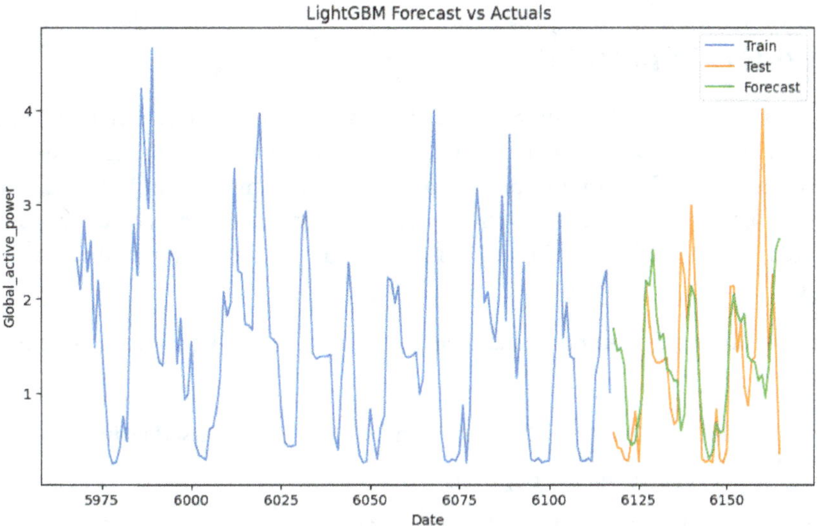

Figure 8.4: XGBoost forecast versus actuals (training and testing)

We zoom in on the testing period in *Figure 8.5* for a visual comparison of the forecast and actuals.

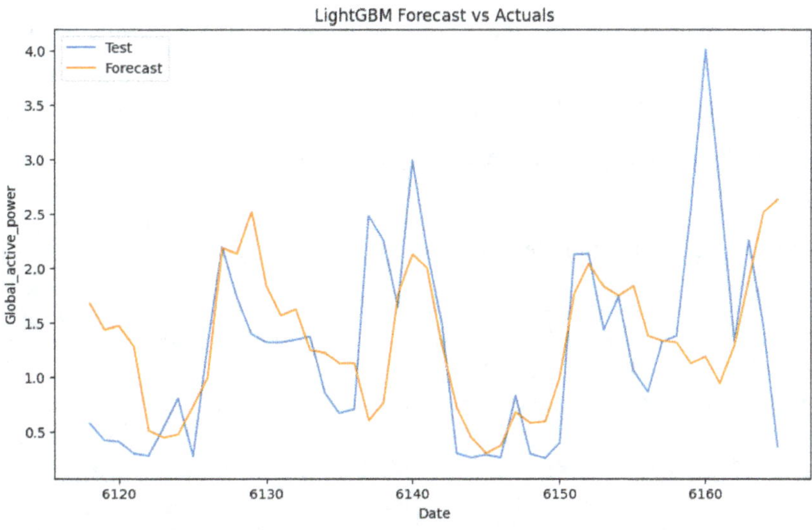

Figure 8.5: XGBoost forecast versus actuals (zoom on test data)

In this section, we have seen parallelism in single-model training. This requires the use of a library, such as XGBoost used here, which supports a multi-node processing backend such as Apache Spark. In addition to ensemble methods, other models, such as deep learning, can benefit from training parallelism.

Multiple models can also be trained in parallel, which we will explore next.

Multiple models in parallel

Earlier in this chapter, we scaled the dataset to represent the household energy consumption of multiple customers. In this section, we will train a different machine learning model for each customer in parallel. This is required if we want to predict the energy consumption of individual customers based on their own historical consumption. There are several other use cases where such multi-model training is required, for example, in the retail industry when doing sales forecasting for individual products or stores.

Coming back to our energy consumption example, the `train_model` function does the following for each customer:

1. Get the customer ID (`cust_id`) from the pandas DataFrame passed as input.

2. Choose the features (`X`) and target (`y`) variables.

3. Split (`train_test_split`) the dataset into training and testing, specifying `shuffle` as `False` to preserve the time order. As discussed in *Chapter 1*, this is an important consideration for time-series datasets.

4. Perform hyperparameter tuning with `GridSearchCV` using `LGBMRegressor` as the model and `TimeSeriesSplit` for the dataset splits.

5. Train (`fit`) the final model with the best hyperparameters (`best_params`) on the full training dataset.

6. Test the final model on the test dataset and calculate the evaluation metrics (`rmse` and `mape`).

7. Return the result of `train_model` in a DataFrame with `cust_id`, `best_params`, `rmse`, and `mape`.

The following code shows the function definition with the preceding steps:

```python
def train_model(df_pandas: pd.DataFrame) -> pd.DataFrame:
    # Extract the customer ID for which the model is being trained
    cust_id = df_pandas["cust_id"].iloc[0]
    # Select features and target variables from the DataFrame
    X = df_pandas[[
        'Global_active_power_lag1', 'Global_active_power_lag2',
        'Global_active_power_lag3', 'Global_active_power_lag4',
        'Global_active_power_lag5', 'Global_active_power_lag12',
        'Global_active_power_lag24', 'Global_active_power_lag168'
    ]]
```

```python
y = df_pandas['Global_active_power']
# Split the dataset into training and testing sets, preserving
# time order
X_train, X_test, y_train, y_test = train_test_split(
    X, y, test_size=0.2, shuffle=False, random_state=12
)
# Define the hyperparameter space for LightGBM model tuning
param_grid = {
    'num_leaves': [30, 50, 100],
    'learning_rate': [0.1, 0.01, 0.001],
    'n_estimators': [50, 100, 200]
}


# Initialize the LightGBM regressor model
lgbm = lgb.LGBMRegressor()


# Initialize TimeSeriesSplit for cross-validation to
#  respect time series data structure
tscv = TimeSeriesSplit(n_splits=10)


# Perform grid search with cross-validation
gsearch = GridSearchCV(
    estimator=lgbm, param_grid=param_grid, cv=tscv)
gsearch.fit(X_train, y_train)


# Extract the best hyperparameters
best_params = gsearch.best_params_


# Train the final model using the best parameters
final_model = lgb.LGBMRegressor(**best_params)
final_model.fit(X_train, y_train)


# Make predictions on the test set
y_pred = final_model.predict(X_test)
# Calculate RMSE and MAPE metrics
rmse = np.sqrt(mean_squared_error(y_test, y_pred))
mape = mean_absolute_percentage_error(y_test, y_pred)


# Prepare the results DataFrame to return
return_df = pd.DataFrame(
    [[cust_id, str(best_params), rmse, mape]],
    columns=["cust_id", "best_params", "rmse", "mape"]
)


return return_df
```

Now that the model training function is defined, we can launch it in parallel for each customer (the `groupBy` function), passing a pandas DataFrame of all the rows for this specific customer to the `applyInPandas` function.

> **pandas UDFs, mapInPandas, and applyInPandas**
>
> Using Spark-enabled libraries, as we did in the previous section with single-model parallel training, is usually faster for large datasets than single-machine libraries. There are, however, cases when we have to use a library that isn't implemented natively for Spark's parallel processing. In these situations, we can use pandas **User-Defined Functions** (**UDFs**), `mapInPandas`, or `applyInPandas`. These methods allow you to call pandas operations in a distributed way from Spark. The common use cases are as follows:
>
> - **pandas UDF**: One input row for one output row
>
> - **mapInPandas**: One input row for multiple output rows
>
> - **applyInPandas**: Multiple input rows for one output row
>
> Note that these are general guidance and that there is great flexibility in how these methods can be used.

In the example in this section, we use `applyInPandas` as we want to execute a pandas-enabled function for all the rows in the dataset corresponding to a specific customer for model training. We want the function to output one row with the result of model training for the specific customer.

Note how, in the following code extract, we specified the `train_model_result_schema` schema of the function's return value. This is a requirement for serializing the result that is added to the `train_model_result_df` pandas DataFrame:

```python
from pyspark.sql.functions import lit


# Group the data by customer ID and apply the
#   train_model function to each group using Pandas UDF
# The schema for the resulting DataFrame is defined by
#   train_model_result_schema
# Cache the resulting DataFrame to optimize performance for
#   subsequent actions
train_model_result_df = (
    data_hr
    .groupby("cust_id")
    .applyInPandas(train_model, schema=train_model_result_schema)
    .cache()
)
```

Figure 8.6 shows the outcome of the multi-model training. It shows the best hyperparameters (the `best_params` column) and evaluation metrics (the `rmse` and `mape` columns) for each customer.

	1^2_3 cust_id	$^{AB}_C$ best_params	1.2 rmse	1.2 mape
1	1	{'learning_rate': 0.1, 'n_estimators': 50, 'num_leaves': 30}	0.64585369825363316	0.43904349207878113
2	2	{'learning_rate': 0.001, 'n_estimators': 50, 'num_leaves': 100}	0.13783085346221924	0.10713604837656021
3	3	{'learning_rate': 0.001, 'n_estimators': 50, 'num_leaves': 30}	0.1413857340812683	0.11260034888982773
4	4	{'learning_rate': 0.001, 'n_estimators': 200, 'num_leaves': 30}	0.13853944838047028	0.11089791357517242
5	5	{'learning_rate': 0.001, 'n_estimators': 100, 'num_leaves': 100}	0.13869743049144745	0.11137434840202332

Figure 8.6: Multi-model training – best hyperparameters and evaluation metrics

With this example, we have trained five different models representing different customers. We have found the best hyperparameters to use for each model, which we are then able to use to do individual energy consumption forecasting.

With this, we conclude the different ways in which we can leverage Apache Spark to scale time-series analysis. Next, we will discuss some of the ways that the training process can be optimized.

Training optimization

When training machine learning models at a large scale, several inefficiencies and overheads can impact resource utilization and performance. These include the following:

- Idle time waiting for resources such as GPU, network, and storage accesses, which can delay the training process.

- Frequent checkpointing, which saves the model during training to avoid restarting in case of failure. This results in additional storage and time during model training.

- Hardware or software failures during the training result in restarts, which waste resources and delay the training.

The following mitigation techniques can be used, depending on the model being trained and the library in use:

- Eliminate the cause of idle wait times by provisioning sufficient compute, network, and storage resources

- Avoid too frequent checkpointing

- Rearrange features based on correlation with the target variable or their importance to facilitate convergence during model training

- Reduce the dimensionality of the dataset, choosing the most informative features

While the implementation details of these techniques are beyond our scope here, we recommend researching and addressing these points when operating at a large scale due to the potentially high impact on cost, efficiency, and scalability.

Summary

In this chapter, we saw the need to scale the processing capacity for bigger datasets. We examined different ways of using Apache Spark to this end. Building on and extending the code examples from *Chapter 7*, we focused on scaling the feature engineering and model training stages. We looked at leveraging Spark to scale transformations, aggregations, lag values calculation, hyperparameter tuning, and single- and multi-model training in parallel.

In the next chapter, we will cover the considerations for going to production with time-series analysis, using and extending what we have learned so far.

Join our community on Discord

Join our community's Discord space for discussions with the authors and other readers:

```
https://packt.link/ds
```

Going to Production

With our time series analysis model built and tested, and the ability to scale seen in the previous chapter, we will now explore the practical considerations and steps involved in deploying time series models into production with the Spark framework. This information is crucial to guide you through the transition from development to real-world implementation, ensuring the reliability and effectiveness of time series models in operational environments. With many machine learning projects stuck in development and proof of concept stages, grasping the nuances of deploying to production enhances your ability to integrate time series analyses seamlessly into decision-making processes.

While in *Chapter 4* we covered the broader end-to-end view of a time series analysis project, in this chapter, we're going to focus on going to production with the following main topics:

- Workflows

- Monitoring and reporting

- Additional considerations

Technical requirements

In this chapter, we will explore with code examples the deployment of a scalable end-to-end workflow for time series analysis in our own container-based environment. A tremendous amount of work goes into building a production-ready environment, which goes way beyond what we can reasonably cover in this chapter. We will focus instead on providing an example as a starting point. We will see how what we have learned so far about time series analysis comes together to create an end-to-end workflow.

The code for this chapter can be found at this URL: `https://github.com/PacktPublishing/Time-Series-Analysis-with-Spark/tree/main/ch9`

Let's start by setting up our environment for the example.

Environment setup

We will be using Docker containers, like in *Chapter 3* and *Chapter 4*, for the platform infrastructure. Follow the instructions in the *Using a container for deployment* section of *Chapter 3* and the *Environment setup* section of *Chapter 4* on setting up the container environment.

Once the environment is set up, download the deployment script from the Git repository for this chapter, which is at the following URL:

```
https://github.com/PacktPublishing/Time-Series-Analysis-with-Spark/
tree/main/ch9
```

You can then start the container environment as per the *Environment startup* section of *Chapter 4*. Do a quick visual validation of the components as per the *Accessing the UIs* section of the same chapter.

Before we get into the nitty-gritty of the code, let's step back with an overview of the workflow to see the big picture of what we will be building in this section.

Workflows

The code example in this chapter includes two workflows. These are implemented as **Directed Acyclic Graphs (DAGs)** in Airflow, like in *Chapter 4*. The best way to visualize the workflows is from the DAG views in Airflow, as per *Figures 9.1* and *9.2*.

The two workflows are as follows:

- `ts-spark_ch9_data-ml-ops`: This is an example of the end-to-end process, shown in *Figure 9.1*, which includes the following tasks:

  - `get_config`

  - `ingest_train_data`

  - `transform_train_data`

  - `train_and_log_model`

  - `forecast`

  - `ingest_eval_data`

  - `transform_eval_data`

  - `eval_forecast`

Figure 9.1: Airflow DAG for the end-to-end workflow

- `ts-spark_ch9_data-ml-ops_runall`: This second workflow, shown in *Figure 9.2*, calls the preceding one multiple times with different ranges of dates. It simulates what happens in the real world whereby the preceding end-to-end workflow is launched at a regular interval, say daily or weekly, with new data.

Figure 9.2: Airflow DAG with multiple calls to the end-to-end workflow

The code for these Airflow DAGs is in the `dags` folder. They are in Python (`.py` files) and can be visualized via a text, or preferably a code, editor.

> **Modularity**
>
> It is worth noting that for the example here, we could have joined up all the code of these individual tasks into one big task. Instead, we have broken the workflow into multiple tasks to illustrate the best practice of modularization. In a real-world situation, this facilitates independent code change, scaling, and task reruns. Different teams may have ownership of the tasks.

> **Workflow separation**
>
> The workflows we are demonstrating in this example can be further separated in your own implementation. For instance, it is common to have the model-training-related tasks, the forecasting, and the model evaluation in their own individual workflows launched at different time intervals.

We will explain each of these DAGs and related tasks in detail in the upcoming sections, starting with `ts-spark_ch9_data-ml-ops_runall`.

Simulation and runs

As we saw in *Figure 9.2*, `ts-spark_ch9_data-ml-ops_runall` has five tasks, which we will explain further here.

The purpose of the `_runall` workflow is to simulate the real-world execution of the cycle of training, forecasting, and evaluation at regular intervals. In our example, each task of the `_runall` workflow corresponds to one cycle of training, forecasting, and evaluation. We will call each task a run and have five runs in all, corresponding to the five tasks of `_runall`. These tasks will be scheduled at regular intervals, daily, weekly, monthly, or so. In the example here, we are just running them sequentially, one after the other.

Each task calls the `ts-spark_ch9_data-ml-ops` workflow with a different set of parameters. They are as follows:

- `runid`: An integer to identify the run

- `START_DATE`: The start date in the time series dataset to use for training

- `TRAIN_END_DATE`: The end date in the time series dataset for training

- `EVAL_END_DATE`: The end date in the time series dataset for evaluation

The way the different runs are configured is with a sliding window of 5 years of training data and 1 year of evaluation data in our example. In a real-world scenario, the evaluation date range is likely to be shorter, corresponding to a shorter forecasting horizon.

The run configurations are as follows:

```python
conf_run1 = {
    'runid':            1,
    'START_DATE':       '1981-01-01',
    'TRAIN_END_DATE': '1985-12-31',
    'EVAL_END_DATE':    '1986-12-31',
}
conf_run2 = {
    'runid':            2,
    'START_DATE':       '1982-01-01',
    'TRAIN_END_DATE': '1986-12-31',
    'EVAL_END_DATE':    '1987-12-31',
}
...
```

The tasks are defined as follows to trigger the `ts-spark_ch9_data-ml-ops` workflow passing the run configuration as a parameter:

```python
# Define tasks
t1 = TriggerDagRunOperator(
    task_id="ts-spark_ch9_data-ml-ops_1",
    trigger_dag_id="ts-spark_ch9_data-ml-ops",
    conf=conf_run1,
    wait_for_completion=True,
    dag=dag,
)


t2 = TriggerDagRunOperator(
    task_id="ts-spark_ch9_data-ml-ops_2",
    trigger_dag_id="ts-spark_ch9_data-ml-ops",
```

```
        conf=conf_run2,
        wait_for_completion=True,
        dag=dag,
    )
...
```

The tasks are then launched sequentially as follows:

```
t1 >> t2 >> t3 >> t4 >> t5
```

You can kick off this `ts-spark_ch9_data-ml-ops_runall` Airflow DAG from the Airflow DAG view as per *Figure 9.3*, by clicking on the run (>) button highlighted in green.

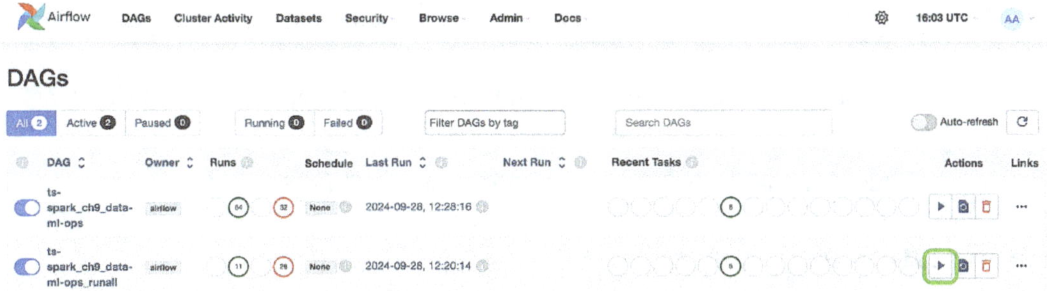

Figure 9.3: Run the Airflow DAG

The outcome of this DAG can be seen in *Figure 9.2*, showing the status of the individual tasks.

We will now discuss the details of these tasks, which, as we have seen, call the `ts-spark_ch9_data-ml-ops` workflow with different parameters. Let's start with the first step, `get_config`, tasked with handling these parameters.

Configuration

The first task in the `ts-spark_ch9_data-ml-ops` workflow is `t0` and it calls the `get_config` function to retrieve the configuration needed to run the workflow. These are passed as parameters when calling the workflow. They are, as mentioned earlier, the run identifier and date ranges of the time series data for which we want to run the workflow. We will see how they are used in the subsequent tasks.

The code that defines task `t0` is as follows:

```
t0 = PythonOperator(
    task_id='get_config',
    python_callable=get_config,
    op_kwargs={'_vars': {
        'runid': "{{ dag_run.conf['runid'] }}",
        'START_DATE': "{{ dag_run.conf['START_DATE'] }}",
```

```
                    'TRAIN_END_DATE': "{{ dag_run.conf['TRAIN_END_DATE'] }}",
                    'EVAL_END_DATE': "{{ dag_run.conf['EVAL_END_DATE'] }}",
                },
        },
        provide_context=True,
        dag=dag,
)
```

The get_config function, which is called by task t0, is as follows:

```
def get_config(_vars, **kwargs):
    print(f"dag_config: {_vars}")


    return _vars
```

All it does is pass through the configuration parameters received at the launch of the Airflow DAG in a _vars variable for use by subsequent tasks.

We can see the status of the task in the DAG view in Airflow as per *Figure 9.1*.

Data ingestion and storage

At this step, after completion of the t0 task, the t1 task is launched by Airflow. It calls the ingest_ train_data function to ingest the training data from the input CSV file as specified by the DATASOURCE variable. In this example, as it is a relatively small file, we ingest the full file every time. You will likely ingest only new data points incrementally at this stage.

The code for this step is as follows:

```
def ingest_train_data(_vars, **kwargs):
    sdf = spark.read.csv(
        DATASOURCE, header=True, inferSchema=True
    )
    sdf = sdf.filter(
        (F.col('date') >= F.lit(_vars['START_DATE'])) &
        (F.col('date') <= F.lit(_vars['TRAIN_END_DATE']))
    )
    data_ingest_count = sdf.count()
    sdf.write.format("delta").mode("overwrite").save(
        f"/data/delta/ts-spark_ch9_bronze_train_{_vars['runid']}"
    )


    _vars['train_ingest_count'] = data_ingest_count
    return _vars
```

The data is ingested using Spark, with the `spark.read.csv` function, into a Spark DataFrame. We then filter the data for the range of dates that fall within the training dataset as per the `START_DATE` and `TRAIN_END_DATE` parameters.

We want to be able to later report on how much data we ingest every time. To enable this, we count the number of rows in the DataFrame.

Finally, in this task, we persist the ingested data with the `write` function to disk storage in `delta` format for use by the next steps of the workflow. As we will parallelize the workflow tasks in the future, and to avoid multiple parallel writes to the same disk location, we store the data for this specific run in its own table appended with `runid`. Note as well how we used the term `bronze` in the name. This corresponds to the **medallion** approach, which we discussed in the *Data processing and storage* section of *Chapter 4*. Persisting the data to storage at this stage can come in handy when we are ingesting a lot of data. This makes it possible in the future to change and rerun the rest of the pipeline without having to re-ingest the data.

The status of the task is visible in the DAG view in Airflow as per *Figure 9.1*.

With the data ingested from the source and persisted, we can move on to the data transformation stage.

Data transformations

This stage corresponds to Airflow task `t2`, which calls the `transform_train_data` function. As its name suggests, this function transforms the training data into the right format for the upcoming training stage.

The code for this step is as follows:

```python
def transform_train_data(_vars, **kwargs):
    sdf = spark.read.format("delta").load(
        f"/data/delta/ts-spark_ch9_bronze_train_{_vars['runid']}"
    )
    sdf = sdf.selectExpr(
        "date as ds",
        "cast(daily_min_temperature as double) as y"
    )
    sdf = sdf.dropna()

    data_transform_count = sdf.count()
    sdf.write.format("delta").mode("overwrite").save(
        f"/data/delta/ts-spark_ch9_silver_train_{_vars['runid']}"
    )


    _vars['train_transform_count'] = data_transform_count
    return _vars
```

We first read the data from `bronze`, where it was stored by the previous task, `t1`. This stored data can then be used as input to run the current task.

In this example, we do the following simple transformations:

- Column level: Rename the `date` column as `ds`

- Column level: Change `daily_min_temperature` to the double data type (the `cast` function) and rename it as `y`

- DataFrame level: Remove all rows with missing values using the `dropna` function

As in the previous stage, we want to collect metrics specific to this stage so that we can later report on the transformations. To do this, we count the number of rows in the DataFrame after the transformations.

> **Note**
>
> This stage is likely to include several data checks and transformations, as discussed in the *Data quality checks, cleaning, and transformations* section of *Chapter 5*.

Finally, in this task, we persist the ingested data with the `write` function to disk storage in `delta` format for use by the next steps of the workflow. We call this data stage `silver`, as per the medallion approach explained previously.

Similarly to the previous tasks, we can see the task's status in the DAG view in Airflow, as per *Figure 9.1*.

With the data curated and persisted, we can move on to the model training stage.

Model training and validation

This stage is the longest in our example and corresponds to Airflow task `t3`, which calls the `train_and_log_model` function. This function trains and validates a Prophet forecasting model using the training data from the previous stage. As we saw in *Chapter 7*, choosing the right model involves a whole process, which we have simplified here to a minimum.

The code extract for this step is as follows:

```python
def train_and_log_model(_vars, **kwargs):
    sdf = spark.read.format("delta").load(
        f"/data/delta/ts-spark_ch9_silver_train_{_vars['runid']}"
    )
    pdf = sdf.toPandas()

    mlflow.set_experiment(
        'ts-spark_ch9_data-ml-ops_time_series_prophet_train'
    )
```

```python
mlflow.start_run()
mlflow.log_param("DAG_NAME", DAG_NAME)
mlflow.log_param("TRAIN_START_DATE", _vars['START_DATE'])
...

mlflow.log_metric(
    'train_ingest_count', _vars['train_ingest_count'])
...

model = Prophet().fit(pdf)
...

cv_metrics_name = [
    "mse", "rmse", "mae", "mdape", "smape", "coverage"]
cv_params = cross_validation(
    ...
)
_cv_metrics = performance_metrics(cv_params)
cv_metrics = {
    n: _cv_metrics[n].mean() for n in cv_metrics_name}
...

signature = infer_signature(train, predictions)

mlflow.prophet.log_model(
    model, artifact_path=ARTIFACT_DIR,
    signature=signature, registered_model_name=model_name,)
mlflow.log_params(param)
mlflow.log_metrics(cv_metrics)
...

mlflow.end_run()
return _vars
```

In this code example, we do the following:

1. We first read the data from `silver`, where it was stored by the previous task, `t2`. Then, we can run the current task using the stored data as input.

2. MLflow Tracking Server is used to save all the parameters and metrics for each run. We group them under an experiment called `ts-spark_ch9_data-ml-ops_time_series_prophet_train` and use `log_param` and `log_metric` functions to capture the parameters and metrics gathered so far in the run.

3. We then train the Prophet model with the training data using the `fit` function.

4. As a model validation step, we use the `cross_validation` function and retrieve the corresponding metrics with the `performance_metrics` function.

5. The final step is to log the model to the MLflow Model Registry, using the `log_model` function, and all the related training and validation metrics with MLflow. Note that we log the model signature as a best practice to document the model in the MLflow Model Registry.

We can see the task's status in the DAG view in Airflow, as per *Figure 9.1*. The logged parameters and metrics are visible in MLflow Tracking server, as shown in *Figure 9.4*.

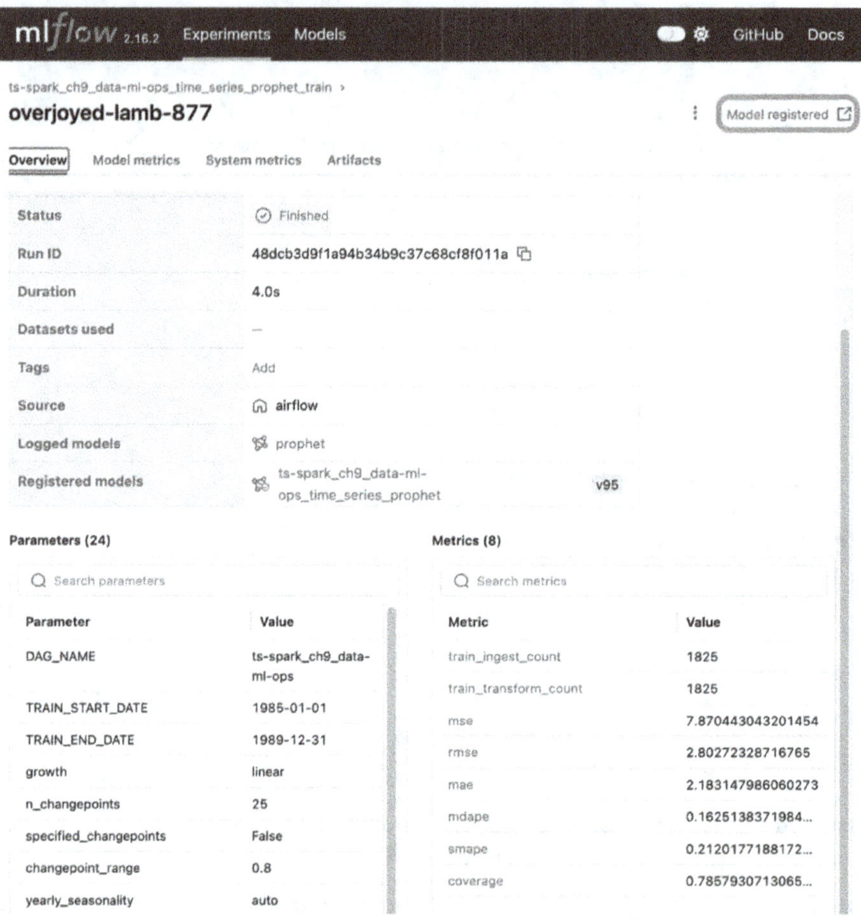

Figure 9.4: MLflow experiment tracking (training)

The model saved in the MLflow Model Registry is shown in *Figure 9.5*.

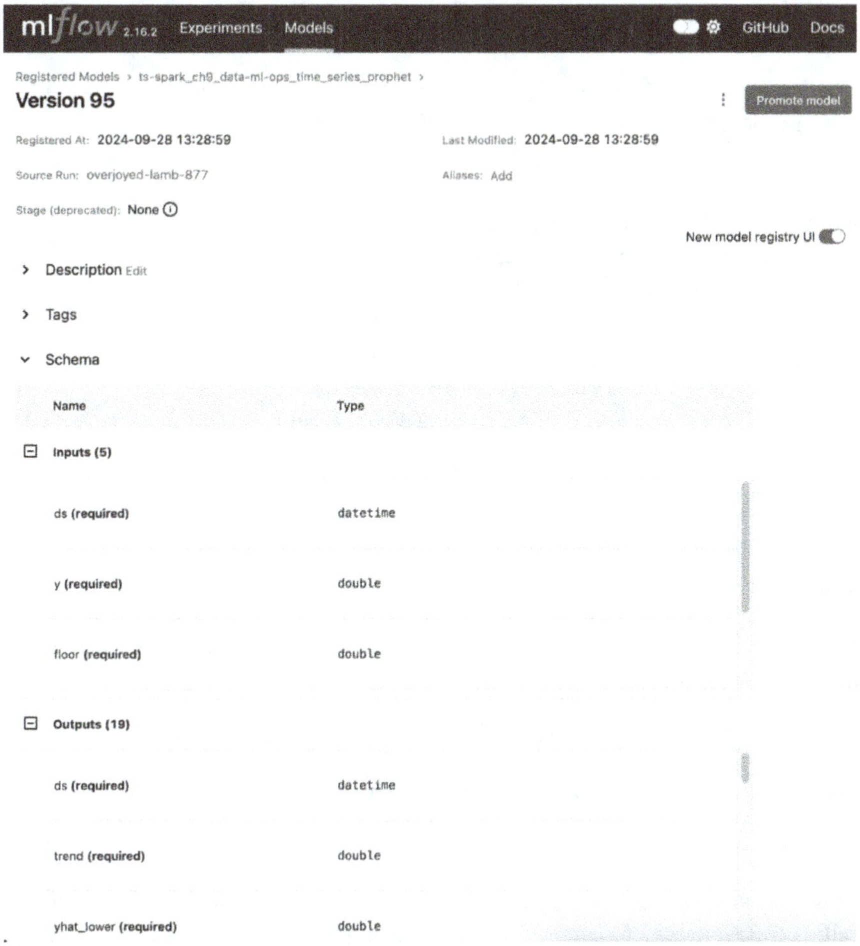

Figure 9.5: MLflow Model Registry

After the conclusion of the model training stage, we can progress to the next stage, where we will use the trained model to do forecasting.

Forecasting

This stage corresponds to Airflow task t4, which calls the forecast function. As its name suggests, this function infers future values of the time series. While we have this task in the same workflow as the prior training tasks, it is common for the forecasting task to be in a separate inferencing pipeline. This separation allows for scheduling the training and inferencing at different times.

The code for this step is as follows:

```python
def forecast(_vars, **kwargs):

    # Load the model from the Model Registry
    model_uri = f"models:/{model_name}/{model_version}"
    _model = mlflow.prophet.load_model(model_uri)

    forecast = _model.predict(
        _model.make_future_dataframe(
            periods=365, include_history = False))
    sdf = spark.createDataFrame(forecast[
        ['ds', 'yhat', 'yhat_lower', 'yhat_upper']])
    sdf.write.format("delta").mode("overwrite").save(
        f"/data/delta/ts-spark_ch9_gold_forecast_{_vars['runid']}")

    print(f"forecast:\n${forecast.tail(30)}")

    mlflow.end_run()
    return _vars
```

We first load the model from the model registry, where it was stored by the previous task, t3. This model can then be used for forecasting in the current task.

In this example, we want to generate a forecast for 365 days in advance by calling the following:

- The make_future_dataframe function to generate the future period

- The predict function to forecast for these future times

Another approach to generating the future period is to get this as input from the user or another application calling the model. As for the 365-day forecasting horizon, this is a relatively long time to forecast. We discussed in the *Forecasting* section of *Chapter 2* how a shorter forecasting horizon is likely to yield better forecasting accuracy. We have used a long period in this example for practical reasons to showcase forecasting over a 5-year period, with 5 runs of 365 days each. These runs were explained in the earlier *Simulation and runs* section. Moving beyond the requirement of the example here, keep the forecasting horizon shorter relative to the span of the training dataset and the level of granularity.

Finally, in this task, we persist the forecasted data with the write function to disk storage in delta format for use by the next steps of the workflow. We call this data stage gold as per the medallion approach explained previously. This delta table, where the forecasting outcome is stored, is also known as the inference table.

With the forecasts persisted, we can move on to the model evaluation stage.

Model evaluation

This stage corresponds to Airflow tasks `t5`, `t6`, and `t7`, which call the `ingest_eval_data`, `transform_eval_data`, and `eval_forecast` functions respectively.

> **Note**
>
> In a production environment, we want to monitor the accuracy of our model's forecast against real data so that we can detect when the model is not accurate enough and needs retraining. In the example here, we have these tasks in the same workflow as the prior forecasting task to keep the example simple enough to fit within this chapter. These tasks will be a separately scheduled workflow, which will be executed a posteriori of the event being forecasted. In the example, we are simulating the post-event evaluation by using the data points following the training data.

The `ingest_eval_data` and `transform_eval_data` functions are very similar to the `ingest_train_data` and `transform_train_data` functions, which we have seen in the previous sections. The main difference, as the name suggests, is that they operate on the evaluation and training data respectively.

We will focus on the `eval_forecast` function in this section, with the code extract as follows:

```python
def eval_forecast(_vars, **kwargs):
    sdf = spark.read.format("delta").load(
        f"/data/delta/ts-spark_ch9_silver_eval_{_vars['runid']}")
    sdf_forecast = spark.read.format("delta").load(
        f"/data/delta/ts-spark_ch9_gold_forecast_{_vars['runid']}")
    sdf_eval = sdf.join(sdf_forecast, 'ds', "inner")
    ...

    evaluator = RegressionEvaluator(
        labelCol='y', predictionCol='yhat', metricName='rmse')
    eval_rmse = evaluator.evaluate(sdf_eval)
    ...

    mlflow.set_experiment('ts-spark_ch9_data-ml-ops_time_series_
prophet_eval')
    mlflow.start_run()
    mlflow.log_param("DAG_NAME", DAG_NAME)
    mlflow.log_param("EVAL_START_DATE", _vars['START_DATE'])
    ...

    mlflow.log_metric('eval_rmse', _vars['eval_rmse'])
    mlflow.end_run()
    return _vars
```

In this code example, we do the following:

1. We first read the evaluation data from `silver`, where it was stored by the previous task, `t6`. We also read the forecasted data from `gold`, where it was stored earlier by the forecasting task, `t4`. We join both datasets with the `join` function so that we can compare the forecasts to the actuals.

2. In this example, we use **Root Mean Squared Error** (**RMSE**) as the evaluation metric. `RegressionEvaluator` from the `pyspark.ml.evaluation` library is used to do the calculation.

3. As a final step, MLflow Tracking Server is used to save all the parameters and metrics for each run. We group them under an experiment called `ts-spark_ch9_data-ml-ops_time_series_prophet_eval` and use the `log_param` and `log_metric` functions to capture the parameters and metrics gathered so far in the run.

We can see the task's status in the DAG view in Airflow, as per *Figure 9.1*. The logged parameters and metrics are visible in MLflow Tracking Server, as shown in *Figure 9.6*.

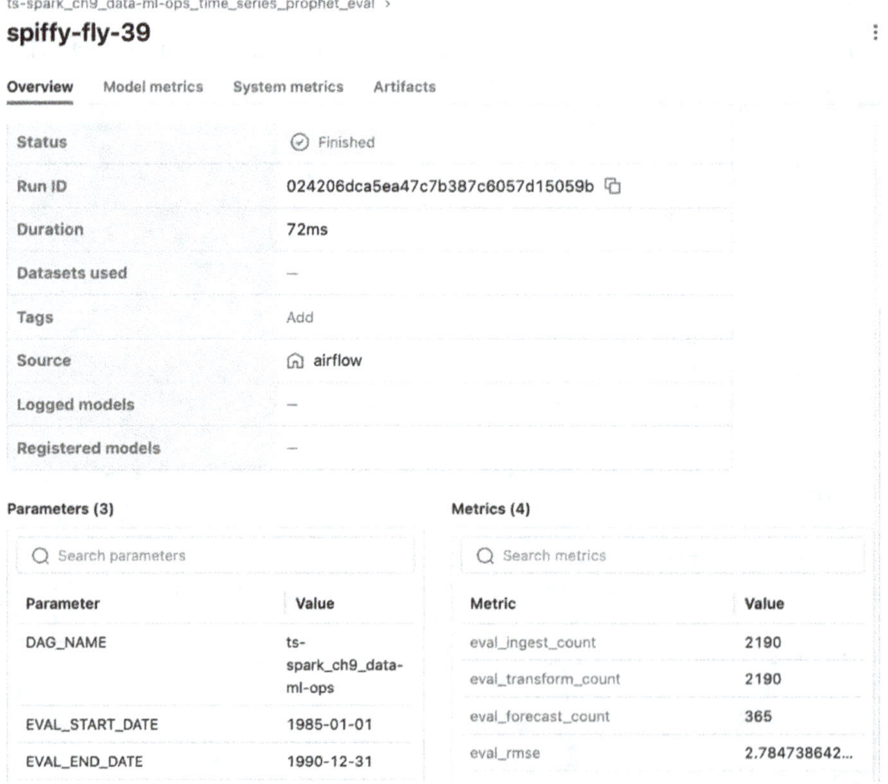

Figure 9.6: MLflow experiment tracking (evaluation)

As with the training experiment tracking shown in *Figure 9.4*, we can see in the evaluation experiment in *Figure 9.6* the ingest, transform, and forecast data counts, as well as the evaluation RMSE.

With this concluding the model evaluation stage, we have seen the end-to-end workflow example. In the next section, we will cover the monitoring and reporting part of the example.

Monitoring and reporting

The workflows we covered in the previous section are the backend processes in our end-to-end time series analysis example. In this section, we will cover the operational monitoring of the runs and the end user reporting of the forecasting outcome.

Monitoring

The work to collect the metrics has been done as part of the code executed by the workflows we have seen in this chapter. Our focus in this section is on the visualizations to monitor the workflows and the metrics.

Workflow

Starting with the workflow, as we have seen in *Figures 9.1* and *9.2*, the Airflow DAG shows the status of the runs. In case a task fails, as shown in *Figure 9.7*, we can select the failed task in Airflow and inspect the event log and logs to troubleshoot.

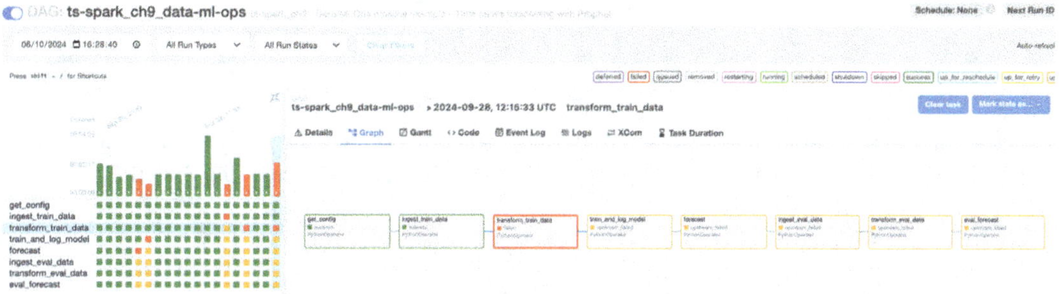

Figure 9.7: Airflow DAG with failed task

Training

We can visualize the training metrics for a specific run in MLflow Tracking Server, as shown in *Figure 9.4*. We can also monitor the metrics across multiple runs and compare them in a table, as per *Figure 9.8*.

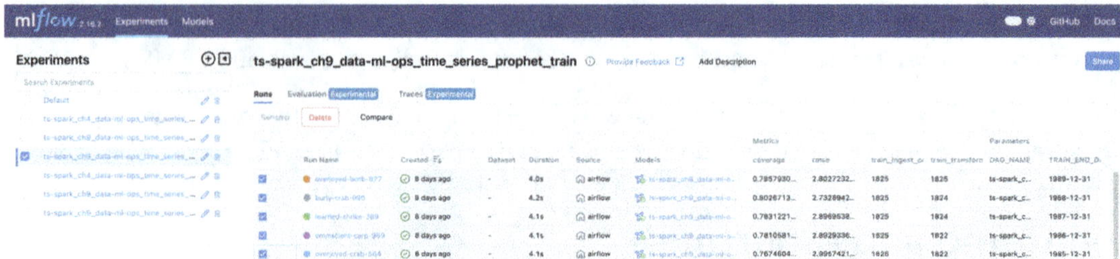

Figure 9.8: MLflow experiments (training) – select and compare

By selecting the five runs of our `_runall` workflow and clicking on the **Compare** button as in *Figure 9.8*, we can create a scatter plot as per *Figure 9.9*. This allows us to see the details for a specific run as well by hovering the mouse pointer over a data point in the graph.

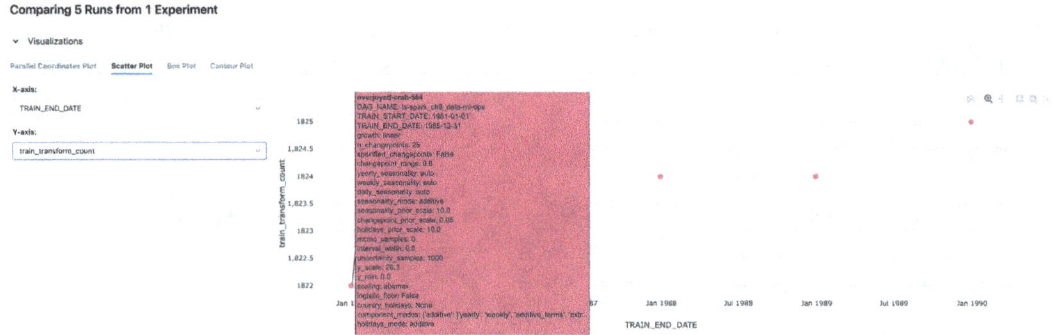

Figure 9.9: Training – plot by runs with details

An interesting metric to monitor is the count of training data transformed and ready for training, as per *Figure 9.10*. We can see here that the first four runs had fewer data points for training than the last run.

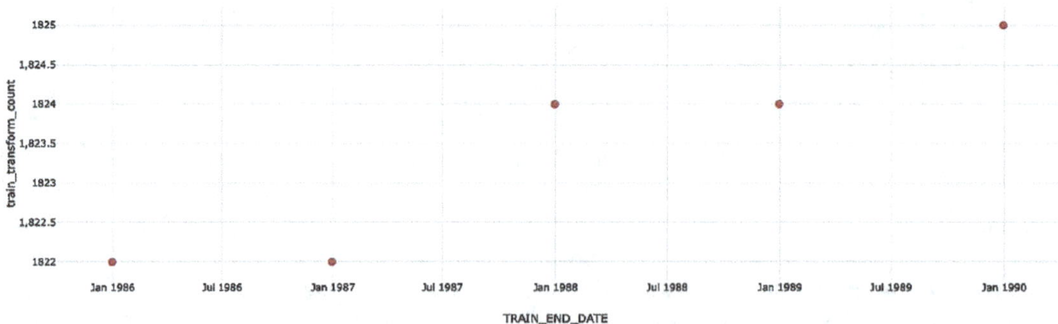

Figure 9.10: Training – transform count by runs

We can similarly monitor the RMSE for each training run, as per *Figure 9.11*. We can see here that the model accuracy has improved (lower RMSE) in the last two runs. If the accuracy had dropped instead, then the question from an operational point of view would have been whether this drop is acceptable or there is a need to develop another model. In this situation, this decision is dependent on your specific requirement and what was agreed as an acceptable drop in accuracy.

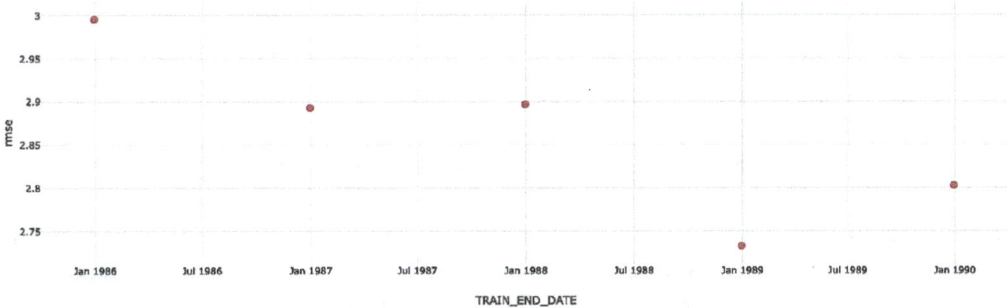

Figure 9.11: Training – RMSE by runs

After the model has been trained and is used for forecasting, we can evaluate the model's forecasted values against actuals. We will cover the monitoring of the evaluation metrics next.

Evaluation

We can visualize the evaluation metrics for a specific run in MLflow Tracking Server, as shown in *Figure 9.6*. We can also monitor the metrics across multiple runs and compare them in a table, as per *Figure 9.12*.

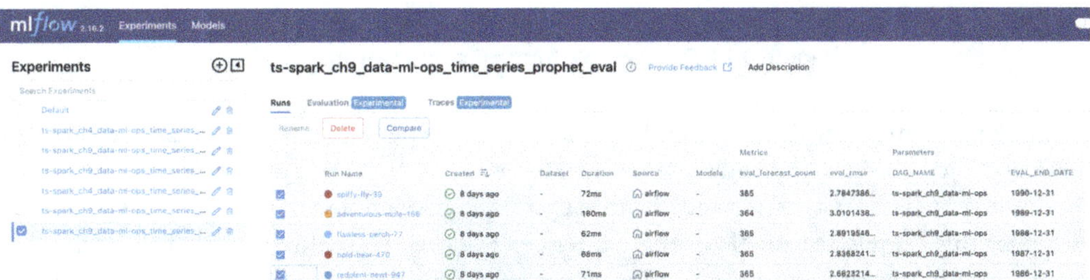

Figure 9.12: MLflow experiments (evaluation) – select and compare

By selecting the five runs of our `_runall` workflow and clicking on the **Compare** button as in *Figure 9.12*, we can create a scatter plot as per *Figure 9.13*. This allows us to also see the details for a specific run by hovering the mouse pointer over a data point in the graph.

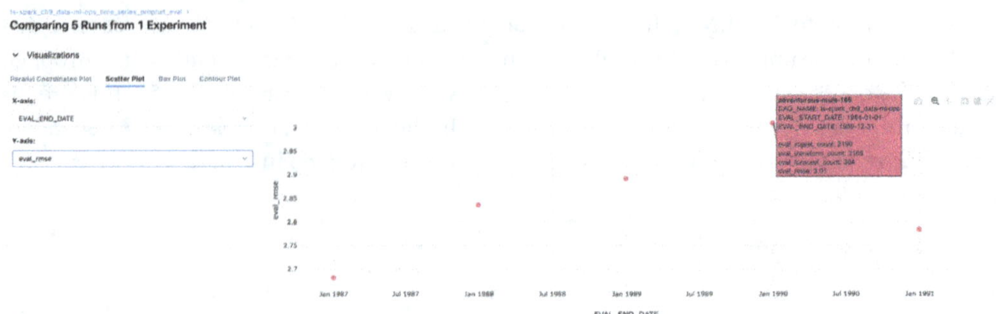

Figure 9.13: Evaluation – RMSE by runs with details

An interesting metric to monitor is the count of forecasted data points, as per *Figure 9.14*. We can see here that all the runs had the expected number of data points, except the fourth run, having one less. This can be explained by the fact that the evaluation dataset missed one data point during this time period.

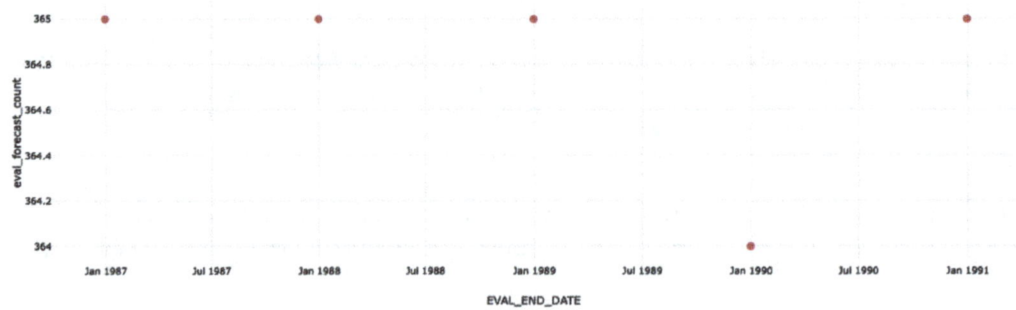

Figure 9.14: Evaluation – forecast count by runs

We can similarly monitor the RMSE for each evaluation run, as per *Figure 9.13*. We can see here that the model accuracy dropped gradually (higher RMSE) until the fourth run and then improved in the last run. If the drop had persisted instead, the question from an operational point of view would have been whether this drop is acceptable or there is a need to develop another model. This decision is dependent on your specific requirement and what has been agreed as an acceptable drop in accuracy.

This concludes the section on monitoring. While using MLflow was sufficient for the example here, most organizations have dedicated monitoring solutions into which MLflow metrics can be integrated. These solutions also include alerting capabilities, which we have not covered here.

We have explored the process to reach an outcome so far, but have not seen the outcome yet. In the next section, we will report on the forecasting outcome.

Reporting

We will use a Jupyter notebook in this example to create a set of graphs to represent the forecasting outcome. The `ts-spark_ch9_data-ml-ops_results.ipynb` notebook can be accessed from the local web location, as shown in *Figure 9.15*. This Jupyter environment was deployed as part of the *Environment setup* section.

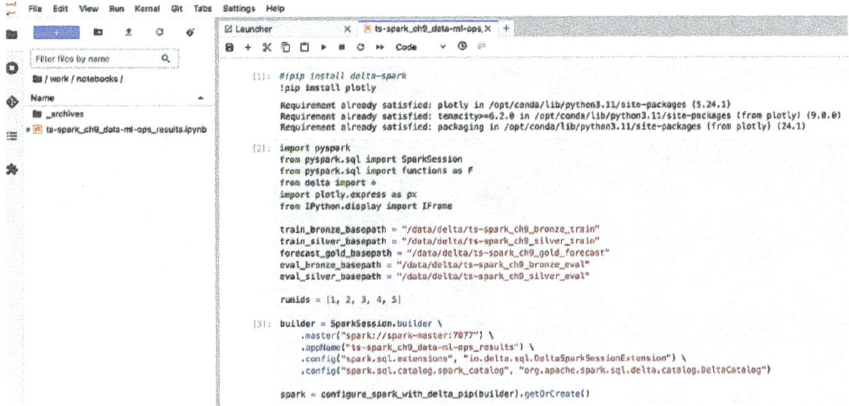

Figure 9.15: Reporting – notebook to create a graph

After running the notebook, we can see at the end of the notebook the graph, as per *Figure 9.16*, of the forecasts (gray lines) and actuals (scatter plot) for the different runs. The forecast captures the seasonality well, and most of the actuals fall within the uncertainty intervals, which are set at 80% by default on Prophet.

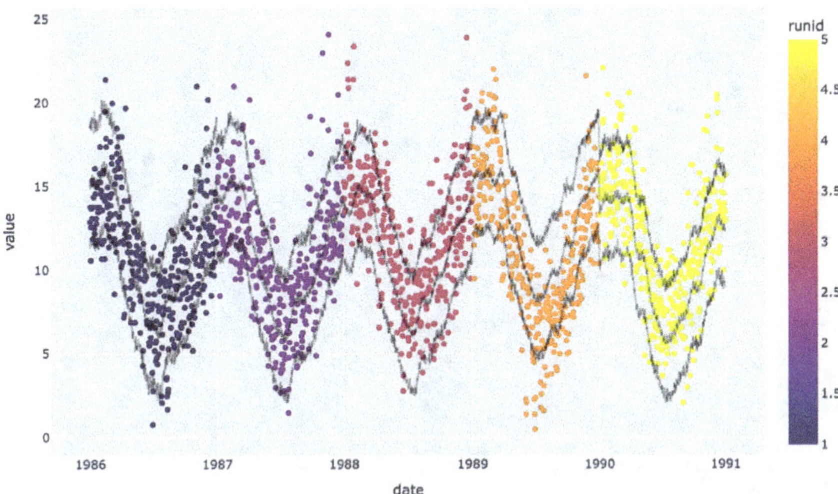

Figure 9.16: Reporting – actuals (scatter plot) compared to forecasts (gray lines)

We can zoom into specific runs as per *Figures 9.17* and *9.18*. These match with the RMSE values we saw in the earlier *Monitoring* section, as we will detail next.

As we can see in *Figure 9.13*, the first run had the lowest RMSE. This is reflected in *Figure 9.17*, with most actuals falling within the forecasting interval.

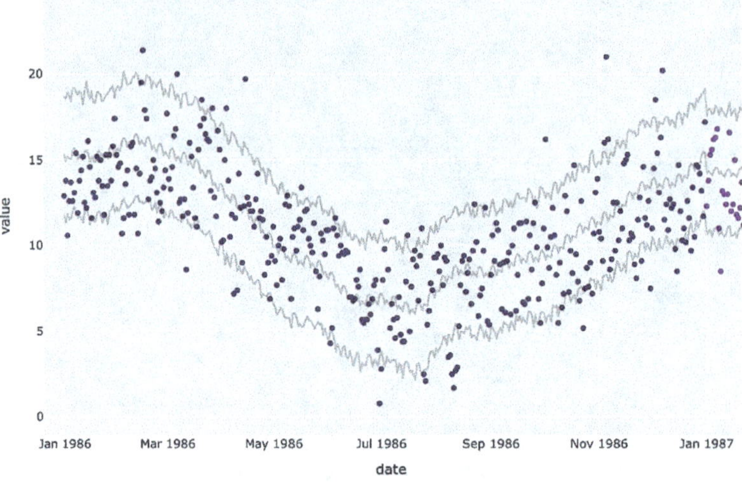

Figure 9.17: Reporting – actuals compared to forecasts (run with lowest RMSE)

In *Figure 9.13*, the fourth run had the highest RMSE. This is reflected in *Figure 9.18*, with many more actuals than in the first run falling outside the forecasting interval.

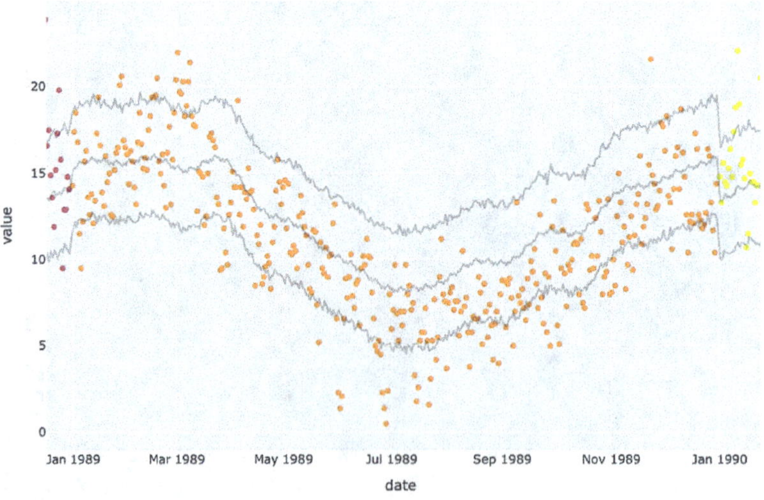

Figure 9.18: Reporting – actuals compared to forecasts (run with highest RMSE)

At this point, the output of the Jupyter notebook can be exported as a report in several formats, such as HTML or PDF. While using Jupyter was sufficient for the example here, most organizations have reporting solutions into which the forecasting outcome can be integrated.

Additional considerations

We will discuss here some of the additional considerations that apply when going to production, in addition to what we already covered in the example in this chapter.

Scaling

We covered scaling extensively in *Chapter 8*. The environment and workflows in this chapter can be scaled as well. At a high level, this can be achieved in the following ways:

- Airflow server: scale up by adding more CPU and memory resources

- Airflow DAG: run the tasks in parallel

- Spark cluster: scale up by adding more CPU and memory resources

- Spark cluster: scale out by adding more workers

- Model: use Spark-enabled models or parallelize the use of pandas, as discussed in the previous chapter

You can find more information about Airflow DAGs, including parallel tasks, here: `https://airflow.apache.org/docs/apache-airflow/stable/core-concepts/dags.html`

To relate this to our Airflow DAG example in this chapter, we defined the tasks as sequential in the following way in the code for `ts-spark_ch9_data-ml-ops_runall`:

```
t1 >> t2 >> t3 >> t4 >> t5
```

The code to run tasks `t3` and `t4` in parallel is as follows:

```
t1 >> t2 >> [t3, t4] >> t5
```

With regard to the considerations for scaling the Spark cluster, refer to *Chapter 3* and, more specifically, the *Driver and worker nodes* section, for a detailed discussion.

Model retraining

We already included retraining in our example workflow at every run using a sliding window of the most recent data. In practice, and to optimize resource utilization, the retraining can be scheduled at a less frequent interval in its own separate workflow. We discussed tracking the model's accuracy metrics across runs of the workflow in the *Monitoring* section. The trigger of this retraining workflow can be based on the accuracy dropping below a predefined threshold. The appropriate value for the threshold depends on your specific requirements.

Governance and security

In *Chapter 4*, in the *From DataOps to ModelOps to DevOps* section, we discussed the considerations for governance and security at various points. Securing your environment and production rollout is beyond the scope of this book. As these are key requirements, and we will not be going into further details here, we highly recommend referring to the following resources to secure the components used in our example:

Apache Spark	`https://spark.apache.org/docs/latest/security.html`

MLflow	`https://mlflow.org/docs/latest/auth/index.html`
	
	`https://github.com/mlflow/mlflow/security`

Airflow	`https://airflow.apache.org/docs/apache-airflow/stable/security/index.html`
Jupyter	`https://jupyter.org/security`
Docker	`https://www.docker.com/blog/container-security-and-why-it-matters/`
Unity Catalog	`https://www.unitycatalog.io/`

Table 9.1: Resources on security and governance for components in use

This concludes the section on the additional considerations before going to production.

Summary

In this chapter, we focused on the crucial phase of moving projects into production, especially given the challenges many projects face in achieving this transition and delivering measurable business results. We saw an example of an end-to-end workflow, covering the stages of data ingestion, storage, data transformations, model training and validation, forecasting, model evaluation, and monitoring. With this example, we brought together what we have learned in this book in view of planning for a production rollout.

In the next chapter, we will explore how to go further with Apache Spark for time series analysis by leveraging the advanced capabilities of a managed cloud platform for data and AI.

Get This Book's PDF Version and Exclusive Extras

Scan the QR code (or go to packtpub.com/unlock). Search for this book by name, confirm the edition, and then follow the steps on the page.

Note: Keep your invoice handly. Purchase made directly from packt don't require one.

10
Going Further with Apache Spark

In the previous chapter, we leveraged open source components to bring time series analysis to production. This requires significant effort to set up and manage the platform. In this chapter, we will answer such challenges by using Databricks as a cloud-based managed **platform-as-a-service (PaaS)** solution to go further with Apache Spark. We will use an end-to-end example of time series analysis built on Databricks using advanced features such as Delta Live Tables with a streaming pipeline, AutoML, Unity Catalog, and AI/BI dashboards.

In this chapter, we're going to cover the following main topics:

- Databricks components and setup

- Workflows

- Monitoring, security, and governance

- The user interface

Technical requirements

In this chapter, we will use code examples to explore the deployment of a scalable end-to-end solution for time series analysis on Databricks, starting with the setup of the environment in the following section.

The code for this chapter is at this URL:

```
https://github.com/PacktPublishing/Time-Series-Analysis-with-Spark/
tree/main/ch10
```

Databricks components and setup

We will be using a Databricks environment, as in *Chapter 8*, for the platform infrastructure. Follow the instructions in the *Technical requirements* section of *Chapter 8* on setting up the Databricks environment.

Workspace, folders, and notebooks

Once the environment is set up, follow the instructions in the links provided here to import the notebooks:

1. Navigate the Databricks workspace: `https://docs.databricks.com/en/workspace/index.html`

2. Create a folder named `ts_spark` and a sub-folder named `ch10`: `https://docs.databricks.com/en/workspace/workspace-objects.html#folders`

3. Import the notebooks for this example into the `ch10` folder: `https://docs.databricks.com/en/notebooks/notebook-export-import.html#import-a-notebook`

    There are eight notebooks in all, and they can be imported from the following URLs:

    *   `https://github.com/PacktPublishing/Time-Series-Analysis-with-Spark/raw/main/ch10/ts_spark_ch10_dlt_features.dbc`

    *   `https://github.com/PacktPublishing/Time-Series-Analysis-with-Spark/raw/main/ch10/ts_spark_ch10_evaluate_forecast.dbc`

    *   `https://github.com/PacktPublishing/Time-Series-Analysis-with-Spark/raw/main/ch10/ts_spark_ch10_generate_forecast.dbc`

    *   `https://github.com/PacktPublishing/Time-Series-Analysis-with-Spark/raw/main/ch10/ts_spark_ch10_model_training.dbc`

    *   `https://github.com/PacktPublishing/Time-Series-Analysis-with-Spark/raw/main/ch10/ts_spark_ch10_model_training_automl.dbc`

    *   `https://github.com/PacktPublishing/Time-Series-Analysis-with-Spark/raw/main/ch10/ts_spark_ch10_reset.dbc`

    *   `https://github.com/PacktPublishing/Time-Series-Analysis-with-Spark/raw/main/ch10/ts_spark_ch10_update_data.dbc`

    *   `https://github.com/PacktPublishing/Time-Series-Analysis-with-Spark/raw/main/ch10/ts_spark_ch10_update_model.dbc`

With the notebooks imported, we can next set up the clusters.

Clusters

We can use the Databricks **Machine Learning Runtime** (**MLR**) or serverless compute for the clusters.

The MLR cluster comes preloaded with common libraries used for **machine learning** (**ML**). It instantiates virtual machines in your cloud provider account. You will be charged for the virtual machine by the cloud provider. Choose a small instance with minimal CPU and memory to minimize this cost when creating the cluster. This will be sufficient for the example in this chapter. Refer to the *Technical requirements* section of *Chapter 8* on setting up the Databricks cluster.

The MLR cluster has libraries required for the AutoML example, which we will cover in a later section. You can skip the code execution for this example if you do not want to incur the MLR-related cloud provider cost for the associated virtual machines. We will provide an alternative workflow that does not use AutoML.

> **Note**
>
> At the time of writing, the cloud provider cost for these virtual machines is above the free allowance that you get with the free cloud provider trial account. This means that you will have to upgrade to a paid cloud provider account and the cost will be charged to the credit card you specified when creating the account. The virtual machines and cloud infrastructure costs are not incurred from the free Databricks trial account.

The serverless cluster is included in your Databricks cost as the underlying virtual machines are fully managed by Databricks. This means it does not incur separate cloud provider costs. Serverless clusters do, however, require the installation of ML libraries at the time of writing, as you will see in the code example. Databricks may provide serverless clusters with pre-loaded ML libraries in the future.

> **Note**
>
> Databricks has started to include serverless in the free trial account at the time of writing. This means that your use of serverless clusters to execute the code in this chapter will be free if within the time and cost limit of the Databricks free trial account. This may be subject to change in the future.

You can find more information on MLR and serverless clusters in the following resources:

- `https://docs.databricks.com/en/machine-learning/databricks-runtime-ml.html`

- `https://docs.databricks.com/en/compute/serverless/index.html`

With the clusters covered, we will next configure the data pipeline using Delta Live Tables.

Streaming with Delta Live Tables

Databricks **Delta Live Tables** (DLT) is a low-code declarative solution to build data pipelines. In our example, we will use DLT for the feature engineering pipeline, getting data from the source files, checking the data quality, and transforming it into features that can be used to train the time series model. You can find more information on DLT at the following link:

```
https://www.databricks.com/discover/pages/getting-started-with-
delta-live-tables
```

We will go into the details of the DLT configuration in the *Implementing workflows* section.

Workflows

Databricks workflows are the equivalent of the Airflow DAGs that we used in *Chapter 4* and *Chapter 9*. You can find more information on workflows, also referred to as **jobs**, at the following link:

```
https://docs.databricks.com/en/jobs/index.html
```

We will now go into the details of *jobs* configuration.

Implementing workflows

The code example in this chapter includes four workflows. These are implemented as jobs in Databricks. The best way to visualize the jobs is from the **Workflows** > **Jobs** > **Tasks** views in Databricks, as per *Figures 10.1, 10.2, 10.3*, and *10.4*.

The jobs are as follows:

- `ts-spark_ch10_1a_ingest_and_train` – This job is for data ingestion, feature engineering, and model training, and is shown in *Figure 10.1*. It includes the following tasks:

  - `reset`

  - `dlt_features`

  - `model_training`

Figure 10.1: Data ingestion, feature engineering, and model training job

- `ts-spark_ch10_1b_ingest_and_train_automl` – The second job, shown in *Figure 10.2*, is another version of the first job, with the difference being the use of AutoML, which will be explained in the *Training with AutoML* section.

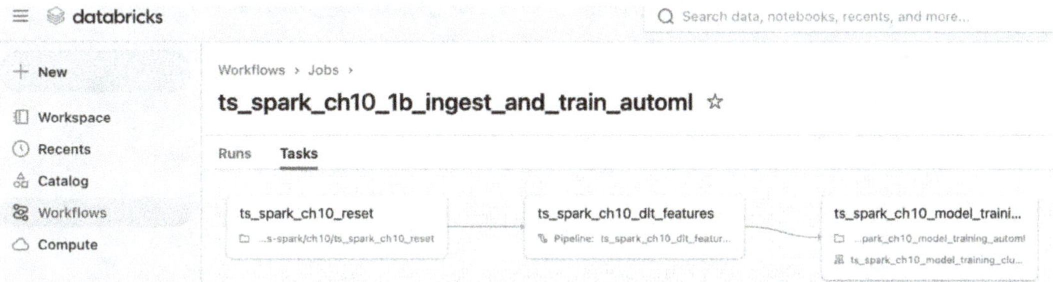

Figure 10.2: Data ingestion, feature engineering, and model training (AutoML) job

- `ts-spark_ch10_2b_ingest_and_forecast` – This job ingests new data, retrains the model, and generates and evaluates forecasts, and is shown in *Figure 10.3*. It includes the following tasks.

  - `dlt_features`

  - `update_model`

  - `generate_forecast`

  - `update_data`

  - `evaluate_forecast`

Figure 10.3: Ingest new data, retrain model, and generate forecasts job

- `ts-spark_ch10_2a_update_iteration` – This job, shown in *Figure 10.4*, calls the preceding one multiple times to ingest new data. It simulates what happens in the real world whereby the previous end-to-end workflow is launched at a regular interval, say, daily or weekly, with new data.

Figure 10.4: Multiple calls to ingest and process new data job

> **Modularity and task separation**
>
> As in *Chapter 9*, we have broken the jobs into multiple tasks to illustrate the best practice of modularization. This facilitates independent code change, scaling, and task reruns. The ownership of the tasks can be with different teams. The jobs in this example can be further split in your own implementation, depending on your requirement to launch the tasks separately.

We will explain each of these jobs and related tasks in detail in the upcoming sections, starting with the ingestion and training job.

To set up the jobs required for this chapter, follow the instructions on creating jobs and configuring tasks at these links:

- `https://docs.databricks.com/en/jobs/configure-job.html#create-a-new-job`

- `https://docs.databricks.com/en/jobs/configure-task.html#configure-and-edit-databricks-tasks`

Refer to the tables in the upcoming sections for the configuration when creating the jobs and related tasks, replacing <USER_LOGIN> with your own Databricks user login.

Ingest and train

The **Tasks** part of the `ts-spark_ch10_1a_ingest_and_train` job, shown in *Figure 10.1*, will be detailed in this section.

Table 10.1 shows the configuration for the `ts_spark_ch10_1a_ingest_and_train` job to use when following the instructions in the previously provided URL. Note that for simplicity, we have given each task the same name as the code notebook or pipeline that it runs.

Job	ts_spark_ch10_1a_ingest_and_train	
Task 1	Task name	ts_spark_ch10_reset
	Type	Notebook
	Source	Workspace
	Path (notebook)	/Workspace/Users/<USER_LOGIN>/ts-spark/ch10/ts_spark_ch10_reset
	Compute	Serverless
Task 2	Task name	ts_spark_ch10_dlt_features
	Type	Pipeline
	Pipeline	ts_spark_ch10_dlt_features
	Trigger a full refresh on the pipeline	☑
	Depends on	ts_spark_ch10_reset
Task 3	Task name	ts_spark_ch10_model_training
	Type	Notebook
	Source	Workspace
	Path (notebook)	/Workspace/Users/<USER_LOGIN>/ts-spark/ch10/ts_spark_ch10_model_training
	Compute	Serverless
	Depends on	ts_spark_ch10_dlt_features

Table 10.1: Job configuration – ts_spark_ch10_1a_ingest_and_train

reset

The `reset` task does the following:

- Resets the Databricks catalog, `ts_spark`, which is used for this example

- Downloads the data files from the GitHub location for this chapter to the volumes created in the `ts_spark` catalog

The code for this task is in the `ts_spark_ch10_reset` notebook.

> **Catalog and volume**
>
> Databricks' Unity Catalog provides data governance and management in Databricks. It organizes data into a three-level hierarchy: catalogs, schemas (equivalent to databases), and tables, views, or volumes. Tabular data is stored in tables and views, while files are stored in volumes. In our code example, we are using a separate catalog, `ts_spark`, and volumes to store the data files.

dlt_features

This task is used for data ingestion and feature engineering. It is implemented as the `ts_spark_ch10_dlt_features` DLT pipeline, as shown in *Figure 10.5*.

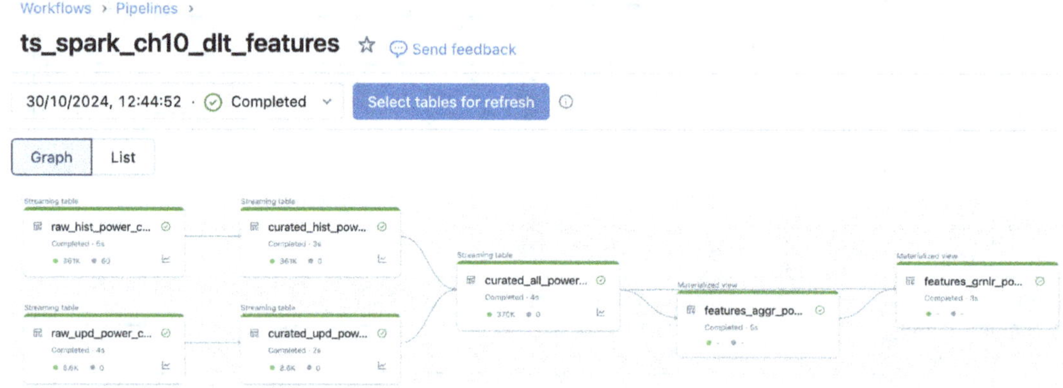

Figure 10.5: Feature engineering pipeline

You can find and zoom in on a digital version of *Figure 10.5* here: `https://packt.link/D9OXb`

To set up the DLT pipeline required for this chapter, follow the instructions on creating the pipeline at the following link:

`https://docs.databricks.com/en/delta-live-tables/configure-pipeline.html#configure-a-new-delta-live-tables-pipeline`

Note that you will have to create the `ts_spark` catalog before you can set up the DLT pipeline. Refer to the following instructions to create the `ts_spark` catalog via the Catalog Explorer: `https://docs.databricks.com/aws/en/catalogs/create-catalog?language=Catalog%C2%A0Explorer`

Refer to *Table 10.2* for the configuration when creating the pipeline, replacing `<USER_LOGIN>` with your own Databricks user login.

Pipeline	`ts_spark_ch10_dlt_features`	
General	Pipeline name	`ts_spark_ch10_dlt_features`
	Serverless	☑
	Pipeline mode	Triggered
Source code	Path (notebook)	`/Workspace/Users/<USER_LOGIN>/ts-spark/ch10/ts_spark_ch10_dlt_features`
Destination	Storage options	`Unity Catalog`
	Default catalog / Default schema	`ts_spark / ch10`

Table 10.2: DLT configuration – ts_spark_ch10_dlt_features

The code for this pipeline task is in the `ts_spark_ch10_dlt_features` notebook. It has the following steps:

1. Read historical data from files in the `vol01_hist` volume using Auto Loader, check the data, and store the data in the `raw_hist_power_consumption` streaming table.

> **Auto Loader**
>
> Databricks Auto Loader, also referred to as `cloudfiles` in code, enables the efficient incremental ingestion of new data files as they arrive in a cloud storage location. You can find more information on Auto Loader at the following link: `https://docs.databricks.com/en/ingestion/cloud-object-storage/auto-loader/index.html`.

> **Data quality checks**
>
> Databricks DLT can include data quality checks to ensure data integrity based on quality constraints within data pipelines. You can find more information on data quality checks in DLT at the following link: `https://docs.databricks.com/en/delta-live-tables/expectations.html`.

2. Read update data from files in the `vol01_upd` volume using Auto Loader, check the data, and store the data in the `raw_upd_power_consumption` streaming table.

3. Read raw historical data from the `raw_hist_power_consumption` streaming table, transform the data, and store the result in the `curated_hist_power_consumption` streaming table.

4. Read raw update data from the `raw_upd_power_consumption` streaming table, transform the data, and store the result in the `curated_upd_power_consumption` streaming table.

5. Append data from the `curated_hist_power_consumption` and `curated_upd_power_consumption` streaming tables, storing the combined result in the `curated_all_power_consumption` streaming table.

6. Read curated data from the `curated_all_power_consumption` streaming table, use Tempo to calculate the **exponential moving average** (**EMA**) over a 5-minute window, and resample the data to hourly means. Then, store the aggregated data in the `features_aggr_power_consumption` materialized view.

> **Tempo**
>
> Databricks Tempo is an open source project simplifying time series data manipulation within Apache Spark. You can find more information on Tempo at the following link: `https://databrickslabs.github.io/tempo/`.

7. Read aggregated data from the `features_aggr_power_consumption` materialized view, and use Tempo to do an `AsOf` join with the `curated_all_power_consumption` streaming table. Then, store the result in the `features_gnlr_power_consumption` materialized view.

These steps correspond to the data transformation stages of the medallion approach, which was discussed in the *Data processing and storage* section of *Chapter 4*.

model_training

This task is used to train a Prophet model using the features calculated in the prior `dlt_features` task. The code for `model_training` is in the `ts_spark_ch10_model_training` notebook. The steps are as follows:

1. Read the features from `features_aggr_power_consumption`.

2. Rename the `Date` column to `ds` and `hourly_Global_active_power` to `y`. These column names are required by Prophet.

3. Start an MLflow run to track the training in MLflow.

4. Fit the Prophet model to the dataset.

5. Register the model to Unity Catalog, setting the alias as `Champion`.

Note that this notebook shows a simplified model training, which is sufficient to illustrate the training step in the example in this chapter. It does not include the full model experimentation process and hyperparameter tuning, which we covered in *Chapter 7*.

Training with AutoML

Another approach to model training is to use Databricks AutoML to find the best model for the given dataset.

AutoML is a feature within Databricks that automates the process of developing ML models. It has tasks such as data profiling, feature engineering, model selection, and hyperparameter tuning. This enables users to quickly generate baseline models for regression, classification, and forecasting problems. With its "glass box" approach, AutoML provides the underlying code for each model, which differs from "black box" approaches that do not show the code details. AutoML can be used from the UI, as shown in *Figure 10.6*, or programmatically, as in the example provided in this chapter.

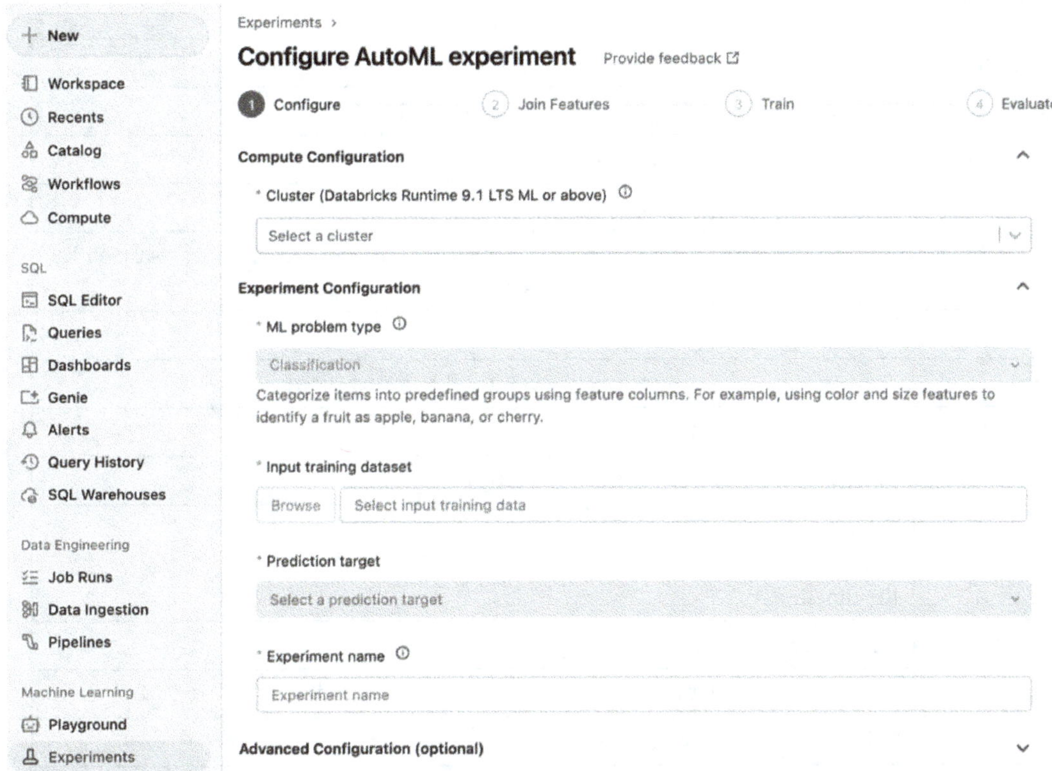

Figure 10.6: Databricks AutoML

You can find more information on AutoML here:

`https://www.databricks.com/product/automl`.

The `ts-spark_ch10_1b_ingest_and_train_automl` job is an example of how to include AutoML programmatically in the training task. The code for this task is in the `ts_spark_ch10_model_training_automl` notebook. The steps are as follows:

1. Read the features from `features_aggr_power_consumption`.
2. Call the `databricks.automl.forecast` function, which takes care of renaming the columns, starting an MLflow run to track the training, and finding the best model for forecasting based on the specified `primary_metric` (mdape is used in the example).
3. Register the model to Unity Catalog, setting the alias as `Champion`.

The configuration for the `ts_spark_ch10_1b_ingest_and_train_automl` job is shown in *Table 10.3*.

Job (optional)	ts_spark_ch10_1b_ingest_and_train_automl	
Task 1	Task name	`ts_spark_ch10_reset`
	Type	Notebook
	Source	Workspace
	Path (notebook)	`/Workspace/Users/<USER_LOGIN>/ts-spark/` `ch10/ts_spark_ch10_reset`
	Compute	Serverless
Task 2	Task name	`ts_spark_ch10_dlt_features`
	Type	Pipeline
	Pipeline	`ts_spark_ch10_dlt_features`
	Trigger a full refresh on the pipeline	☑
	Depends on	`ts_spark_ch10_reset`
Task 3	Task name	`ts_spark_ch10_model_training_automl`
	Type	Notebook
	Source	Workspace
	Path (notebook)	`/Workspace/Users/<USER_LOGIN>/ts-spark/` `ch10/ts_spark_ch10_model_training_automl`

Job (optional)	ts_spark_ch10_1b_ingest_and_train_automl	
	Compute	*Refer to the earlier section on clusters to choose the compute
	Depends on	ts_spark_ch10_dlt_features

Table 10.3: Job configuration – ts_spark_ch10_1b_ingest_and_train_automl

Note that in addition to simplifying the steps compared to the previous training approach without AutoML, we also get to find the best model.

Ingest and forecast

The **Tasks** part of the `ts-spark_ch10_2b_ingest_and_forecast` job, shown in *Figure 10.3*, will be detailed in this section.

The configuration for the `ts_spark_ch10_2b_ingest_and_forecast` job is shown in *Table 10.4*.

Job	ts_spark_ch10_2b_ingest_and_forecast	
	Job parameters	Key: upd_iter Value: 1
Task 1	Task name	ts_spark_ch10_dlt_features
	Type	Pipeline
	Pipeline	ts_spark_ch10_dlt_features
	Trigger a full refresh on the pipeline	☑
Task 2	Task name	ts_spark_ch10_update_model
	Type	Notebook
	Source	Workspace
	Path (notebook)	/Workspace/Users/<USER_LOGIN>/ts-spark/ch10/ ts_spark_ch10_update_model
	Compute	Serverless
	Depends on	ts_spark_ch10_dlt_features

Job		ts_spark_ch10_2b_ingest_and_forecast
Task 3	Task name	ts_spark_ch10_generate_forecast
	Type	Notebook
	Source	Workspace
	Path (notebook)	/Workspace/Users/<USER_LOGIN>/ts-spark/ch10/ ts_spark_ch10_generate_forecast
	Compute	Serverless
	Depends on	ts_spark_ch10_update_model
Task 4	Task name	ts_spark_ch10_update_data
	Type	Notebook
	Source	Workspace
	Path (notebook)	/Workspace/Users/<USER_LOGIN>/ts-spark/ch10/ ts_spark_ch10_update_data
	Compute	Serverless
	Depends on	ts_spark_ch10_generate_forecast
Task 5	Task name	ts_spark_ch10_evaluate_forecast
	Type	Notebook
	Source	Workspace
	Path (notebook)	/Workspace/Users/<USER_LOGIN>/ts-spark/ch10/ ts_spark_ch10_ evaluate_forecast
	Compute	Serverless
	Depends on	ts_spark_ch10_update_data

Table 10.4: Job configuration – ts_spark_ch10_2b_ingest_and_forecast

dlt_features

This task is the same `ts_spark_ch10_dlt_features` DLT pipeline, shown in *Figure 10.5*, as used in the earlier *Ingest and train* section, where it was used to process historical data. The difference is here we will be calling this pipeline to process new data files from the `vol01_upd` volume.

update_model

This task is used to train a Prophet model using the features calculated in the prior `dlt_features` task. The code for `update_model` is in the `ts_spark_ch10_update_model` notebook. This task is similar to the task discussed in the *model_training* section, the difference being that we now have new data to include in the training. The steps are as follows:

1. Read the features from `features_aggr_power_consumption`.
2. Rename the `Date` column to `ds` and `hourly_Global_active_power` to `y`. These column names are required by Prophet.
3. Fit the Prophet model to the dataset.
4. Register the model to Unity Catalog, setting the alias as `Champion`.

With the latest model updated, we can use it to forecast next.

generate_forecast

This task uses the previously trained model to generate and store forecasts. The code for `generate_forecast` is in the `ts_spark_ch10_generate_forecast` notebook. The steps are as follows:

1. Load the `Champion` model from Unity Catalog.
2. Generate a forecast for the next 24 hours.
3. Store the forecasts, together with the model's name and version, in the `forecast` table.

With the forecast generated, we can compare the forecasted time period against the actuals, which we will get next.

update_data

This task simply copies the data file for the new time period from the `vol01_upd_src` volume to `vol01_upd`. The code for `update_data` is in the `ts_spark_ch10_update_data` notebook.

evaluate_forecast

This task calculates and stores the forecasting accuracy metrics. The code for `evaluate_forecast` is in the `ts_spark_ch10_evaluate_forecast` notebook. The steps are as follows:

1. Join the `features_aggr_power_consumption` actuals table to the previously created `forecast` table.
2. Calculate the `mdape` metrics.
3. Store the calculated metrics with the model's name and version in the `forecast_metrics` table.
4. Store the data quality check results in the `dq_results` table.

With the forecast evaluated, we can report on the outcome and metrics. We will cover this in the *User interface* section. Before we get to this, let's detail how we will orchestrate the multiple iterations of new data arrival and corresponding processing.

Updating iterations

The `ts-spark_ch10_2a_update_iteration` job, shown in *Figure 10.4*, simulates what happens in the real world whereby we have new data to process at a regular interval, say, daily or weekly. It calls the `ts-spark_ch10_2b_ingest_and_forecast` job seven times, corresponding to one week of daily new data. Every call results in the end-to-end processing of a new data file, as described in the previous *Ingest and forecast* section.

The configuration for the `ts_spark_ch10_2a_update_iterations` job is shown in *Table 10.5*.

Job	`ts_spark_ch10_2a_update_iterations`	
Task 1	Task name	`ts_spark_ch10_update_iterations`
	Type	For each
	Inputs	[1,2,3,4,5,6,7]
Task 2 (Add a task to loop over)	Task name	`ts_spark_ch10_update_iterations_iteration`
	Type	Run Job
	Job	`ts_spark_ch10_2b_ingest_and_forecast`
	Job Parameters	Key: `upd_iter` Value: `{{input}}`

Table 10.5: Job configuration – ts_spark_ch10_2a_update_iterations

Starting the jobs

With the jobs configured and explained, we will now start these jobs, which will execute the code for this chapter. You can find more information on running jobs here:

`https://docs.databricks.com/en/jobs/run-now.html`

Proceed in the following order:

1. Click on **Run Now** for `ts-spark_ch10_1a_ingest_and_train`. Wait for the job to complete.

2. Click on **Run Now** for `ts-spark_ch10_2a_update_iteration`.

With the jobs launched and executed, we can review their status, as will be explained in the next section.

Monitoring, security, and governance

As we discussed in *Chapter 4* in the *From DataOps to ModelOps to DevOps* section and in *Chapter 9* in the *Governance and security* section, a key requirement for workloads in a production environment and with sensitive data is to have proper monitoring, security, and governance in place. This is greatly facilitated by leveraging the built-in functionalities of a managed platform such as Databricks with Unity Catalog. The alternative approach, if we were to develop and test our own custom-built platform, requires considerable time and effort to robustly meet these requirements.

Monitoring

The monitoring of the jobs can be done from the **Workflows** > **Jobs** > **Runs** page, as shown in *Figure 10.7* for the `ts-spark_ch10_2b_ingest_and_forecast` job. We can see the different runs, their parameters, durations, and statuses, among other information useful for monitoring.

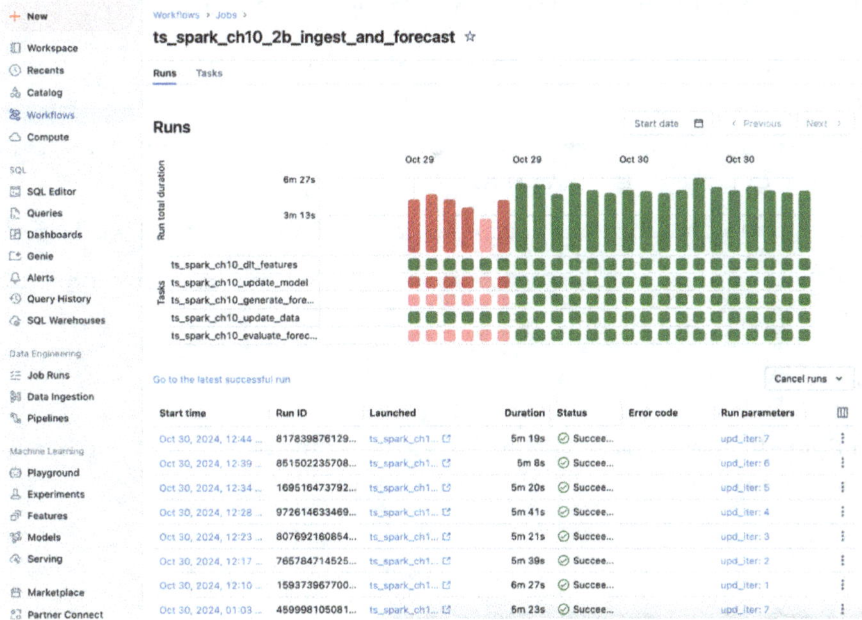

Figure 10.7: Databricks Workflows – Jobs – Runs

The monitoring of the `ts_spark_ch10_dlt_features` DLT pipeline can be done from the **Workflows** > **Pipelines** page, as shown in *Figure 10.8*. We can see the different stages, data checks, durations, and statuses, among other information useful for monitoring.

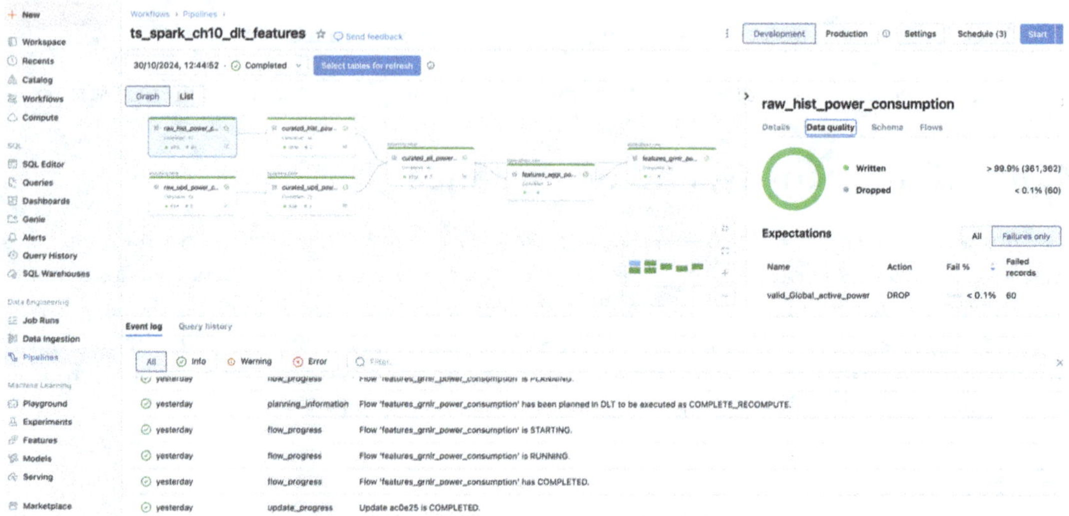

Figure 10.8: Databricks DLT pipelines

You can find more information on observability, monitoring, and alerting here:

- `https://docs.databricks.com/en/delta-live-tables/observability.html`

- `https://www.databricks.com/blog/lakehouse-monitoring-unified-solution-quality-data-and-ai`

- `https://docs.databricks.com/en/lakehouse-monitoring/index.html`

- `https://docs.databricks.com/aws/en/lakehouse-monitoring/monitor-alerts`

Security

As shown in *Figure 10.9*, setting access permissions to tables and other objects requires just a few clicks when using Unity Catalog.

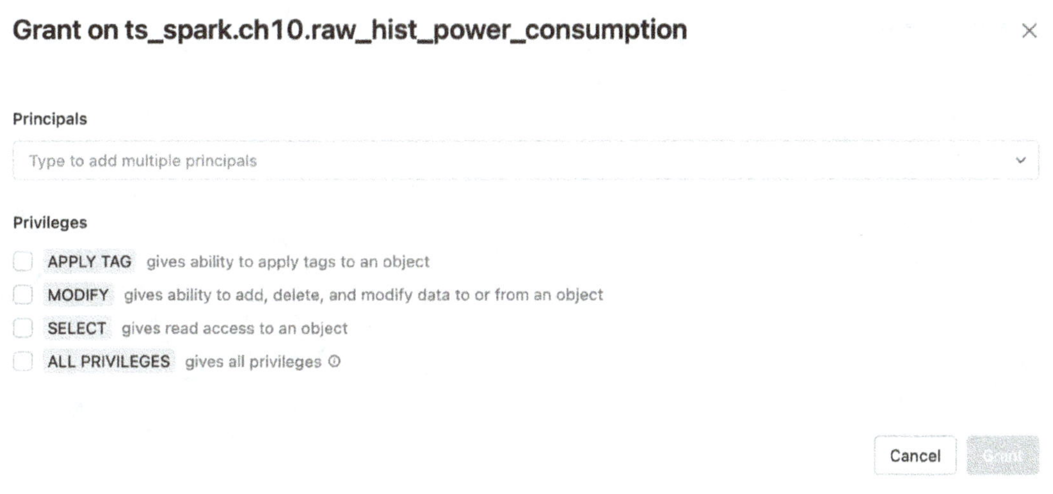

Grant on ts_spark.ch10.raw_hist_power_consumption   ✕

Principals

Type to add multiple principals   ⌄

Privileges

☐ **APPLY TAG**   gives ability to apply tags to an object

☐ **MODIFY**   gives ability to add, delete, and modify data to or from an object

☐ **SELECT**   gives read access to an object

☐ **ALL PRIVILEGES**   gives all privileges ⓘ

Cancel   Grant

Figure 10.9: Databricks Unity Catalog – setting permission

It is also possible to define fine-grained access control at a more granular row or column level within tables, as per the following resources:

```
https://www.databricks.com/resources/demos/videos/governance/access-controls-with-unity-catalog
```

You can find more information on security here:

```
https://docs.databricks.com/en/security/index.html
```

Governance

An important consideration for governance is being able to track the lineage of data assets, as shown in *Figure 10.10*. We can see here the source of the data, the multiple intermediate stages, and the final tables where the data is stored. Unity Catalog tracks this automatically in Databricks to give us real-time visibility into the data flows.

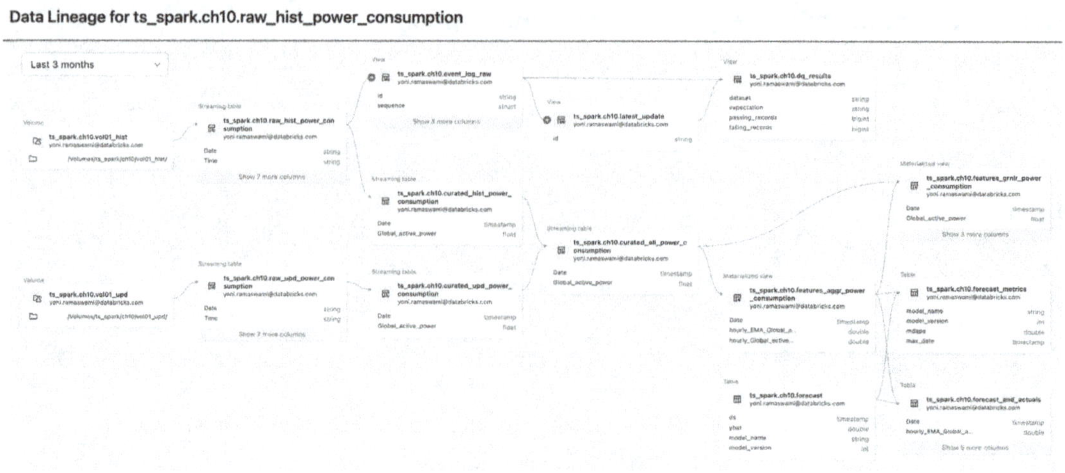

Data Lineage for ts_spark.ch10.raw_hist_power_consumption

Figure 10.10: Databricks Unity Catalog – lineage view

You can find and zoom in on a digital version of *Figure 10.10* here:

`https://packt.link/D6DyC`

We have touched only briefly on governance and security with Databricks Unity Catalog. You can find more information here:

`https://www.databricks.com/product/unity-catalog`

With an understanding of how to leverage a platform such as Databricks for monitoring, security, and governance, we will next uncover how to present the outcome of time series analysis.

Databricks UI — AI/BI dashboards

When it comes to presenting the outcome of the time series analysis we have done so far, Databricks provides a few options for the user interface with AI/BI dashboards, Genie spaces, AI-based chatbots, and Lakehouse Apps. We will cover AI/BI dashboards in this section and the other options in the next chapter.

We have been using various graphs extensively throughout this book to represent data and the outcome of analysis. This has required us to execute code in notebooks to create the graphs. This works well when we are able to write code and have an execution environment. When this is not the case, a common way to present the data and the outcome of the analysis is with a reporting dashboard. This is possible with Databricks AI/BI dashboards, as shown in *Figure 10.11*.

The Databricks AI/BI dashboard is a solution integrated into the Databricks platform to create reports and dashboards. It has AI-powered capabilities to assist with the creation of queries and data visualizations. The dashboards can be published and shared for consumption.

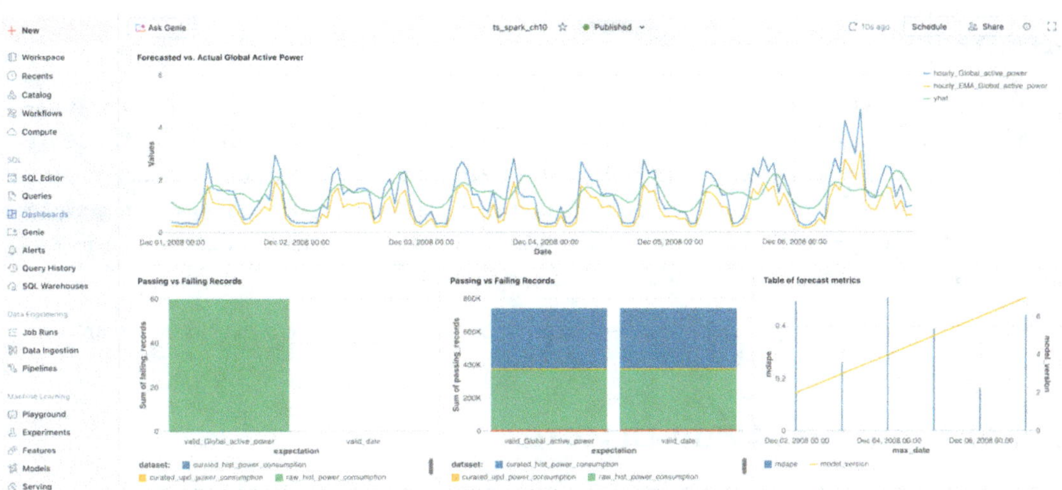

Figure 10.11: Databricks AI/BI dashboard

To install this dashboard in your own environment, first, download it from the following location:

```
https://github.com/PacktPublishing/Time-Series-Analysis-with-Spark/
blob/main/ch10/ts_spark_ch10.lvdash.json
```

The dashboard file can then be imported into your own environment by following the instructions here:

```
https://docs.databricks.com/en/dashboards/index.html#import-a-
dashboard-file
```

> **Note**
>
> You will need a SQL Warehouse in order to run the dashboard. Refer to the following instructions to create a SQL Warehouse:
>
> ```
> https://docs.databricks.com/aws/en/compute/sql-warehouse/create.
> ```

In this dashboard, we have brought together, in a combined view, the following:

- Graph of the actual and forecasted values

- Number of records that failed and passed the data quality checks

- Metrics for different model versions

You can find more information on AI/BI dashboards at the following links:

- ```
  https://www.databricks.com/blog/introducing-aibi-intelligent-
  analytics-real-world-data
  ```

- ```
  https://docs.databricks.com/en/dashboards/index.html
  ```

Summary

With the end-to-end example of time series analysis on a managed Spark platform, this chapter has shown how to leverage the out-of-the-box features of Databricks to go further with Apache Spark. We have gone from data ingestion with a streaming pipeline to feature engineering and model training and to inferencing and reporting while ensuring that monitoring, security, and governance are in place. By combining pre-built features on Databricks with our own custom code, we were able to implement a solution that can be extended to further use cases.

This brings us to our last chapter, where we will expand on some of the recent developments in time series analysis.

Join our community on Discord

Join our community's Discord space for discussions with the authors and other readers:

`https://packt.link/ds`

11

Recent Developments in Time Series Analysis

As we reach the last chapter of this book, let's do a brief recap of the journey we have been through. Starting with an introduction to time series and its components in *Chapter 1*, we looked at the different use cases for time series analysis in *Chapter 2*. We were then introduced to Apache Spark, its architecture, and how it works in *Chapter 3*. Before delving into the details of how Apache Spark is used for time series analysis, we stepped back, in *Chapter 4*, to look at the big picture of an end-to-end time series project. We then turned our focus to each of the main stages of a project from *Chapter 5* to *Chapter 9*, covering data preparation, exploratory data analysis, model development, testing, scaling, and going to production. In *Chapter 10*, we covered ways to go further with Apache Spark by using a managed data and AI platform such as Databricks.

In this concluding chapter, we will explore recent developments in the field of time series analysis, covering emerging methodologies, tools, and trends. We will cover an approach from the exciting field of generative AI applied to time series forecasting. Having a forecasting mechanism in place is great but not enough. Another area of interesting development is how forecasting is served and made available on demand to data analysts and applications. End users can also benefit from new approaches to making the outcome of time series analysis accessible to them in non-technical ways.

In this chapter, we're going to cover the following main topics:

- Generative AI for time series

- Serving forecasts via API

- Democratizing access to time series analysis

Technical requirements

We will be using a Databricks environment for the platform infrastructure. To set up the environment, follow the instructions in the *Environment setup* section of *Chapter 10*.

The code for this chapter can be found at this URL:

```
https://github.com/PacktPublishing/Time-Series-Analysis-with-Spark/
tree/main/ch11
```

Generative AI for time series analysis

While effective, traditional time series models have limitations in performance and accuracy, especially with large-scale data or complex patterns.

Generative AI, and particularly **time series transformers** (**TSTs**), offers a solution to these challenges. Similar to the transformer models in **natural language processing** (**NLP**), TSTs are adept at capturing complex, non-linear dependencies over long sequences. This capability makes them suitable for real-world data that includes missing values, seasonality, and irregular patterns. TSTs use a self-attention mechanism to analyze time series data and identify seasonal patterns. These models are pre-trained on vast datasets to create foundation models, which can then be fine-tuned for specific time series applications.

Recently, several pre-built TSTs have been released enabling us to leverage their capabilities without requiring effort to engineer such solutions. Examples include Chronos, Moira, TimesFM, and TimeGPT, among others.

In the next section, we will examine the practicalities of using one of these with TimesFM.

Introduction to TimesFM

TimesFM, short for **Time Series Foundation Model**, is an open source forecasting model developed by Google Research, designed specifically for time series data. Built on a transformer-based architecture, TimesFM is versatile, handling a wide range of forecasting tasks from short-term to long-term predictions. Unlike models such as Chronos, which treat time series similarly to natural language, TimesFM includes specialized mechanisms for time series data, such as seasonality handling, support for missing values, and capturing multivariate dependencies.

Pre-trained on over 100 billion real-world time series points, TimesFM generalizes effectively to new datasets, often providing accurate zero-shot predictions without additional training. This extensive pre-training allows TimesFM to recognize both short- and long-term dependencies in time series data, making it highly useful for applications requiring an understanding of seasonal patterns and trends.

For an overview of the TimesFM architecture and a detailed explanation, we recommend consulting the original research paper, *A decoder-only foundation model for time-series forecasting*, here:

```
https://research.google/blog/a-decoder-only-foundation-model-for-
time-series-forecasting/
```

We will see TimesFM in action with a forecasting example in the next section.

Forecasting

For the time series forecasting example in this section, we will be using the Databricks environment as set up in the *Technical requirements* section. The code for this section can be uploaded into the Databricks workspace from the following URL:

```
https://github.com/PacktPublishing/Time-Series-Analysis-with-Spark/
raw/main/ch11/ts_spark_ch11_timesFM.dbc
```

You can use the Databricks serverless compute to execute the code, as we did in *Chapter 10*. Alternatively, you can use the Databricks Runtime for ML. Version 14.3 is required for compatibility with the version of Python supported by TimesFM at the time of writing.

We will go through the steps to install and use TimesFM here, with code extracts. Refer to the notebook for the full code:

1. Install the following necessary libraries: `timesfm[torch]`, `torch`, and `sktime`.

2. Specify the hyperparameters (`hparams`) and load the TimesFM model from a checkpoint in Hugging Face (`huggingface_repos_id`). Note that `500m` refers to the 500 million parameters supported by the model, and we will use the `pytorch` version due to compatibility with Databricks:

```python
# Initialize the TimesFm model with specified hyperparameters
# and load from checkpoint
model = timesfm.TimesFm(
    hparams = timesfm.TimesFmHparams(
        backend="gpu",
        per_core_batch_size=32,
        horizon_len=128,
        num_layers=50,
        use_positional_embedding=False,
        context_len=2048,
    ),
    checkpoint = timesfm.TimesFmCheckpoint(
        huggingface_repo_id="google/timesfm-2.0-500m-pytorch"
    )
)
```

While we have used the default values for the hyperparameters, you will need to experiment to find the best ones to use depending on your forecasting requirement.

With the TimesFM model loaded, we can bring in the dataset for forecasting. We will reuse the energy consumption dataset from *Chapter 10*. Before proceeding with the next step, you must execute the code example, including the feature engineering pipeline from the previous chapter.

3. We will read from the `features_aggr_power_consumption` table and convert the Spark DataFrame into a pandas DataFrame, which is required by TimesFM. The `Date` column is renamed to `date` and converted to the `datetime` format, as expected by the model:

```python
# Define catalog, schema, and table names
CATALOG_NAME = "ts_spark"
SCHEMA_NAME = "ch10"
ACTUALS_TABLE_NAME = f"{CATALOG_NAME}.{SCHEMA_NAME}.features_
aggr_power_consumption"
FORECAST_TABLE_NAME = f"{CATALOG_NAME}.{SCHEMA_NAME}.forecast"


# Load data from the actuals table into a Spark DataFrame
sdf = spark.sql(f"""
    SELECT * FROM {ACTUALS_TABLE_NAME}
""")


# Convert Spark DataFrame to Pandas DataFrame
df = sdf.toPandas()


# Convert 'Date' column to datetime format
df['date'] = pd.to_datetime(df['Date'])
```

4. As the forecasting is done in batches, we must convert the DataFrame using the `get_batched_data_fn` function. The important part, shown in the following code extract, is the mapping of `inputs` and `outputs`. The code is based on an adaptation of an example from TimesFM

(`https://github.com/google-research/timesfm/blob/master/notebooks/covariates.ipynb`):

```python
# Function to create a data pipeline for batching time series
# data
def get_batched_data_fn(
    ...
    examples["inputs"].append(
        sub_df["hourly_Global_active_power"][
            start:(context_end := start + context_len)
        ].tolist())

    ...
    examples["outputs"].append(
```

```
        sub_df["hourly_Global_active_power"][
            context_end:(context_end + horizon_len)
        ].tolist())

    ...
```

5. We can then iterate over the batches of input data to generate the forecast using the `forecast` function, as in the following code extract:

```
# Iterate over the batches of data
for i, example in enumerate(input_data()):
    # Generate raw forecast using the model
    raw_forecast, _ = model.forecast(
        inputs=example["inputs"],
        freq=[0] * len(example["inputs"])
    )
```

6. We evaluate the forecast using the `mdape` metric, as we have done in the previous chapters. This is comparable to *Chapter 10*:

```
# Calculate and store the evaluation metric for the forecast
metrics["eval_mdape_timesfm"].extend([
    mdape(
        pd.DavtaFrame(raw_forecast[:, :horizon_len]),
        pd.DataFrame(example["outputs"])
    )
])
```

This gives the following result:

```
eval_mdape_timesfm: 0.36983413500008916
```

As we have seen in this section, using a pre-trained transformer-based foundation model such as TimesFM, with default hyperparameters, gives us comparable accuracy to the different approaches we have used in the previous chapters. With hyperparameter tuning and the use of covariates, which will be discussed next, we can seek to further improve accuracy.

Support for covariates

An important feature of TimesFM is its support for external **covariates**, as time series rarely occur in isolation. Various factors, such as economic indicators or weather conditions, can correlate with a time series, and incorporating these into the analysis can improve prediction accuracy. Put simply, a covariate is a separate variable that can help us forecast a time series.

TimesFM accommodates both univariate and multivariate forecasting with covariates, enabling it to capture correlations between the target series and these external variables. By inputting covariates as parallel sequences, the model learns how they relate to future values over time, enhancing its adaptability to real-world scenarios where external factors significantly impact outcomes. For example, we can investigate using the estimation of road traffic to forecast pollution levels. This capability to support covariates gives TimesFM a predictive edge over traditional time series models and other foundational models that do not incorporate these variables.

You can find more information on covariates support with an example here:

```
https://community.databricks.com/t5/technical-blog/genai-for-time-
series-analysis-with-timesfm/ba-p/95507
```

Other generative AI models and Many Model Forecasting

You can test other generative models to find the best one for your use case. One way to do this is with the **Many Model Forecasting** (**MMF**) Solution Accelerator by Databricks. This offers a solution for organizations needing to create forecasts across numerous time series, such as for sales, demand, or inventory predictions. The repository provides a scalable approach using Databricks to deploy and manage many forecasting models simultaneously. It includes resources such as notebooks, model templates, and data pipelines that streamline the process of training, evaluating, and deploying time series models on a large scale.

You can find more information here:

```
https://github.com/databricks-industry-solutions/many-model-forecasting
```

With generative AI and MMF now part of our time series analysis toolkit, let's explore how we can enhance the availability of forecasts for applications and data analysts.

Serving forecasts via API

The main part of this book has focused on preparing and analyzing a time series dataset. We also covered presenting the analysis's outcomes in tables and graphs in notebooks and reporting dashboards. However, in many cases, forecasts must be served on-demand to data analysts and applications. We will now explore ways to achieve this.

Forecasting simplified with ai_forecast

In this situation, the data analyst has access to time series data and wants to provide this as input to get a forecast without first having to develop a model. By abstracting the forecast behind a function such as the `ai_forecast` function on the Databricks platform, the ability to forecast can be greatly simplified for someone without knowledge of forecasting models and algorithms.

You can see this action with a simple example at the following URL:

```
https://github.com/PacktPublishing/Time-Series-Analysis-with-Spark/
raw/main/ch11/ts_spark_ch11_aiforecast.dbc
```

This code is based on the example in the documentation, the link to which is provided at the end of this section:

```
SELECT *
FROM AI_FORECAST(
    TABLE(aggregated),
    horizon => '2016-03-31',
    time_col => 'ds',
    value_col => 'revenue'
)
```

The output of running this example is shown in *Figure 11.1*.

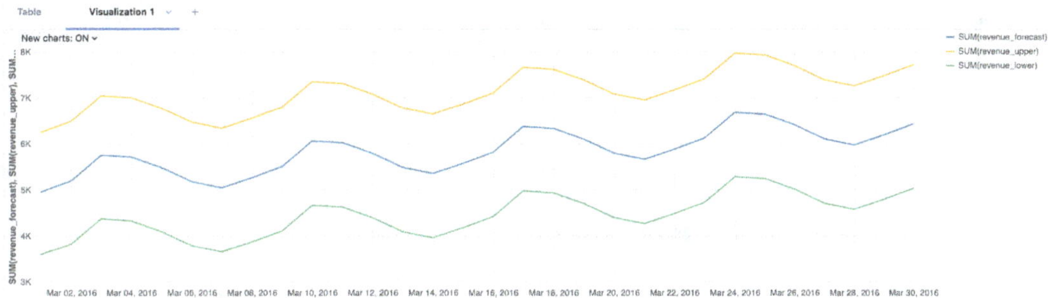

Figure 11.1: Example output of ai_forecast

You can find and zoom in on a digital version of *Figure 11.1* here:

```
https://packt.link/vg87q
```

Note that this feature is in public preview at the time of this writing, so you may need to request access from Databricks to try it.

You can find more information here:

```
https://docs.databricks.com/en/sql/language-manual/functions/ai_
forecast.html
```

While a simplified and predefined function such as `ai_function` is a great way to quickly generate a forecast, we may want to make our own custom-developed forecasting model accessible easily to other applications, as we will cover next.

Model Serving

In some cases, we need to programmatically get a forecast from our model from another application. For such application-to-application integration, the use of a REST API is a common practice. One way to provide a REST API interface to our model is by using Databricks' **Model Serving**.

Databricks' Model Serving provides the functionality for deploying, governing, and querying ML and AI models, for both real-time and batch inference. The deployed model is accessible via a REST API, which enables integration into web or client applications. Various model types are supported, including custom Python models packaged in the MLflow format and open foundation models provided. This service is designed for high availability and low latency, automatically scaling to changing demand.

Here's an overview of the steps to serve a model. Note that this is not a working example. The screenshots shown here are to illustrate the steps only:

1. Access the model in Unity Catalog as per *Figure 11.2* and click the **Serve this model** button at the top right.

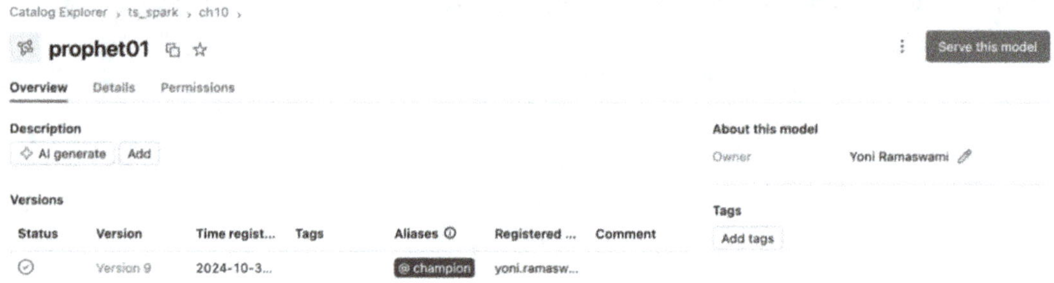

Figure 11.2: Model in Unity Catalog

2. Create a serving endpoint as per *Figure 11.3*. This will show the URL to use to access the REST API to invoke the model.

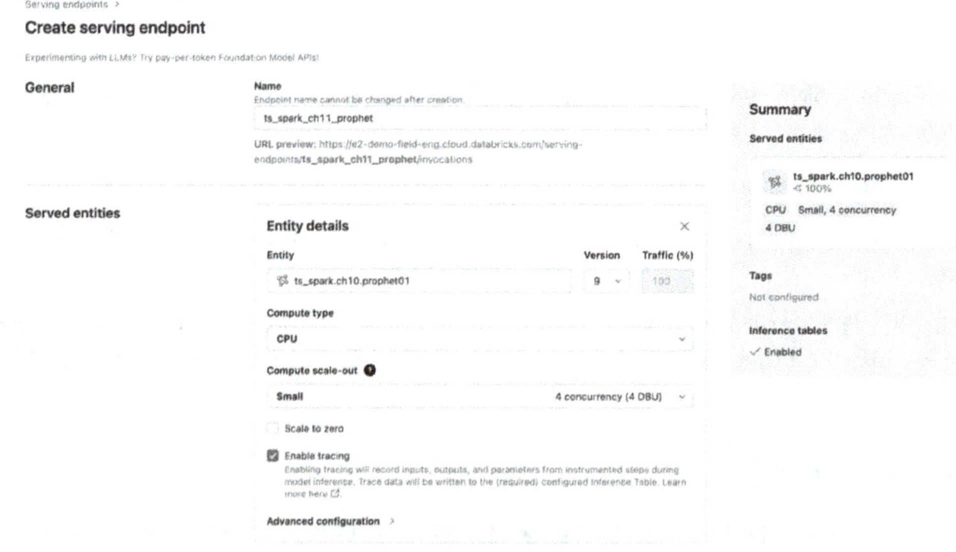

Figure 11.3: Create serving endpoint

3. When creating the serving endpoint, we can enable an inference table, as per *Figure 11.4*, to store all the input and output of interactions with the model REST API.

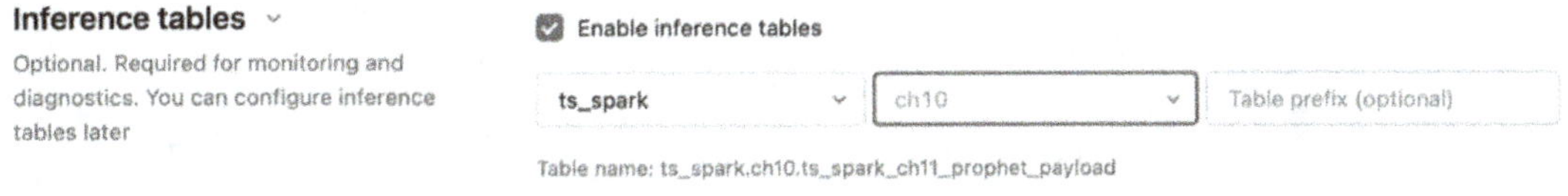

Figure 11.4: Inference tables

4. Once created, the serving endpoint will be shown with the status of **Ready**, as per *Figure 11.5*, and can be used.

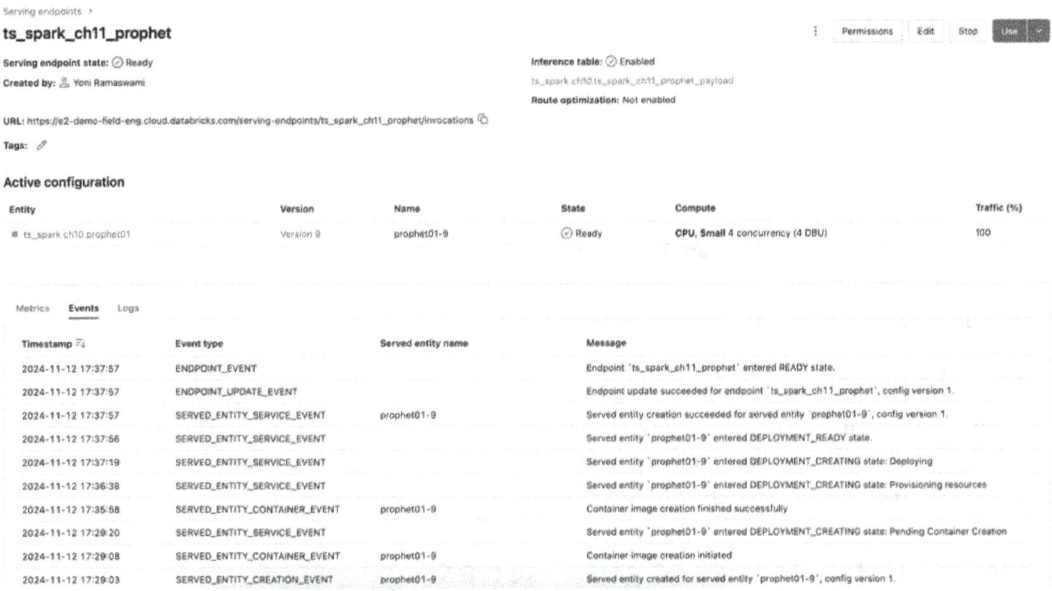

Figure 11.5: Serving endpoint is ready

5. As the serving endpoint is used, its metrics can be monitored, as per *Figure 11.6*.

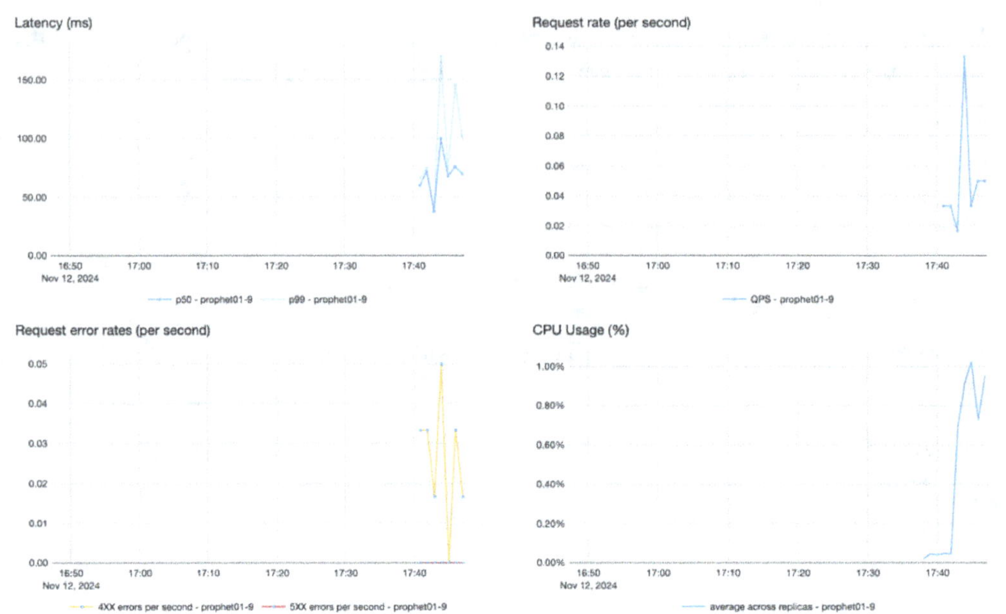

Figure 11.6: Service endpoint metrics

You can find more information on Model Serving here:

```
https://docs.databricks.com/en/machine-learning/serve-models.html
```

As we have seen in this section, exposing our time series analysis model via a REST API makes it easier to integrate the analysis with other applications. Continuing on the accessibility of time series analysis, we will look next at how to facilitate this for end users as well.

Democratizing access to time series analysis

In this section, we will explore how innovative approaches to accessing the outcome of time series can benefit non-technical users. This allows us to democratize time series analysis for the benefit of an even broader audience.

Genie spaces

In the first approach, we will be using a natural language chatbot-like interface on Databricks called **Genie spaces**.

The Databricks Genie spaces is a conversational UI enabling business users to ask questions in natural language and receive analytical insights without requiring technical expertise. This works by configuring Genie spaces with relevant datasets, sample queries, and instructions. Users can then interact in natural language, asking questions and visualizations about the data. Genie uses annotated table and column metadata to translate the user queries into SQL statements. These are used to query the data so that Genie can provide responses to users.

To see this in practice, we will use the dashboard that we created in *Chapter 10*, as shown in *Figure 11.7*. This is one way to access Genie – from the dashboard, we can click on the top-left **Ask Genie** button. This opens a chatbot-like interface at the bottom right, where we can start typing questions in natural language. Alternatively, we can choose to open the Genie space in a full screen.

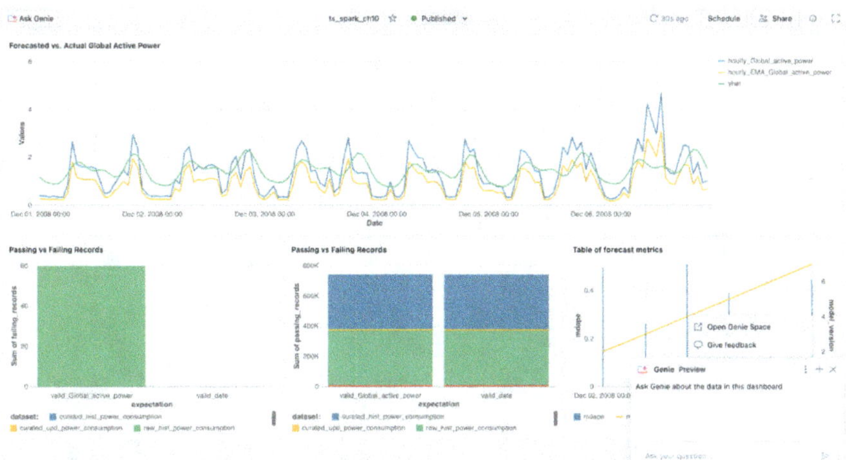

Figure 11.7: Access to Genie space from the dashboard

In *Figure 11.8*, we can see the complete Genie space with a query, the results, and the generated SQL used to get the results.

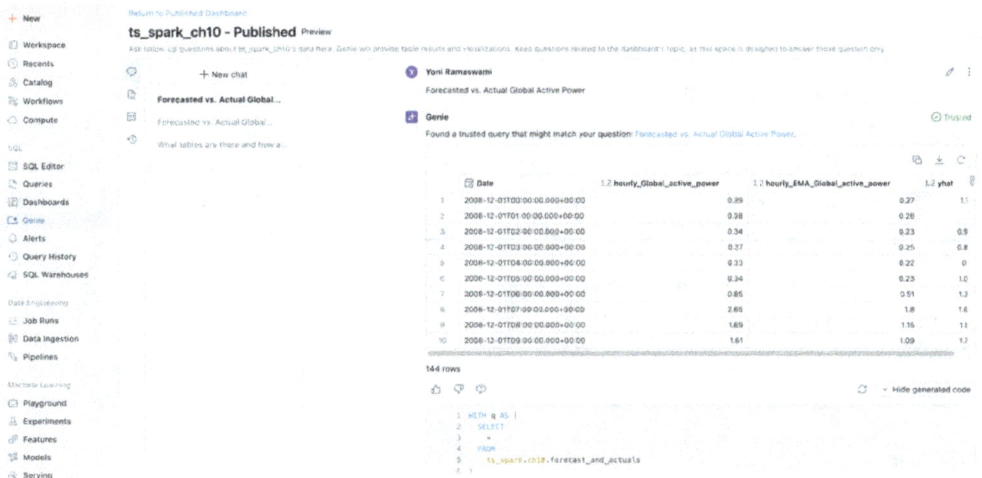

Figure 11.8: Genie spaces query and results

The query in this example is to show **Forecasted vs. Actual**, which can also be requested as a visualization, as shown in *Figure 11.9*.

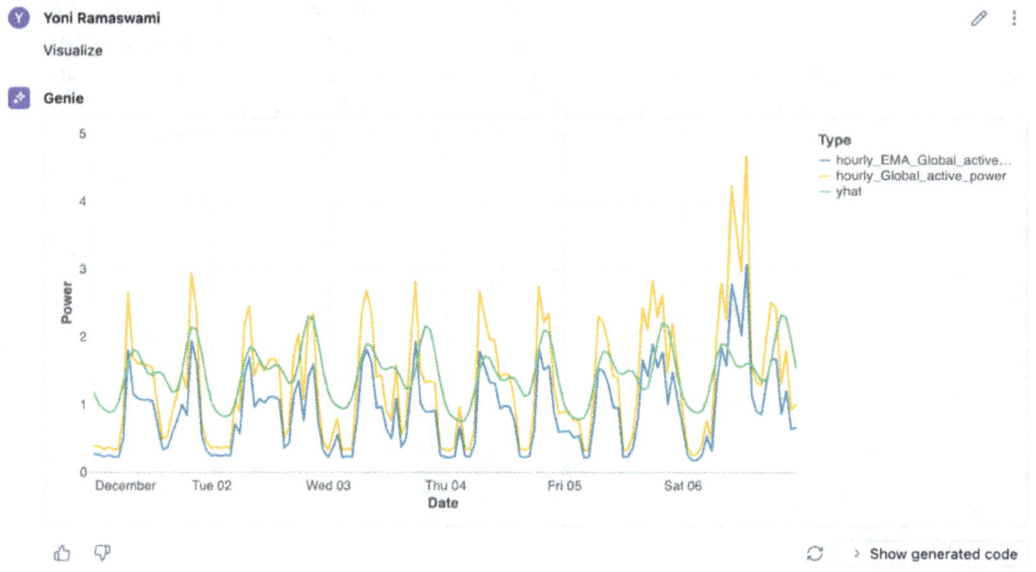

Figure 11.9: Genie spaces visualization

You can find more information on Databricks Genie spaces here: `https://docs.databricks.com/en/genie/index.html`

Apps

In cases where more application-like interactivity is required, a dashboard or chatbot interface is not sufficient to meet the users' needs. Databricks Apps provides a platform to build and deploy applications directly within the Databricks environment. Currently in public preview, Databricks Apps supports development frameworks such as Dash, Shiny, Gradio, Streamlit, and Flask, for the creation of data visualizations, AI applications, self-service analytics, and other data applications.

You can find more information on Databricks Apps here: `https://www.databricks.com/blog/introducing-databricks-apps`

Summary

In this final chapter, we delved into recent advancements in time series analysis, focusing on emerging methodologies, tools, and trends. We tried the innovative approach from the dynamic field of generative AI applied to time series forecasting. To answer the growing requirement for forecasts via API, we explored ways to provide on-demand forecasting to data analysts and applications. We concluded with the use of an AI chatbot and Databricks Apps to democratize access to time series analysis for non-technical users.

As we arrive at the end of the book, looking back at our journey and the skills we acquired, we have built a solid foundation on the multiple stages of time series analysis projects with Apache Spark and other components. Armed with the multiple use cases discussed in *Chapter 2*, the practical skills gained throughout the book, and the recent advancements in this chapter, we have the necessary ingredients to succeed in production-ready, scalable, and future-proofed time series analysis projects across industries.

We began this book with Pericles' wise counsel on the importance of time—now, at the end of this book, we have the ability to uncover the valuable insights hidden in time series and use them to our benefit. May this knowledge empower you to tackle challenges with new ideas and confidence. Wishing you happy learning and success on your journey with time series analysis and Apache Spark!

12
Unlock Your Exclusive Benefits

Your copy of this book includes the following exclusive benefit:

- ⟳ Next-gen Packt Reader
- 📄 DRM-free PDF/ePub downloads

Follow the guide below to unlock them. The process takes only a few minutes and needs to be completed once.

Unlock this Book's Free Benefits in 3 Easy Steps

Step 1

Keep your purchase invoice ready for *Step 3*. If you have a physical copy, scan it using your phone and save it as a PDF, JPG, or PNG.

For more help on finding your invoice, visit `https://www.packtpub.com/unlock-benefits/help`.

> **Note**
>
> If you bought this book directly from Packt, no invoice is required. After *Step 2*, you can access your exclusive content right away.

Step 2

Scan the QR code or go to `packtpub.com/unlock`.

On the page that opens (similar to *Figure 11.1* on desktop), search for this book by name and select the correct edition.

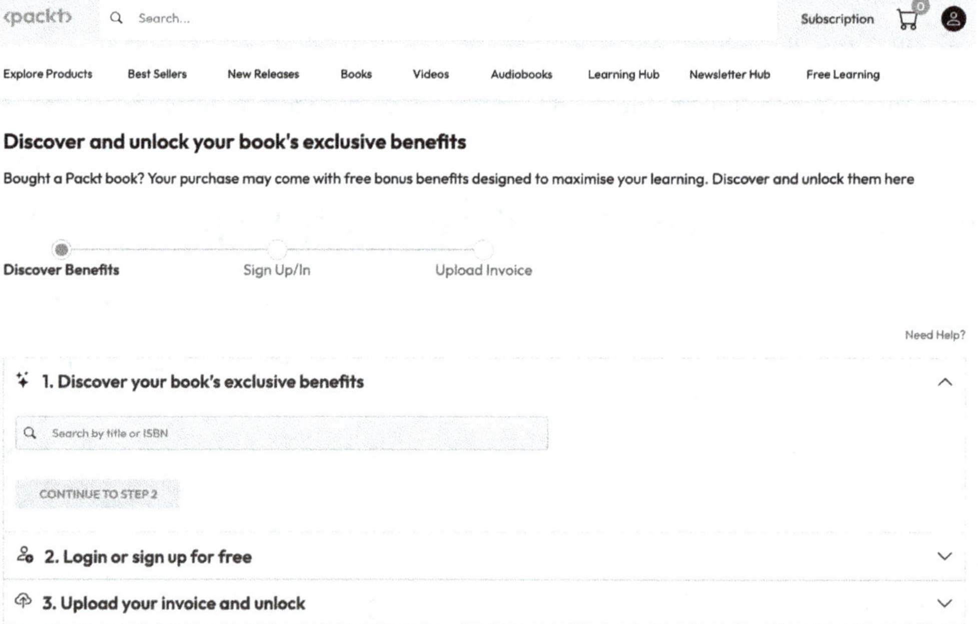

Figure 11.1: Packt unlock landing page on desktop

Step 3

After selecting your book, sign in to your Packt account or create one for free. Then upload your invoice (PDF, PNG, or JPG, up to 10 MB). Follow the on-screen instructions to finish the process.

Need help?

If you get stuck and need help, visit
`https://www.packtpub.com/unlock-benefits/help`
for a detailed FAQ on how to find your invoices and more. This QR
code will take you to the help page.

Note

If you are still facing issues, reach out to `customercare@packt.com`.

Index

I

O

observability
  reference link 242
orchestrator approach 94
  benefits 94, 95
  workflow authorization 95
  workflow, running 98, 99
orchestrator approach, workflow authorization 95
  DAG definition 96, 97
  DAG tasks 97, 98
  Python code 95, 96
Ordinary Least Squares (OLS) 15
outliers 118
  handling 116

P

Pandas 156
pandas UDFs 198
PapermillOperator operator 98
ParameterGrid approach 162, 163
partial autocorrelation 160
Partial AutoCorrelation Function (PACF) 141
pattern classification
  use case 41-43
pattern classification 151
pattern detection and categorization 31
  deep learning 33
  dictionary-based 32
  distance-based 31
  ensembles 33
  frequency-based 32
  interval-based 32
  shapelets 32

pattern recognition 151
Personally Identifiable Information (PII) 22
Photon 52
Platform as a Service (PaaS) 8, 60, 225
Podman
  reference link 61
Postgres 87
PySpark 51
Python development environment 8
  PaaS 8

R

RandOm Convolutional KErnel Transform (ROCKET) 32
Random Interval Spectral Ensemble (RISE) 32
RDD 54
Recurrent Neural Networks (RNNs) 33, 35
regular time series 131
resampling 135, 136
Resilient Distributed Datasets (RDDs) 50
retail, time series analysis
  customer behavior analysis 38
  inventory management 38
  marketing planning 38
  price optimization 38
  product life cycle management 38
  revenue prediction 38
  sales forecasting 38
  store performance analysis 38
  supply chain optimization 38
  workforce planning 38
Return on investment (ROI) 74
Root Mean Squared Error (RMSE) 214

S

T

task 57

Temporal Convolutional Networks (TCNs) 150

testing and forecasting, SARIMA 164, 165

TimeNet 33

time series

time series analysis 4, 5

time series analysis model

time series analysis model, considerations

time series analysis model, monitoring 215

time series analysis models

time series analysis model, workflows

time series analysis project

time series components 15

packtpub.com

Subscribe to our online digital library for full access to over 7,000 books and videos, as well as industry leading tools to help you plan your personal development and advance your career. For more information, please visit our website.

Why subscribe?

Spend less time learning and more time coding with practical eBooks and Videos from over 4,000 industry professionals

- Improve your learning with Skill Plans built especially for you

- Get a free eBook or video every month

- Fully searchable for easy access to vital information

- Copy and paste, print, and bookmark content

At www.packtpub.com, you can also read a collection of free technical articles, sign up for a range of free newsletters, and receive exclusive discounts and offers on Packt books and eBooks.

Other Books You May Enjoy

If you enjoyed this book, you may be interested in these other books by Packt:

Modern Time Series Forecasting with Python

Manu Joseph, Jeffrey Tackes

ISBN: 978-1-83588-318-1

- Build machine learning models for regression-based time series forecasting
- Apply powerful feature engineering techniques to enhance prediction accuracy
- Tackle common challenges like non-stationarity and seasonality
- Combine multiple forecasts using ensembling and stacking for superior results
- Explore cutting-edge advancements in probabilistic forecasting and handle intermittent or sparse time series
- Evaluate and validate your forecasts using best practices and statistical metrics

Time Series Analysis with Python Cookbook

Tarek A. Atwan

ISBN: 978-1-80107-554-1

- Understand what makes time series data different from other data
- Apply various imputation and interpolation strategies for missing data
- Implement different models for univariate and multivariate time series
- Use different deep learning libraries such as TensorFlow, Keras, and PyTorch
- Plot interactive time series visualizations using hvPlot
- Explore state-space models and the unobserved components model (UCM)
- Detect anomalies using statistical and machine learning methods
- Forecast complex time series with multiple seasonal patterns

Packt is searching for authors like you

If you're interested in becoming an author for Packt, please visit `authors.packtpub.com` and apply today. We have worked with thousands of developers and tech professionals, just like you, to help them share their insight with the global tech community. You can make a general application, apply for a specific hot topic that we are recruiting an author for, or submit your own idea.

Share Your Thoughts

Now you've finished *Time Series Analysis with Spark*, we'd love to hear your thoughts! Scan the QR code below to go straight to the Amazon review page for this book and share your feedback or leave a review on the site that you purchased it from.

`https://packt.link/r/1803232250`

Your review is important to us and the tech community and will help us make sure we're delivering excellent quality content.